REVELL'S DICTIONARY OF BIBLE TIMES

REVELL'S DICTIONARY OF BIBLE TIMES

Herbert Sundemo

Translated by Birgitta Sharpe

FLEMING H. REVELL COMPANY
Old Tappan, New Jersey

Published in Swedish by Leif Stegeland
Förlag AB
Published in England by Scripture Union
47 Marylebone Lane
London W1M 6AX

Text and illustrations © Leif Stegeland
Förlag AB
English translation © 1979 Scripture Union
ISBN 0-8007 1058-4

Printed in the United States of America

Introduction

The Bible stands at the centre of Christian faith and experience and plays a vital part in the life of every Christian. The reader is, however, presented with a problem – he finds that the Bible was written in a totally different culture to his own. There are customs he does not understand, unfamiliar metaphors, strange images; all set in a foreign geographical and historical setting. If we are to understand correctly the meaning of the Bible we will need to know something about these background details.

This is where Bible Times can help. It contains a wealth of information covering just the areas which will present problems. The lively articles and clear illustrations make this a book that will be of great value not only for personal Bible study but also for those teaching in school or Sunday school or leading Bible study groups.

It was originally written by Herbert Sundemo, who works at the experimental and demonstration unit of the Swedish Advanced College of Education where some of the material in this book was first used. The English translation has been specially revised by Canon J. Stafford Wright and others to make it even more suitable for the English reader.

REVELL'S DICTIONARY OF BIBLE TIMES

A

A

The initial letter in most alphabets. In Scripture *alpha* and *omega*, the first and last letters of the Greek alphabet, are used as a title of God himself and of Jesus Christ in particular as the beginning and end of all that is (Revelation 1:8; 21:6; 22:13). The title is actually a quotation of Isaiah 41:4; 44:6.

ĀΩ AѠ

ABYSS

The abyss, or 'the bottomless pit', is in the New Testament another word for Hell.

See Luke 8:31; Romans 10:7; Revelation 20:1.
See also Kingdom of the Dead, Gehenna.

ACACIA SEE TREES

ACROPOLIS SEE ATHENS, GREECE

ACTS OF THE APOSTLES

Written by the author of the Gospel of Luke, Luke the physician, who accompanied Paul on many of his journeys in the Roman empire.

In the Acts of the Apostles Luke gives important information about life in the first Christian congregations. The book also tells us how the Christian message was spread throughout the Roman empire.

ADRIATIC SEA

A gulf of the Mediterranean, east of Italy.

AGE

There are times in the course of history when God acts decisively. When Jesus preached that the time is fulfilled (Mark 1:15), he was referring to all that had gone before, culminating and climaxing in his unique life and ministry. For the Christian the time of God's action has come, and now we live awaiting the age to come, the final consummation. (See Day of the Lord.) There is a distinction between this time and the age to come (see Mark 10:30; Ephesians 1:21). Jesus has done everything to conquer sin and death, but their persistence and the continued work of Satan is the mark of a waiting period, or a mopping-up time. Their days are numbered as Revelation clearly says (Revelation 20:14; 21:8).

The gift of the Holy Spirit is the Christian's pledge or guarantee of what is to come in the age to come (see Spirit). (2 Corinthians 1:22). So in Christ the time is fulfilled and God's intervention seen. The present age is an interim, a middle waiting period when Christians live in certain hope of the age to come. In that future age we shall see the final, visible end to sin, death and the works of the Devil. In anticipation of that we are to live Christlike lives of preparation, like the wise virgins awaiting the bridegroom (Matthew 25). Christ's instructions to us are to watch and pray.

See Matthew 24; Luke 21; Mark 13; 1 Corinthians 15; Romans 8:18–23; 1 Corinthians 10:11.
See also: Day Of The Lord.

AGRICULTURE

The Canaanites, who lived in Palestine before the arrival of the Israelites, were excellent farmers. The Israelites learnt agriculture from them.

It was not feasible to cultivate the soil everywhere in Palestine. It was impossible in the mountain and desert regions. It was difficult to irrigate the dry areas with water from the river Jordan, because the course of this river was low in

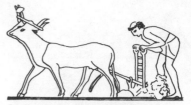
Egyptian ploughman from about 1400 BC

relation to the level of the surrounding countryside.

The most commonly grown cereals were wheat and barley. Of the various fruit trees, olives, vines and figs were especially valued. In October–November the first winter rains came. They were called autumn rains or early rains. They softened the hard and dry soil. A simple, wooden plough turned the topsoil. A pair of oxen yoked together pulled the plough. Hard lumps of soil were broken up with a pointed stick. No fertilizer was used on the soil.

The grain was sown by hand. After the sowing, the grains were ploughed into the soil.

Unless the winter rains continued, there would be a failure of crops and lack of food. The patriarch Jacob was forced to buy grain from abroad during a long period of drought and bad harvests (Genesis 42:1–5).

In April the grain in the lowlands ripened, first the barley, and a few weeks later the wheat (Deuteronomy 16:9). In May the harvest was ripe in the high-

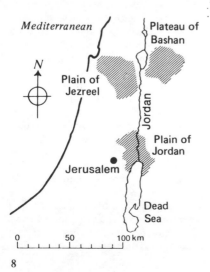

Mediterranean

N

Plain of Jezreel

Plateau of Bashan

Jordan

Plain of Jordan

Jerusalem

Dead Sea

0   50   100 km

Donkeys carrying wheat to the threshing floor

lands. The crops were cut with a sickle (Joel 3:13, Mark 4:29) which was sometimes toothed, like a saw. The stalks were bound together in sheaves. A small part of the grain was often left growing as food for strangers and poor people (Leviticus 23:22).

Sometimes the growing wheat was destroyed by locusts, drought or enemies.

The wheat was bound in sheaves, which were carried to the threshing-floor. If that was some distance away, the wheat was carried by donkeys or transported on carts (Genesis 37:7, Psalm 129:7). The threshing-floor was out in the open, since there was no rain in the summer. The wheat was spread out on the ground, and the oxen trod the grains out of the ears of wheat. Often a heavy sledge was pulled round and round the

Oxen pulling a threshing cart

threshing-floor by the oxen. This threshing-sledge was made from planks of wood, with sharp pieces of stone or iron on the underside. In order to make the cart heavier, the driver of the oxen stood on top of it (Isaiah 28:27, 28).

After the threshing, the wheat had to be winnowed. It was thrown several

times into the air with closely set pitchforks. If the wind conditions were right, the grains would fall to the ground in a heap, near the feet of the workers. The chaff, which was lighter, was blown further away. The straw was collected for fodder and bedding for the cattle.

Finally the grains were winnowed

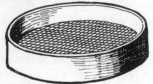

Sieve for winnowing wheat

again, by being riddled in a sieve. Then they were carried in sacks to the village. Other crops are listed in Isaiah 28:25–28.

Pentecost, or the Feast of Weeks, was originally a time of joy and a harvest festival. People showed their joy and gratitude to God through an offering from the new harvest (Leviticus 23:15–21; Deuteronomy 16:9–12).

Many of the parables of Jesus are taken from the life of farmers, e.g. Matthew 13:3–9; Mark 4:26–29.
See also: Climate, Bread, Wine

ALABASTER

is a kind of stone, which is light in colour and easily worked. Before glass was commonly available, bottles were made of alabaster. Perfumes and ointments were kept in them. Most of the alabaster came from Egypt and North Africa.
See Mark 14:3; Luke 7:37.

ALEXANDRIA

was a large port in the north of Egypt on the Mediterranean coast. It was founded by Alexander the Great in 332 BC and became a centre of culture and of world trade, and also of Jewish settlement. The Greek translation of the Old Testament known as the Septuagint was made here from about 250 BC onwards (Acts 18:24; 27:6; 28:11).

ALMIGHTY, OMNIPOTENT

To be omnipotent ('all-mighty') is to have unlimited power to do everything that one wants to do. The Bible speaks of God as omnipotent, as Almighty God. He has power to do that which is his holy will. Jesus Christ shares God's omnipotence.
See Genesis 17:1; Psalm 91:1; Matthew 28:18; Revelation 4:8.

ALMOND-TREE SEE TREES

ALMS

The word alms comes from a Greek word meaning mercy. Alms were gifts to the poor. In New Testament times, almsgiving was a major Jewish religious activity, a duty to be performed. Money was collected in the synagogue chest on the Sabbath and given to the poor, so that to give alms was a sign of righteousness. Jesus condemned those who showed off and boasted by their giving. 'When you give alms, do not let your left hand know what your right hand is doing, so that your alms may be in secret' (Matthew 6:1–4). The early church placed great importance on caring for the needy and the poor (Acts 4:32; 11:30; 1 Corinthians 16:1–4). Cornelius is praised because he feared God, gave alms liberally and prayed constantly (Acts 10:1). Paul quotes Jesus in Acts 20:35, 'It is more blessed to give than to receive' as he urges the Ephesians to help the weak.

ALOE

is a tree from which a pleasant perfume was produced. Aloe was also used as incense. The tree grows in India and China. Nicodemus brought a large quantity to bind up with the grave-clothes round the body of Jesus. (100 Roman pounds = about 30 kilogrammes).
See Psalm 45:9; Proverbs 7:17; John 19:39.

ALTAR

After the Holy of Holies, the most important place in the temple was the bronze altar, filled with stones and earth. On the altar the sacrificial animal was killed and burnt. The most important element of the sacrifice was the animal's blood, which was sprinkled or smeared on the altar. The Israelites were instructed that the animal's life or soul was in the blood (Leviticus 17:11).

The earliest altars were made of stones or soil (Exodus 20:24–25). The patriarchs built such altars at Shechem (Genesis 12:6–7), near Bethel (Genesis 12:8), at Hebron (Genesis 13:18) and at Beersheba (Genesis 26:23–25). Later, altars were made from hewn and dressed stones.

Smaller altars of dressed stone gradually became more common. These had four raised corners, like horns (Exodus 27:2; 1 Kings 1:50–51).

In the Tabernacle and in Solomon's Temple the altar of burnt offering was made of bronze, probably filled with stones and earth (Exodus 27:1–8; 2 Chronicles 4:1). Solomon's altar was so high that it must have needed steps, as described in Ezekiel 43:13–17.

In the temple there were also altars for incense, where various fragrant substances were burnt (Exodus 30:1–10).

See also: Sacrifice, Incense, Temple, High Place

An early altar made of stones

Horned altar about 2 ft (55 cm) high found at Megiddo

An artist's reconstruction of the large altar in the Temple at Jerusalem

AMMONITES

The Ammonites were a people east of the Jordan, who fought with the Israelites on several occasions (e.g. Judges 11; 1 Samuel 11).

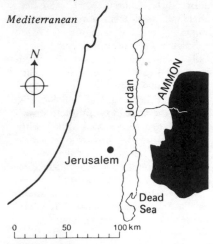

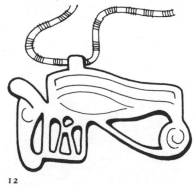

AMOS, BOOK OF

The Book of Amos is dated about 750 BC. It contains Amos' prophecies of judgement directed, in the first instance, towards the northern kingdom of Israel, but also including Judah and the neighbouring pagan countries. Amos himself was a shepherd before his call to be a prophet (1:1; 7:14).

AMULET

A small object or charm, which a person wears (usually on a string around his neck) and which he believes is able to protect him against accidents or to bring him good fortune. Isaiah includes them among the women's ornaments in 3:18–24.

ANATHOTH

was a city situated about three miles (5 km) north of Jerusalem. The prophet Jeremiah came from here (Jeremiah 1:1) and was persecuted by his fellow townsmen (11:21).

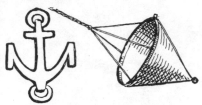

ANCHOR

The anchor was part of a ship's equipment in Bible times, just as it is today. Often there were several anchors, both in the fore and aft of the ship. (Acts 27:29, 40).

The sea-anchor was used at sea, for reducing the ship's speed. It was a large cone made of sail-cloth with an iron ring round the edge, which was dragged in the water behind the ship.

The anchor was used as an old Christian symbol, representing Christian hope (Hebrews 6:19).

ANGELS

The Bible frequently speaks of angels as the messengers of God, spirits who go on God's errands between heaven and earth. Although they are naturally glorious beings (Luke 2:9–13) they sometimes appeared in human form (Genesis 19:1, 2; Judges 6:11–18).

Some of the angels mentioned in the Bible have names: Gabriel, Luke 1:19, and Michael, Daniel 12:1. In the Apocrypha Raphael and Uriel are also mentioned (Tobit 3:17; 12:15; 2 Esdras 5:20).

Cherubs and seraphs (or cherubim and seraphim) are particular kinds of angels. They belong to the hosts of angels surrounding the Lord. In Isaiah chapter 6 they are described as winged, half-human beings (Genesis 3:24, Isaiah 6:2).

See also: Genesis 28:12; Psalm 34:7; Matthew 1:20; 13:41; Luke 2:9, 13; John 20:12; Acts 12:7; Revelation 7:11.

Hunting dogs from an Assyrian relief

Dogs were used in hunting in Middle Eastern countries, but in Palestine they are mentioned as assisting the shepherds in guarding the flocks. Wild and half-wild dogs collected everywhere near people's houses, scavenging among the household rubbish. The Jews regarded the dog as an unclean animal, so that to call someone a 'dog' was an expression of contempt and an insult. When Jesus used the word to the Canaanite woman, he used a word which described small pet dogs.

See Job 30:1; 2 Kings 8:13; Luke 16:21; Philippians 3:2.

Fox with a fish, as shown on an Egyptian ointment spoon

A cherub found on an ivory plaque found at Megiddo

ANIMALS

Larger animals are rare nowadays in Palestine, due to the sparse vegetation. Some of the animals which were common in Bible times are now extinct.

Bears are no longer to be found in Palestine. In Bible times the Syrian Bear was fairly common.

See 1 Samuel 17:34; 2 Kings 2:24; Amos 5:19.

Deer. Fallow Deer were very common in Palestine in the past but numbers gradually declined. In the Bible the deer is a symbol of beauty and speed. The male deer is called a hart or a stag, and the female deer a hind.

See Psalm 18:33; 42:1; Song of Solomon 2:7.

Foxes. There were a large number of foxes in Palestine in Old Testament times. It is still quite a common animal there. The Egyptian fox is smaller and lighter in colour than ours, and lives in the south of Palestine. The Syrian fox is larger than ours and lives in the north.

See Judges 15:4; Nehemiah 4:3; Luke 9:58; 13:32

Gazelles as shown on an Assyrian relief from Nineveh

Gazelles are frequently mentioned in the Old Testament. They were known for their beauty and swiftness (1 Chronicles 12:8; Song of Solomon 2:9-17).

Jackals were among the common animals of Palestine. They were a yellowish grey colour and looked like foxes. They lived in the desert regions as scavengers, eating the scraps of food left behind by the larger predators (Isaiah 13:22; Jeremiah 9:11).

Leopards were once to be found in Palestine, but are now extinct. They lived in the mountains. The prophets mentioned the leopard in their preaching (Song of Solomon 4:8; Jeremiah 13:23; Hosea 13:7).

Lion hunting a deer as shown on an Assyrian relief

Lions are no longer to be found in Palestine. In the past they lived near the river Jordan. They could hide in the dense vegetation by the river.

The shepherds had to be prepared to defend their flocks against attacks from lions. The lion was a symbol of courage and strength (1 Samuel 17:34; Amos 3:12).

Wolves were a great trouble to the shepherd and his flock. They were numerous, fearless, swift and dangerous.

Wolves often lay hidden near the enclosures where sheep were kept during the night. The wall of the enclosure was high, in order to protect the sheep. On top of the wall shrubs with thorns and spikes were planted. There are still wolves in Palestine (Isaiah 11:6; John 10:12).

The ant. The Harvester Ant collects grains and seeds in summer and is quoted as a symbol of diligence and hard work (Proverbs 6:6; 30:25).

Gnats (midges). One of the plagues inflicted on Egypt, when Pharaoh prevented the Israelites from leaving the country, was a plague of gnats, or perhaps mosquitoes. Formerly, Palestine had richer supplies of water than it has now, and probably suffered a great deal more from gnats and midges (Exodus 8:16–18; Psalm 105:31; Matthew 23:24).

Moths. Clothes moths are mentioned in the Bible, in order to show how things on earth are destroyed and soon finished. The moth grubs spoil and eat all kinds of clothes and foodstuffs. In the same way, man's life on earth is impermanent and moves quickly towards its end (Job 4:19; 13:28; Psalm 39:11; Luke 12:33).

Silk (Revelation 18:12) comes from the silk moth, and was probably imported from China in New Testament times. It is doubtful whether the translations are correct in Ezekiel 16:10, 13, rather than 'fine linen'. Silk farming did not reach the Mediterranean area until about the sixth century AD.

Locusts usually came in large swarms, like clouds, and where they landed they devoured all plants. The locusts laid their eggs in the soil, and when they were hatched, the larvae too, ate all vegetation within reach (Joel 1:4).

The locusts had several natural enemies: birds, foxes, jackals and other animals. People still catch and eat locusts, either dried or fried.

John the Baptist ate locusts and wild honey, among other things (Joel 1:2–7; 2:4–9; Matthew 3:4).

Grasshopper. It is not easy to say whether some Hebrew words refer to grasshoppers rather than locusts, but it is likely that grasshoppers are singled out for their small size in Numbers 13:33; Ecclesiastes 12:5 mg.; Isaiah 40:22.

Egyptian bracelet with a scarab made of gold and enamel

Scarab or Dung Beetle is a beetle which lives in countries with a warm climate. The Egyptians regarded it as sacred.

Scorpions are of the spider family, but look like small lobsters. The largest species can grow to a length of 10 to 12 cm (4 to 5 inches). The scorpion carries a poisonous sting at the point of its tail, but does not attack humans except when threatened. The scorpion enjoys heat. It finds its way into houses, hides inside beds, under carpets, among clothes and in shoes (Ezekiel 2:6; Luke 10:19; Revelation 9:3–5).
See also: Domestic Animals, Fish, Birds, Snakes

ANTICHRIST

The word 'antichrist' occurs only in the letters of John, but the idea behind the word is found elsewhere in the Bible. The 'antichrist' is one who is opposed to God. Daniel 7:7 and 2 Thessalonians 2 describe the strong opposition that the forces of evil will raise against Christ in the last days, as does Revelation 13. The letters of John describe the Antichrist in personal terms as one who denies the Father and the Son (1 John 2:22) 'this is the spirit of antichrist', and as one who denies that Jesus Christ is come in the flesh (1 John 4:3). 'Many antichrists are already in the world' (1 John 2:18), but there will come one who will strongly oppose Jesus Christ in the last days, empowered by Satan. But his opposition will fail.
See 2 Thessalonians 2; 1 John 2; Matthew 24:24.

ANTIOCH

1. A city in Syria. A large Christian congregation was formed here. It was in Antioch that the disciples of Jesus were first called Christians (Acts 11:26). Paul began many of his missionary travels at Antioch (Acts 13:1–3).
2. A city in Asia Minor which Paul visited on his first missionary journey (Acts 13:14; Acts 14:19).

A Syrian coin with a portrait of Antiochus Epiphanes

ANTIOCHUS EPIPHANES

was a king of Syria, 220–163 BC. He attacked Jerusalem and plundered the Temple in about 167 BC. The Temple at Jerusalem was made into a Temple of the Greek god Zeus. The Jews revolted. The leaders of the revolt came of a family called the Maccabees, who successfully freed and restored the Temple. Their success is celebrated by the Jewish Feast of Hanukkah or Dedication (John 10:22).

ANTONIA

was the name of a fort situated north-west of the temple area in Jerusalem. In the time of Jesus there was a battalion of Roman soldiers in the fort. It is believed that the governor, Pontius Pilate, lived here, and this was probably the place where he condemned Jesus to death.

See Matthew 27:27; John 18:28, 33; 19:9; Acts 21:31.
See also: Praetorium

APOCRYPHA

The word means *hidden*, and is used of certain sacred books which are not clearly part of the inspired Canon. In particular the Apocrypha comprises a set of Jewish writings which exist only in Greek. They were not accepted by the Palestinian Jews, among whom Jesus Christ was brought up, but they circulated primarily in Alexandria. The Protestant churches do not rank them with the Canon of Scripture, but the Church of Rome, and some Eastern churches, include them. When Jerome made his Latin translation, the Vulgate, in the fourth century AD, he included the books, although he recognized that they were of secondary authority, and the Roman church until recently has regarded the Vulgate as the authoritative version of the Bible.

Modern translations of the Bible frequently include the Apocrypha in a separate section, but originally some of the books were attached to, or incorporated in, the Hebrew books of the Old Testament. They are entitled as follows: 1 Esdras, 2 Esdras, Tobit, Judith, The rest of the chapters of Esther, The Wisdom of Solomon, Ecclesiasticus or the Wisdom of Jesus son of Sirach, Baruch, Letter of Jeremiah, Song of the Three, Susanna, Bel and the Dragon, Prayer of Manasseh, 1 Maccabees, 2 Maccabees.

There are some other books which are not included in any Bible, with one exception, the Book of Enoch, which is incorporated in the Ethiopian Bible. These other books include the Psalms of Solomon, the Testaments of the Twelve Patriarchs, the Book of Jubilees, the Martyrdom of Isaiah, the Apocalypse of Ezra, the Apocalypse of Baruch, and the Sibylline Oracles. These books are commonly referred to as Pseudepigrapha, or writings under assumed names. Other Jewish writings come from the Qumran Community.

There are also a few apocryphal and pseudepigraphal Christian books, including fragments of rather strange gospels, a book called The Acts of Paul and Thecla, fragments of apocalypses, and a few doctrinal pieces that come from the early second century. Some obviously emanate from heretical groups, and it is universally agreed that none deserves to be included among the New Testament scriptures.

See also: Bible, Canon, Dead Sea Scrolls

APOSTLE

means literally 'sent out', i.e. a messenger.

The word 'apostle' usually refers to one of the twelve men whom Jesus chose from among the large group of disciples who gathered around him. (Matthew 10:2-4; Luke 6:13-16; Acts 1:13).

Jesus gave the apostles particular duties and powers: They were to preach the gospel (Luke 9:6; Romans 1:1). They were to cast out evil spirits and heal the sick (Matthew 10:1). They were to be able to bind men in their sins and to absolve (forgive) them (Matthew 16:19; 18:18; John 20:23; Acts 10:43). They were to be witnesses to the acts and words, and especially the resurrection, of Jesus (Acts 1:21-22).

The Twelve Apostles:

Andrew (Matthew 4:18): Brother of Peter.

Bartholomew (Matthew 10:3): May be identical with Nathanael (John 1:45–51).
Philip (Mark 3:18).
James the Elder (Matthew 4:21): Son of Zebedee, and brother of John.
James the Younger (Matthew 10:3); son of Alphaeus.
John (Matthew 4:21): Son of Zebedee and brother of James the Elder.
Judas (Luke 6:16): Also called Thaddeus or Lebbaeus. Son or brother of James.
Judas Iscariot (Matthew 10:4).
Matthew (Matthew 10:3; Mark 2:14): Also called Levi, the tax collector.
Peter (Matthew 4:18; 10:2): Andrew's brother.
Simon the Zealot (Matthew 10:4).
Thomas (Matthew 10:3; John 20:24, 25).
Matthias (Acts 1:26): The successor of Judas Iscariot.
Paul describes himself as the Apostle to the Gentiles (Romans 1:1).

ARABIA

A peninsula between the Red Sea and the Persian Gulf, now occupied by several Arab states. The country is rich in oil. The two holy cities of Islam, Mecca and Medina, are situated in a fertile mountain region on the west coast. In Bible times the Arabians included Ishmaelites, Amalekites, Midianites and Sabeans (probably the kingdom of the Queen of Sheba).

ARAMAIC

A Semitic language akin to Hebrew. In the Old Testament Ezra 4–7 and Daniel 2–7 are in Aramaic, which had become the language of officialdom in Asia Minor. Eventually it became the normal language spoken by the Jews of Palestine in Jesus' day, although the Greek speaks of it as Hebrew and it is so translated (John 5:2; Acts 21:40). The following Aramaic phrases are quoted in their original form: *Talitha cumi* (Mark 5:41), *Ephphatha* (Mark 7:34), *Eloi, Eloi, lama sabachthani* (Mark 15:34), *Maranatha* (1 Corinthians 16:22), *Abba* (Mark 14:36; Romans 8:15; Galatians 4:6).
See also Language.

ARARAT

is the name of an area near the Black Sea and the Caspian Sea. Noah's ark landed on the mountains of Ararat (Genesis 8:4; 2 Kings 19:37).

AREOPAGUS

The Areopagus (or Mars Hill) was a hill in the Greek city of Athens. Steps hewn out of the rock led to the summit, where the High Court of Athens met. Paul the Apostle was taken before the Court of the Areopagus. One of its sections exercised particular control over the care and education of young people. This section usually investigated the teachings of wandering preachers and philosophers such as Paul. It was before this Court that Paul made his famous Areopagus speech (Acts 17:19–34).

ARIMATHEA

A small place about 18 miles (30 km) northwest of Jerusalem. Joseph, the councillor, to whom Pilate gave permission to bury Jesus, lived here. (Matthew 27:57; Mark 15:43; John 19:38).

ARK SEE NOAH

ARK OF THE COVENANT

The Ark of the Covenant or the Ark of God was a rectangular box made of acacia wood and measured $4 \times 2\frac{1}{2} \times 2\frac{1}{2}$ ft ($2\frac{1}{2}$ by $1\frac{1}{2}$ cubits). It was covered in gold and was carried on poles inserted into rings on the bottom corners. The lid was gold-plated with two winged cherubs and was called the 'mercy seat' (Exodus 25:10–22).

The Ark contained the two tablets of Moses' law (Exodus 25:16), Aaron's rod (Numbers 17:10) and a pot of manna (Exodus 16:33, 34). It was placed in the inner sanctuary or holy of holies where God spoke to his servants and was present in a special way (e.g. Exodus 25:22; Joshua 7:6).

It was the symbol of God's guidance and presence with the Israelites and was prominent at the crossing of the Jordan (Joshua 3:4) and the fall of Jericho (Joshua 6). It was captured by the Philistines at Ebenezer (1 Samuel 4) but the Philistines returned it after seven months of plagues. David placed it in a tent or tabernacle at Jerusalem (2 Samuel 6:12–17), and Solomon installed it in his magnificent temple (1 Kings 8:1). It

was evidently lost when the Babylonians destroyed Jerusalem in 587 BC (Jeremiah 3:16). There was no Ark in the second Temple in the time of Jesus.

ARMOUR SEE WEAPONS

ASHDOD

was one of the five cities of the Philistines. It was situated about 36 miles (60 km) west of Jerusalem, near the Mediterranean. The ark of the Covenant, which had been taken away from the Israelites for a time, was first brought to Ashdod, and placed in the temple of Dagon (1 Samuel 5:1–7).

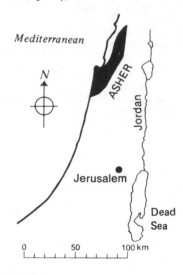

ASHER

was one of the sons of the patriarch Jacob. The tribe of Asher was one of the least important among the tribes of Israel. The home of the tribe was the country between Lake Gennesaret and the Mediterranean (Genesis 30:13; Joshua 19:24–31; Luke 2:36).

ASHERAH

Although the AV translates this as

'grove' or 'groves' Asherah is now known to be a Canaanite goddess. Her symbol was a wooden pole, probably roughly carved (Judges 6:25, 26; 1 Kings 14:15).
See also Deities, High Place

ASHKELON

was one of the five cities of the Philistines. It was situated due west of Jerusalem on the Mediterranean coast.

The city is mentioned in the story of Samson (Judges 14:19; Amos 1:8). It has given its name to a local term for spring onions, i.e. Scallions.

ASIA

When the name Asia is used in the New Testament, it means a much smaller area than the present continent of Asia. The area called Asia was a province of the Roman empire and comprised the western part of what is now Asia Minor.
See Romans 16:5; 1 Corinthians 16:19; Revelation 1:4.

ASIA MINOR

is the mountainous area of land between the Black Sea and the Eastern Mediterranean. The travel routes between the countries in the East and West went across Asia Minor.

Christianity came early to Asia Minor. The apostle Paul himself came from the city of Tarsus in Asia Minor, and his first missionary journeys went to and across Asia Minor.

In our day most of the population are Muslims.

ASS SEE DOMESTIC ANIMALS

ASSASSINS

The assassins (in Latin *sicarii*, 'dagger men') were an extremist group within the Zealot party. They were active during the time of the apostle Paul. They worked for a free Israel and wanted to remove the Romans from Palestine. They used to murder their opponents with daggers hidden under their cloaks (Acts 21:38).

ASSHURBANIPAL (Ashurbanipal)

was the best known king of Assyria, who reigned 668–626 BC. The Greeks called him Sardanapalus. His library of over 20,000 tablets has given scholars a vast amount of information about Assyrian and Babylonian history and mythology.

Asshurbanipal in his chariot as shown on a relief in Nineveh

ASSYRIA

Date (approx.)	King	Important events
1116–1090 BC	Tiglath Pileser I	Conquers Babylon This is followed by a period of weakness lasting 200 years. The kingdom of Israel is a great power under David and Solomon
884–859 BC	Asshurnasirpal	Assyria becomes a leading world power and stretches as far as the Mediterranean
858–824 BC	Shalmaneser III	Made war on Israel, according to Assyrian records
745–727 BC	Tiglath-Pileser III or Pul	The Assyrian empire is extended. The first Assyrian king to remove entire peoples into captivity (2 Kings 15:29; 16:7–9)
727–722 BC	Shalmaneser V	Samaria under siege for three years
722–705 BC	Sargon II	The city of Samaria falls and its inhabitants are taken into captivity. 722 BC (2 Kings 17)
705–681 BC	Sennacherib	Invaded Palestine and besieged Jerusalem, 701 BC (2 Kings 18:13–19:37)
668–626 BC	Asshurbanipal	The king is highly interested in architecture, literature and art and collects a very large library in Nineveh
612 BC		The fall of the Assyrian kingdom. Nineveh is destroyed by the Chaldaeans and Medes. (Jonah and Nahum are significant)

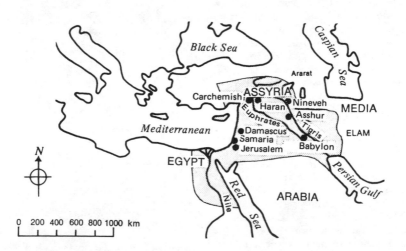

A picture from a Assyrian palace showing people from an Israelite city being taken captive to Assyria

ATHENS

The apostle Paul arrived in Athens in Greece during one of his journeys (Acts 17; 1 Thessalonians 3:1). At that time Athens was no longer of great importance in world trade, but it was still a great centre of art and learning. Paul did not succeed in forming a Christian congregation in the city.
See also Greece, Areopagus

ASSYRIA

was a country watered by the rivers Euphrates and Tigris. The Assyrians were a warlike people and for about 700 years the leading nation of the Orient.

ASTARTE

was another name for Baalat, the consort (wife) of the Canaanite god Baal. The plural, Ashtaroth, denotes the many local representations (e.g. 1 Samuel 7:3).
See also Baal, Deities

A coin from Athens showing a picture of Athena, patron goddess of the city

The Acropolis at Athens in about 430 BC, showing 1. The Parthenon, 2. A giant statue of Pallas Athena patron goddess of Athens, 3. Two other temples, 4. Entrance.

21

AUGUSTUS

Augustus, meaning 'Majesty', was a name conferred on Octavius Caesar in 27 BC, just four years after his victory at Actium over Mark Antony and Cleopatra of Egypt in the greatest sea battle of ancient times. He was Emperor when Christ was born, and Joseph and Mary had to go to Jerusalem for a census. His reign was a period of great stability and strength for the Roman Empire. He lived from 63 BC to AD 14 (Luke 2:1).

Drawing of a statue of Caesar Augustus

BAAL

The Hebrew word 'Baal' means master or possessor. Every piece of land in Canaan had its own god or Baal who was the 'owner', so the gods of Baal encountered by the Israelites were pagan earth gods. There was, however, a Canaanite

A picture of Baal found in Phoenicia

god, Baal, and it was one of his manifestations, the Tyrian Melkart-Baal, whom Jezebel tried to impose on Israel; and whose prophets were defeated by Elijah in the contest on Mount Carmel.
See also Deities, High Place

BABYLON

(or Babel) was the capital of Babylonia from about 1800 BC. The name of the city means 'The gate of God'. Babylon was destroyed, but was rebuilt by King Nebuchadnezzar II. The greatest part of the archaeological finds in excavations of the city dates from his reign. In the time of Christ Babylon was in ruins.

Babylon was built on both sides of the Euphrates, and was defended by a moat, double walls with towers, and eight city gates. The best known of these was called the Gate of Ishtar. There were numerous temples in the city. In the temple which

The Ishtar Gate at Babylon

was consecrated to Bel-Marduk, the god of the city, there was a tower, often identified with the Tower of Babel. The sides of its base were about 325 ft (100 m), and its height 295 ft (90 m). One of the seven wonders of the ancient world was found in Babylon. It was the palace with the 'hanging gardens', so-called because they were constructed on a mound and were consequently seen above the street level.

See also Tower of Babel

BABYLONIA

The kingdom of Babylonia consisted of the plains around the lower course of the rivers Euphrates and Tigris. It was situated approximately where the country of Iraq is now. The land was fertile, thanks to irrigation channels from the rivers. The climate was hot. In the spring the country was often threatened by huge floods, due to the rapid melting of the snow in the hills of Armenia, where the rivers had their source. The farmers grew wheat, barley, figs, olives and dates.

The capital of the country was Babylon. The city of Ur, which was Abraham's home, was in Babylonia.

The Babylonians were interested in literature, art and religion. They were skilled builders, merchants, craftsmen and farmers.

The Babylonians, as well as the

Assyrians, used a form of writing called cuneiform script. The writing signs are wedge-shaped. To begin with, the cuneiform script was pictorial, but it gradually became alphabetical. People wrote this script by impressing the signs into tablets of damp clay with a wedge-shaped stick, called a stylus. Large numbers of these tablets have been found, and scholars have been able to interpret the script.

Babylonia is regarded as the home of astrology; the interpretation of the stars. It was thought that one could read future events on earth from the movements of the stars and planets. The knowledge of stars and celestial bodies, i.e. the science of astronomy, increased at the same time as people attempted to interpret the movement of the stars. They learnt to predict eclipses of the moon and to determine the length of the orbits of the planets around the sun.

See also Babylon, Writing

Cunieform writing

Date (approx.)	King	Particular events
1700 BC	Hammurabi	Babylonia is unified into one kingdom. Hammurabi drew up a detailed legal code, which has been translated
1600–626 BC		Babylonia has a period of weakness, and is conquered by Assyria. Merodach-Baladan (2 Kings 20:12) made an unsuccessful attempt at rebellion about 715 BC
626–605 BC	Nabopolassar	Babylonia again becomes a great power (the New Babylonian kingdom)
605–562 BC	Nebuchadnezzar II	A great conqueror. His conquests included Egypt and Palestine. He captured Jerusalem in 597 BC and took the best of its people to Babylon (2 Kings 24; Daniel 1:1–7). In a second invasion he destroyed Jerusalem and deported most of the people to Babylon (2 Kings 25)
539 BC		Babylonia is conquered by the Persian king Cyrus, who allowed the exiles to return (Ezra 1)

BALM

was the sweetly scented resin of a small shrublike tree. This tree grew in Palestine, especially around the city of Jericho, where the climate was warm and humid. The resin was used in various ointments, in medicines, as incense, scent and in embalming substances (Genesis 37:25; 43:11; Jeremiah 8:22; 51:8; Ezekiel 27:17).
See also Embalming

BATH SEE MEASURES

BEAR SEE ANIMALS

BEAUTIFUL GATE

The Beautiful Gate (or 'the gate called Beautiful') was a gate in Herod's Temple. This gate led from the outer Temple court to the women's court (Acts 3:2, 10).
See also Temple

BED SEE FURNITURE

BEER-SHEBA

was an oasis near the southern border of Palestine. The name means 'The Well of the Seven' or 'The Well of Swearing' (Genesis 21:31). People sometimes used the expression 'from Dan to Beer-Sheba', which meant 'from the northern to the southern border of Palestine', like the expression 'from Land's End to John o' Groats'.

The patriarchs Abraham, Isaac and Jacob visited Beer-Sheba. Isaac built an altar there, and later there was a temple on the site.
See Genesis 21:31; 26:23; Amos 5:5; 8:14

BEKA SEE MONEY

BENJAMIN

Jacob's youngest son, whose mother, Rachel, died in giving him birth. He was the only son born in Canaan (Genesis 35:16–20). The tribe of Benjamin were settled on the northern boundary of Judah, by whom it was eventually

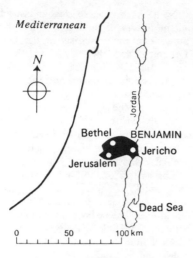

up to heaven (Genesis 28:11–19). For a time the ark of the covenant, containing the tables of the Law, was kept at Bethel (Judges 20:26–28).

The prophet and judge Samuel spent some time here each year, in order to pass judgement in legal controversies between Israelites (1 Samuel 7:16).

King Jeroboam, who reigned over the northern kingdom after the division of the country, made Bethel into the Jerusalem of the north. He set up an altar and a golden calf, which was supposed to be the image of the God of Israel (1 Kings 12:26–30), and it was not until some 300 years later that King Josiah of Judah destroyed it (2 Kings 23:15–20) together with the temple that had been built there (Amos 7:10).

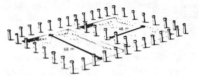

The pool at Bethesda as suggested by archaeological discoveries

absorbed. Three famous men of Benjamin were King Saul (1 Samuel 9:1), the prophet Jeremiah (Jeremiah 1:1) and the apostle Paul (Romans 11:1).

BEROEA

A minor city in Macedonia, visited by the apostle Paul during his journeys. In Beroea many people came to believe in Christ through Paul's preaching (Acts 17:10–12).

BETHANY

was a village slightly less than 2 miles (3 km) east of Jerusalem, where the two sisters Martha and Mary lived with their brother Lazarus. Jesus visited their home on several occasions.
See Matthew 21:17; 26:6; Luke 24:50; John 11:1; 11:18.

BETHEL

is a very old city, which was in existence even at the time of Abraham. It is situated about 12 miles (19 km) north of Jerusalem.

Abraham built an altar to the Lord there (Genesis 12:8) and it was here that Jacob dreamt about the ladder reaching

BETHESDA or BETH-ZATHA

was the name of a pool in Jerusalem, where Jesus healed a man who had been a cripple for 38 years (John 5:1–9). Archaeologists have identified it with a large pool with colonnades north of the site of the Temple in Jerusalem.

BETHLEHEM

A town approximately 5 miles (8 km) south of Jerusalem. Its name in Hebrew means 'House of Bread'. The patriarch Jacob buried his wife Rachel near Bethlehem (Genesis 35:19, 20). It was the city where King David was born (Ruth 4:11–22; 1 Samuel 16:1; Luke 2:4).

The Messiah was to be born in Bethlehem according to the prophecy of Micah. Jesus was born in Bethlehem, as had been indicated by Micah 5:2. A church, called the Church of the Nativity, was built in AD 330 over the spot where, according to the Church's tradition, Jesus was born. Under the church there are several caves. In one of these crypts there is a silver star on the floor, marking the site on which Jesus' manger is supposed to have stood.

BETHPHAGE

A place mentioned in connection with Jesus' going up to Jerusalem. Bethphage was situated on the Mount of Olives, but its exact location is not known (Matthew 21:1; Mark 11:1; Luke 19:29).

BETHSAIDA

was a town close to the Sea of Tiberias, but it is disputed whether it was to the west or east. The apostles Peter, Andrew and Philip were from Bethsaida, and Jesus often visited the town (Matthew 11:21; Mark 6:45; 8:22; Luke 9:10; John 1:44; 12:21).

BETROTHAL SEE MARRIAGE, WEDDING

BIBLE

The word 'Bible' comes from the Greek word *biblia*, which means 'books'. It has become the word most commonly used to describe the Holy Scriptures of the Christian Church.

No book has made so great an impact on the history of the world as has the Bible. The Bible consists of the Old Testament and the New Testament, which might be translated, more precisely, the Old Covenant and the New Covenant.

Most of the Old Testament was originally written in Hebrew, though some few parts were written in Aramaic, a language closely related to Hebrew. See ARAMAIC.

The writers of the New Testament used Greek, a language which at that time was used over the entire Mediterranean area. The 66 books found in most editions of the Bible are called 'canonical' books. 'Canon' is a Greek word meaning 'rule', and is applied to those books which various councils of the Church considered should form the Old and New Testaments. The canon of the Old Testament was preserved on separate scrolls, but in more or less its present form dates from about 130 BC, and that of the New Testament from about AD 397 in the west at the Council of Carthage.

For many centuries the contents of the books of the Old Testament were passed on by word of mouth from one generation to another. Eventually they were written down on papyrus or parchment scrolls. The Old Testament was written in Hebrew, and was later translated into Greek. The most important of these translations is known as the Sep-

| 1. Hebrew, | 2. Aramaic, | 3. Greek |

The languages of the Bible.

tuagint, or LXX (according to tradition the work was carried out by 70 – in Roman numerals LXX – translators) and dates from about 250 BC onwards at intervals. The New Testament was written in Greek, and was also written on papyrus or parchment. The oldest of the books of the New Testament is Paul's First Letter to the Thessalonians. Altogether the New Testament dates from AD 50 to 100, approximately.

Perhaps during the second century AD, and certainly during the third century, leaves of papyrus began to be bound together in book form. This was the so-called codex. One of the oldest of these which has been preserved dates from about AD 300 and is called the Codex Sinaiticus, since it was found in a monastery on Mount Sinai.

Among the earliest translations of the Bible were those into the Latin language. One of these is called the Vulgate, 'the common version' which was completed in the 4th century by Jerome, and which forms the basis for all later translations approved by the Roman Catholic Church. Jerome included the apocryphal books with some hesitation. (See APOCRYPHA.)

The first attempted translation of the Bible into English was made in the 1380's by John Wycliffe. The first translation into German, made by Martin Luther, was published in 1522. William Tyndale produced the first English translation of the New Testament in 1525 and a large portion of the Old Testament before his death in 1536.

The translation of the Bible into new languages, and the improvement and revision of existing versions, is a continuous process. At present, the Bible or parts of the Bible have been translated into some 1,200 languages. These languages are spoken by about 95% of the population of the world.

There are Bible societies, the work of which is mainly concerned with the translating, printing, selling and giving away of Bibles in all parts of the world. During one year recently, these societies together printed almost 40 million Bibles and parts of the Bible.

See also Apocrypha, Canon

BIRDS

There are great numbers of birds in Palestine and in the neighbouring countries. Some species, especially pigeons, but later also hens, were kept for domestic purposes.

Bird catching, a drawing from an old Egyptian painting

Nineteen species of birds were unclean to the Israelites, and therefore could not be used for food (Leviticus 11:13–19). Those wild birds which were regarded as clean were commonly caught in snares or nets (Psalm 124:7; Ecclesiastes 9:12).

Dove, turtle-dove, pigeon. Pigeons were kept as domestic animals in Old Testament times in pigeon houses (Isaiah 60:8). Pigeon was the only meat the poor could afford to eat. Pigeons or doves were used as the poor man's sacrifices (Leviticus 5:7; Luke 2:24). The migration of the turtle-dove is a welcome sign of spring (Song of Solomon 2:12).
See also: Genesis 8:8; Psalm 55:6; Matthew 3:16; Mark 11:15; Luke 2:24.

Eagle. The eagle was an unclean bird (Leviticus 11:13). It was praised for its swiftness and strength (Jeremiah 4:13; Ezekiel 17:3) and for its care of its young (Exodus 19:4; Deuteronomy 32:11).

The eagle could reach a great age and keep its vigour and strength for a very long time (Psalm 103:5; Isaiah 40:31).

The falcon, hawk and kite were counted as unclean birds, and therefore could not be eaten (Leviticus 11:14, 16).

Fighting cocks, an Assyrian picture from the 16th century BC

Hen. The Israelites learnt from the Persians to use the hen as a domestic animal (Nehemiah 5:18; Matthew 23:37; 26:34).

Owl. The owl was an unclean bird. To see an owl was also regarded as an omen of ill fortune and death (Leviticus 11:17; Psalm 102:6).

Partridge. This bird was found from the mountains of Lebanon southwards, and was often hunted (1 Samuel 26:20).

Peacock. The peacock was traditionally supposed to have been introduced into Palestine by King Solomon, through trade with India (1 Kings 10:22).

Pelican. The pelican was an unclean bird, mostly migratory (Leviticus 11:18).

Catching quails in Egypt. A tomb painting from the 15th century BC

Quail is a migrant bird, related to the domestic fowl. The Israelites were allowed to use them as food. During the desert wanderings God provided quails driven by the wind which were caught by the Israelites. Migrant birds can still be caught in nets in this way, by the thousand, and in 1920 three million were caught in Egypt. The bird is about 8 inches long (Exodus 16:12–13; Numbers 11:31–32).

Raven. The first bird mentioned in the Bible, the raven is common in Palestine. It is counted among the unclean birds (Genesis 8:7; Leviticus 11:15; 1 Kings 17:4–6; Job 38:41; Luke 12:24).

Sparrow. According to the Law of Moses, it was permissible to eat sparrows as food. They were accordingly caught in nets on the cornfields after the harvest, and were sold very cheaply in the market place (Psalm 84:3; 124:7; Matthew 10:29; Luke 12:6).

Vulture. An unclean bird, the vulture lived by scavenging, mainly on carrion and rubbish from towns and villages (Leviticus 11:13). In Micah 1:16 and Matthew 24:28 the description shows that the translation 'eagle' should be 'vulture', which flies to feed on dead bodies and is bald round the neck (so NEB).

BIRTHRIGHT

In a Jewish family, the first-born or eldest son became the head of the family when his father died or was absent from home. On his father's death, by right of birth or birthright he inherited twice as much as every other son (Deuteronomy 21:17). In Genesis 25:29–34, we are told how Esau sold his birthright to his younger brother Jacob in exchange for some bread and a bowl of lentil soup. Hebrews 12:16 describes Esau's action as immoral and irreligious. He cared for immediate satisfaction for his stomach rather than being in the line of God's promise.
See Inheritance

BISHOP

The Greek word *episkopos* is translated bishop or overseer. (The American Episcopal Church, like the Church of England, calls its overseers bishops.) In the New Testament, the word is used in two ways. It describes Christ's concern for his followers as Shepherd of the sheep and Guardian of the souls of Christians (1 Peter 2:25). More commonly it describes the leaders of local churches responsible for maintaining the quality of the church. 1 Timothy 3 and Titus 1:7 list the qualifications of a bishop. He must be morally upright in character, respected, hospitable, patient, gentle, mature in faith and married – quite a list! 1 Timothy 5:17 implies that another name for bishops is elders.

BITHYNIA

was a district in Asia Minor, on the shore of the Black Sea. Paul intended to visit Bithynia during his second missionary journey, but was prevented from doing so by an act of God (Acts 16:6, 7).

BITTER HERBS

formed, and still form, part of the Jews' Passover feast (Exodus 12:8; Numbers 9:11). They are eaten together with lamb and unleavened bread; and are meant to remind those taking part of the great sufferings of the Israelites in Egypt. The unleavened bread and bitter herbs could be prepared quickly; and this reminded the Israelites of the haste with which their flight out of Egypt took place.

BLASPHEME/BLASPHEMY

To blaspheme is to mock and insult God and his name, perhaps the most serious sin any man can commit. The penalty for blasphemy in Old and New Testament times was to be stoned (Leviticus 24:10–23; 1 Kings 21:10; Acts 6:11). God can also be blasphemed against when people blaspheme his representatives. In Mark 14:61–64 Jesus was accused of blasphemy by the High Priest. Any charge against God's Son is directed against God. Blasphemy against the Holy Spirit is called the unforgivable sin in Matthew 12:32 and Mark 3:29. This probably means to reject Christ by deliberately rejecting the work of his Spirit in oneself, a sin which might be committed only when there is continued resistance and opposition to God.

BLESSING

In the Old Testament there is a special formula of benediction which is to be given by the priests (Numbers 6:23–26).

BLOOD

The law of Moses prohibited the drinking of blood or the eating of meat with blood remaining in it. This remains the Jewish rule up to the present day.

Some people think that blood in the Old Testament, which the Israelites sprinkled on the altar as a sacrifice to atone for sin, speaks of life as it is in the body. But the evidence links blood with death more than life. Out of 362 references to blood, 203 link it with death and sacrifice.

In addition to the regular offering of the blood for purification of the people and atonement, the covenant or promise given by God at Sinai was sealed with a blood sacrifice (Exodus 24:3–8).

The death of Jesus Christ is the New Testament conclusion and fulfilment of all the Old Testament blood rituals. Romans 5:9 shows that through Jesus' death and shed blood, we are justified and made right with God. Colossians 1:20 reaffirms this. In Matthew 26:28 Jesus says that his blood is shed for the sake of our sins.

All that the sacrifices of the Old Testament foreshadowed, Jesus fulfilled, and he himself referred to his death as the blood of the covenant (Mark 14:24), symbolized by the wine in communion services. Out of death came life – the resurrection life of Jesus. The blood of the Passover lamb in the Old Testament, when God freed the Israelites from slavery in Egypt, becomes in the New Testament the blood of Jesus whose death brought life to the world (1 Corinthians 5:7). The blood as a symbol of death was the agent for bringing life. 'Behold, the Lamb of God, who takes away the sin of the world!' (John 1:29). See also: Communion, Soul

BLOOD VENGEANCE

meant that the relatives of a murdered man had the right to kill the murderer. Blood vengeance was not allowed if the murder had been committed in self-

defence. Some think that later the relatives might receive a sum of ransom money instead of avenging the dead man, as, e.g. the Koran later allows. In the New Testament the use of blood vengeance appears to have ceased (Genesis 9:5–6; Exodus 21:12–14; Numbers 35:16–25).
See also: Murder

A typical scroll

BOOK

The art of writing dates back several thousand years. It was known in Egypt as early as 2000 BC.

People wrote on blocks of wet clay, with a stylus made of bone or wood; on pieces of pottery; or on papyrus, a thick Egyptian sedge, which was split into thin slices so that they could be glued together to form sheets (see illustration under Birds). At a later date people began to use parchment, made out of the skin of sheep or goats. Both papyrus and parchment writings were made up in long rolls or scrolls. Books with pages were rare. They may well have become more common when Christians, who were too poor to be able to afford scrolls, began to use fragments of parchment for their copies of the Gospels and Acts. When these fragments were fastened together along one edge, the result was a book with pages.

An early book

barley were most common, but bread made from wheat was used, too. Early in the morning the women began to grind

Pestle and Mortar

Handmill

BRAZIER

A metal heater that burned charcoal (Jeremiah 36:22).

the flour. They would use a mortar and pestle or various kinds of handmills (Deuteronomy 24:6; Judges 16:21; Lamentations 5:13; Matthew 24:41).

BREAD

The saying 'Bread is the staff of life' is based on Leviticus 26:26; Psalm 105:16; Isaiah 3:1; Ezekiel 4:16. It was the most important food item for the Israelites. The women made bread every day. Round loaves of coarsely ground

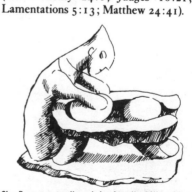

Clay figure representing a baker from the 10th or 9th century BC, from northern Palestine

Women grinding

The coarsely textured flour was mixed with water and salt and worked into a dough. Sometimes leftovers of old dough, 'leaven', were used in order to make the new dough rise (Matthew 13:33). But if the women were in a hurry they would make unleavened bread.

The dough was shaped into thin rounds of bread. The simplest way of baking the loaves of bread was to place them on hot ashes or heated stones, or on a griddle over the fire (Leviticus 2:5).

Oven made with a clay dish

A simple oven was made from an inverted clay dish or shallow bowl, which was put on top of the fire, with its rim resting on a few stones. The thin round loaves of bread were placed on top of the dish. Because bread was so essential to basic life and survival, Jesus used it as a picture of spiritual life. God gave physical life to the starving Israelites in the desert with manna, or bread from heaven. So, too, Jesus offers eternal

A large clay oven in which a fire was lit, when the fire was burning low, pieces of dough were placed inside the oven.

spiritual life to those who receive the Bread of Life which is Jesus himself (John 6:31–50): Jesus said he was the living bread, 'If anyone eats of this bread, he will live for ever, and the bread which I shall give for the life of the world is my flesh.'
See also: Communion

BREAD OF THE PRESENCE (AV Shewbread)

The twelve cakes of wheat bread which were placed on a particular gilded table in the Holy Place in the Tabernacle and the Temple at Jerusalem were called the Bread of the Presence (Exodus 25:30; 1 Chronicles 9:32). They were to be changed on every Sabbath, when the priests would eat the old cakes of bread (Leviticus 24:5–9).

The Bread of the Presence was probably originally some form of offering. In an emergency the high priest allowed David and his men to eat the loaves (1 Samuel 21:1–6; Matthew 12:4)

BREAKING OF BREAD SEE COMMUNION

Foreign brick workers in Egypt as shown on a mural at Thebes

BRICK

was used as a building material in Palestine. A worker would mix straw and clay by treading and kneading them together with his bare feet (Exodus 5:7). The mixture was then pressed into a mould, in order to make all the bricks of a regular size. These bricks were then

dried in the sun. More durable bricks were fired in a kiln (2 Samuel 12:31). See Genesis 11:3; Exodus 5:7; Isaiah 9:10; Nahum 3:14.
See also Crafts

C

BRONZE SEE COPPER

BRONZE SERPENT

During their wandering in the wilderness the Israelites became impatient and complained against God and Moses. The Lord sent poisonous snakes in among the people, and many died of snakebites. Then Moses was told to make a snake (or serpent) of bronze and put it on a pole. If those who had received deadly snake-bites looked up at the bronze serpent, they would live (Numbers 21:6–9). Very many years later, King Hezekiah had the bronze snake destroyed. He knew that many Israelites worshipped the bronze serpent instead of the God of Israel (2 Kings 18:4).

In the New Testament, Jesus compares himself to the 'serpent in the wilderness'. In the same way as the snake was hung on a pole to give life to the dying, Christ himself had to be hung on the cross to give life to and save those who were lost (John 3:14, 15).

BURNT OFFERING SEE SACRIFICE, ALTAR

BUSHEL SEE MEASURES

BYBLOS

or Gebal was a city on the coast of the Mediterranean in the country of Phoenicia. Byblos was famous for shipbuilding. It was above all a city of commerce and seafaring. The Greeks named it Byblos (papyrus) because it was a centre of papyrus import from Egypt. (See BOOK.) Gebal is mentioned in Joshua 13:5; 1 Kings 5:18; Ezekiel 27:9.

CAESAR SEE AUGUSTUS, ROME

CAESAREA

A magnificent city built by Herod the Great on the shores of the Mediterranean 65 miles to the north-west of Jerusalem. It was noted for its palace and temple and was the official residence of the Herodian line of kings and of the Roman governors or 'procurators'. It was a central trading town between Tyre and Egypt and had a large harbour. The Temple was dedicated to Caesar and Rome and contained vast statues of Augustus Caesar. Pontius Pilate lived in this city of mixed population. The Roman centurion Cornelius lived in Caesarea, and his conversion and baptism described in Acts 10 was a turning point in the history of the Church. Peter understood for the first time through a dream, that 'God shows no partiality' and that the gospel was intended for non-Jews (Gentiles) as well as Jews. Cornelius' conversion was the proof of this to Peter.

Caesarea also played an important part in the life of Paul. He landed at the port at the end of his second and third missionary journeys. His fateful decision to visit Jerusalem was made here, and it was to Caesarea that he was sent for trial by Felix, before being imprisoned for two years (Acts 23:23–26:32).

CAESAREA PHILIPPI

was a town situated near the source of the River Jordan. The town was expanded by the tetrarch (ruler) Philip. It

33

was at Caesarea Philippi that Peter confessed before Christ: 'You are the Christ, the Son of the living God.' (Matthew 16:13–16; Mark 8:27–29.)

CALENDAR SEE FESTIVALS, TIMES AND SEASONS

CAMEL

A four-legged animal famous for its ability to cross deserts because it can carry in its hump enough water supply for days and even weeks. In Arabia lives the one-humped or dromedary camel, not to be confused with the two-humped Bactrian camel of Turkey, Iran and Afghanistan. In Bible times camels were not just a means of transport but also a symbol of wealth. Abraham's herd and that of Job were particularly renowned. In the period of the Judges, Israel was troubled by camel-riding Midianites, repelled by Gideon (Judges 6 to 8). Saul and David fought similar battles against camel-riding Amalekites (1 Samuel 15:3; 27:9; 30:17). Elisha was given 40 camel-loads of gifts (2 Kings 8:9). In New Testament times, John the Baptist was clothed in camel's hair and Jesus used the camel for a word-picture in Matthew 19:24.

CANA

was a village in Galilee where Jesus performed his first miracle. When the wine gave out during a wedding celebration, Jesus changed water into wine. Cana's modern identification is uncer-

tain, but it was probably a few miles north of Nazareth (John 2:1–11; 4:46; 21:2).

CANAAN SEE PALESTINE

CANAANITES

The word is used in the Old Testament with two different meanings.

(a) The whole of the population living between the river Jordan and the Mediterranean, when the Israelites began to penetrate into Canaan after their wandering in the wilderness, were called Canaanites (Genesis 12:6; 24:3; 50:11).

(b) The word also referred to a well-defined group of peoples who had settled on the coast and in the fortified cities on the plain (Numbers 13:29; 14:25; Joshua 11:3; 17:16).

The Canaanites followed many gods, from El the high god to Baal and Hadad the storm god. Others included Dagan and goddesses like Astarte and Asherah. Relics of temples have survived and texts from Ugarit mention many animals sacrificed to the gods.
See: Deities

CANDLESTICKS SEE LAMP

CANON

is a Greek work which meant 'reed', 'rule', or 'standard'. The word 'canon' is used about those books and writings which were generally considered worthy of being included in the Old and New

A camel train

Testaments to form the rule of faith and practice and the measurement of truth. The Old Testament canon, in roughly its present form, was determined by about 100 BC and finalized in AD 90, that of the New Testament in or a few years after AD 390.

See also: Bible

CAPERNAUM

A city on the north-western shore of the Sea of Galilee. Jesus made it his headquarters for some time (Matthew 4:13; Mark 1:21–2:14) and here called Matthew to be his disciple (Mark 2:13–17), but eventually condemned it for its lack of faith (Luke 10:15).

CARMEL

is a mountain on the coast of the Mediterranean in western Galilee. Oak, laurel, almond and olive trees grow on the slopes of the mountain. In the Old Testament Carmel is referred to as being rich in forests. The prophet Elijah built an altar to the Lord on Mount Carmel, and demonstrated to Israel that the Lord, and not Baal, was God (1 Kings 18:19–39).

CAROB TREE SEE TREES

CARPENTER SEE CRAFTS

CASSIA SEE HERBS AND SPICES

CASTOR OIL PLANT

The castor oil plant (AV 'gourd') is a shrub which grows exceptionally quickly and dies if the least little damage is done to it. It has large leaves, similar to chestnut leaves, which give a pleasant shade. Its fruit is a thorny pod with three large seeds, which contain oil. The prophet Jonah sought refuge from the sun under a castor oil plant. The Book of Jonah tells us that God made the shrub grow in order to provide shade for the prophet (Jonah 4:6, 7).

The wild gourds of 2 Kings 4:39 were probably colocynths, which resemble cucumbers, but have an irritant and purgative effect, which may actually prove fatal.

CATACOMBS

On the outskirts of the city of Rome there were subterranean grave vaults,

The catacombs at Rome

several storeys deep. They were called catacombs. Along long and dark corridors, graves had been hewn out of the soft rock, where people laid their dead. The total length of these corridors below ground is about 560 miles (900 km).

From the end of the first century into the fourth century, the Christians were able to hide in the catacombs in times of persecution. They used them as burial places and they would also hold services there.

In the catacombs there are wall paintings and pictures which have sometimes been hewn into the rock. These pictures often show events and persons from the Bible. By studying the catacombs scholars have been able to find out a great deal about the Christians of the early Church.

CAVES

are often mentioned in the Bible. There are great numbers of caves in the hills of Palestine. People would use caves occasionally as dwellings (Genesis 19:30; Ezekiel 33:27), for hiding (1 Kings 18:4) and for burial (Genesis 23).

CEDAR SEE TREES

CENTURION

A centurion was a Roman army officer in command of one hundred (a century of) foot soldiers. He usually had great experience of and responsibility for command, and performed a key function in the organization of the army throughout the Roman Empire.

In the gospels of Matthew and Luke the first Gentile who meets Jesus is a centurion (Matthew 8:5-13; Luke 7:2-10). It is the centurion in charge of Jesus' execution who says 'Truly this was the Son of God!' – the first Gentile recorded in the Gospels to have made this witness (Matthew 27:54; Mark 15:39).

The conversion of the centurion

Cornelius is described in Acts 10. A centurion was in charge of the apostle Paul and some other prisoners on the voyage to Rome (Acts 27:1).

CHALDAEA, CHALDAEANS

The Chaldaeans lived on the Persian Gulf. They were one of the peoples who together with others created the Babylonian empire. Several of the powerful rulers of Babylonia were Chaldaeans. One of these was Nebuchadnezzar, 605-562 BC, who in 586 BC conquered Jerusalem and took away the inhabitants of Judah to captivity in Babylon. For the history of the Chaldaeans, see under Babylonia.

The Chaldaeans were highly interested in the knowledge and interpretation of the stars and the word Chaldaean itself came to mean 'wise man', or 'astrologer'.

CHAPTER

The oldest biblical manuscripts have no divisions into chapters and verses. The present arrangement into chapters was made by an English priest, Stephen Langton, in AD 1206.

The division into verses of the Old Testament was done by learned Jewish scribes. The printer Robert Stephanus in Paris divided the New Testament into verses in 1551. The Bible contains 1,189 chapters and 31,173 verses.

CHERUBIM SEE ANGEL

CHORAZIN

was a city northwest of the Sea of Galilee. Jesus appears to have worked miracles in Chorazin, which are not written down in the New Testament. In excavations of the city, archaeologists have found the ruins of a synagogue with a type of ornamentation which was unusual among the Jews. Jesus condemned the city in Luke 10 for its failure to repent (Matthew 11:20–21; Luke 10:13).

CHOSEN PEOPLE

This expression is used as a name of Israel, to indicate that Israel was especially chosen by God from among all the nations, and is his 'own possession among all peoples' (Exodus 19:5; Deuteronomy 7:6–11). The phrase is also used of the body of Christians (1 Peter 2:9).

CHRIST SEE JESUS CHRIST

CHRISTIANS

It was in Antioch that the disciples of Jesus were first called Christians (Acts 11:26). It was not common for the followers of Christ to use the words Christian or Christians about themselves until the second century, although it appears from Tacitus to have been a common description of them in Rome in AD 60.

See also: Acts 26:28; 1 Peter 4:16

CHRONICLES, BOOKS OF THE

Jewish tradition suggests that the author of the Chronicles was Ezra, but this view contains certain problems although the approach of the book suggests he was a priest. The Chronicler probably had access to a book called 'the book of the kings of Judah and Israel' (2 Chronicles 16:11) – perhaps official annals of the kings – and to writings linked with certain prophets like Samuel, Nathan, Gad (1 Chronicles 29:29), Iddo (2 Chronicles 12:15), Jehu (2 Chronicles 20:34) and Hozai (2 Chronicles 33:19, RSV mg). He gives a history from the rise and fall of the monarchy of David's house to the history of the Temple and priesthood. Therefore he has a special interest in the theological and religious

history of Israel, and doubtless had access to priestly records.

Outline of contents	Chapter
The history of Israel up to King Saul	1 Chronicles 1–9
Saul's death	1 Chronicles 10
The story of King David	1 Chronicles 11–29
The story of King Solomon	2 Chronicles 1–9
The history of the kingdom of Judah up to the end of the Exile	2 Chronicles 10–36

CHURCH

In the New Testament, the Greek word for 'church' is *ekklesia*, which means a local congregation of believers and never a building. It is used to describe a church meeting (1 Corinthians 11:18; 14:4; 3 John 6). Also to describe a group of Christians living in one place (Matthew 18:17; Acts 5:11; Romans 16:1,5; 1 Corinthians 1:2; Galatians 1:22; Philemon 2).

As a general name of Christians in a collective sense, *ekklesia* is found in Matthew 16:18; Acts 9:31; 1 Corinthians 12:28; Ephesians 1:22; 3:10. This is often called the church 'universal' or the body of Christ. In 1 Corinthians 10:32 and 1 Thessalonians 1:1; 2:14, we read of the Church of God or Christ to which all believers belong. Whereas today people think of the Church as a building or institution, this kind of thinking is unknown in the Bible.

CILICIA

was a coastal area in S.E. Asia Minor. The district capital was Tarsus, where the apostle Paul was born and grew up.

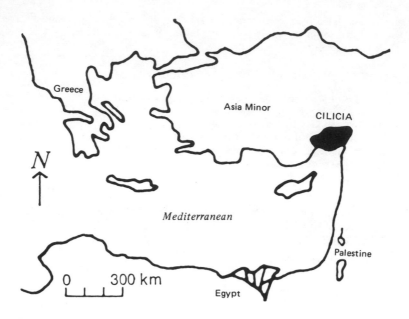

Greece

Asia Minor

CILICIA

N
↑

Mediterranean

Palestine

0   300 km

Egypt

Many Jews lived in Cilicia. Christianity came to the area at an early date. See Acts 15:23; 15:41; Galatians 1:21.

CINNAMON SEE HERBS

CIRCUMCISION

is an operation whereby the foreskin on the male sexual organ is removed. In Israel the circumcision usually took place when the boy was one week old (Genesis 21:4). At this time he was also given his name (Luke 1:59; 2:21). Circumcision meant that the boy was brought into God's covenant with Abraham (Genesis 17:9–14). It was the sign which showed that he belonged to Israel (Joshua 5:2–7). In the New Testament it was especially the apostle Paul who stressed that the Gentiles did not have to be circumcised in order to become Christians (Galatians 5:2–6). The circumcision was something which was part of the Jewish tradition, but not of

Christianity. Even in the Old Testament inward circumcision of the heart is the essential meaning of circumcision (Deuteronomy 30:6; Jeremiah 4:4).

There are some similarities between what circumcision means in Judaism and what baptism means in the Christian church (e.g. Colossians 2:11, 12), but there are also differences.

CLIMATE

Palestine has hot summers without rain, and cool winters with perpetual rain (a sub-tropical climate). There the year only really has two seasons: the rainy season during November to April, and the dry season during May to October. The winters are not very cold and snow seldom falls. There are usually not more than five or six nights during the year when the temperature goes below freezing point. There is also a great difference between day and night temperatures (Exodus 22:26, 27).

See also: Agriculture

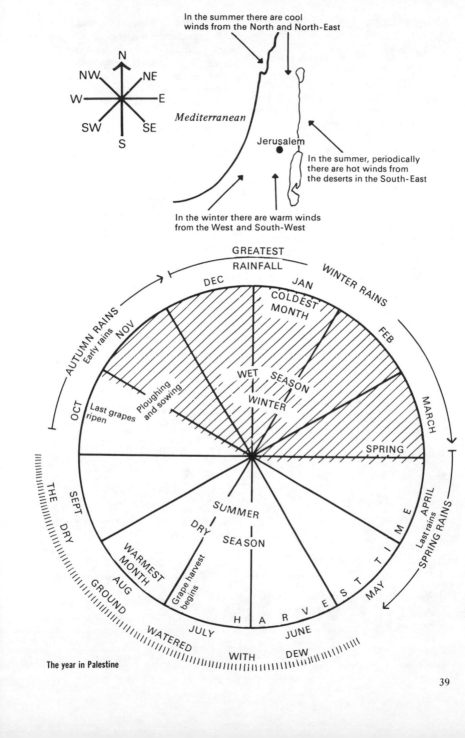

In the summer there are cool
winds from the North and North-East

N

NW   NE

W————E

SW   SE

S

Mediterranean

Jerusalem

In the summer, periodically
there are hot winds from
the deserts in the South-East

In the winter there are warm winds
from the West and South-West

GREATEST
RAINFALL

WINTER RAINS

AUTUMN RAINS

DEC   JAN

COLDEST
MONTH

Early rains NOV   FEB

OCT   Ploughing
and sowing

WET   SEASON

Last grapes   WINTER
ripen

SPRING

MARCH

THE

SEPT   SUMMER   APRIL

DRY   Last rains   SPRING RAINS

DRY   SEASON   HARVEST TIME

WARMEST
MONTH

MAY

GROUND   AUG   Grape harvest
begins

WATERED   JULY   H A R V E S T   JUNE

WITH   DEW

The year in Palestine

COINS SEE MONEY

COLOSSAE

was a small city in the province of Phrygia in Asia Minor. In Colossae, there was a Christian church, to the members of which the apostle Paul addressed one of his letters. Paul himself was not the founder of this church (Colossians 2:1), but a man named Epaphras (Colossians 1:7).

COLOSSEUM

The Colosseum was the largest amphitheatre of the ancient world, and was so named because it was indeed colossal. It was opened in AD 80 in Rome. The amphitheatre was a round or oval building around an arena with ascending rows of seats, and without a roof. The Colosseum theatre was 205 yds (188 m) long, 170 yds (156 m) wide and 52½ yds (48 m) high. It seated approximately 50,000 people.

Here men with swords fought to the death, animals were made to fight each other and many of the early Christians were put into the arena to be torn to pieces by ferocious, starving animals.

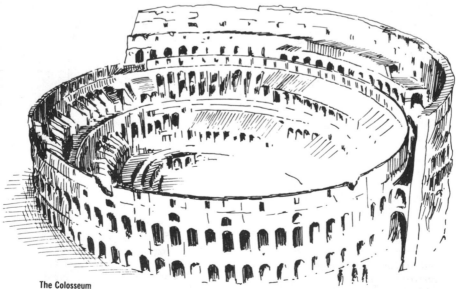

The Colosseum

COLOSSIANS

The letter to the Colossians was written by Paul from prison, almost certainly when in Rome around AD 61. There were two reasons why the letter was written. First, Paul was sending a messenger to Philemon in Colossae in connection with the Christian runaway slave Onesimus (Colossians 4:7–9 and Philemon). Secondly, Epaphras, who founded the church there (Colossians 1:7) had reported to Paul some disturbing news about false teaching within the church which was threatening to lead people away from the truth. This false teaching included near worship of the spirit world, to which Paul replied by stating the fullness of Christ and of the power of God in him. The false teachers also placed wrong importance on outward rites and observances (feasts and fasts, new moons and sabbaths). Paul instructs the Colossian Christians to set their minds on the person of Christ. The false teachers also concentrated on a man-centred philosophy which Paul condemns (2:8). Paul's concern was that the Colossian church should hold fast to what they were first taught: 'As therefore you received Christ Jesus the Lord, so live in Him ...' (2:6).

COMING OF THE LORD SEE DAY OF THE LORD

COMMUNION (GREEK *KOINŌNIA*)

This word, often translated as 'fellowship', is used in two senses in the New Testament. First, to describe the fellowship and sharing that existed in the early church (Acts 2:42). This included one local congregation giving financial help to another (2 Corinthians 8:4, translated 'taking part in'), the caring for widows and orphans, and the community life enjoyed by the early church and described at the end of Acts 2. The second sense of the word has given rise to our term the Holy Communion, to describe the Lord's Supper or Breaking of Bread. It occurs in 1 Corinthians 10:16, translated 'participation in'. These phrases describe the special fellowship meal instituted by Jesus Christ just before his death. Bread was broken and eaten to signify and recall his body, and wine poured out and drunk to recall his blood which was the means of forgiving our sins. (See Bread and Blood.) It is a way of remembering the work of Christ for us and worshipping him. 1 Corinthians 11:23–34 shows how Paul looked on this feast, which for the early church was a special love feast or meal to remember Christ. Today it forms the central part of all Christian worship, as it did in the more informal life of the early church. Communion (fellowship) is also with God (1 John 1:3, 6).

CONCUBINE SEE MARRIAGE

CONGREGATION

In the Old Testament the word 'congregation' is used especially to describe the Israelites when they were gathered for worship (Numbers 16:3; Psalms 22:22; 40:10; 149:1). In the New Testament the equivalent word is used for the group of believers in Jesus and is translated 'church'.

See: Church

CONVERSION, CONVERT SEE TURN

COPPER

There were no copper mines in Palestine itself, but the copper ore was mined in adjacent countries. Usually the copper was combined with other metals and made into bronze. In the Old Testament we are told that bronze was used for many different objects in the temple (Exodus 27:2; 1 Kings 7:14–17).

COR SEE MEASURES

CORIANDER SEE HERBS AND SPICES

CORINTH

was the largest seaport in ancient Greece, with extensive trade and industry. Corinth was one of the largest cities in Greece and known for its immoral social life.

Corinth was also the capital of the Roman province of Achaia. Now the city is in ruins, after an earthquake in 1858. In Corinth there was a Christian church, which the apostle Paul founded during his second missionary journey, in about AD 50–51 (Acts 18:1–18). He stayed in Corinth for two years. Later he wrote letters to this church, two of which have been preserved in the New Testament: the First and Second Letters to the Corinthians.

See also: Asia Minor

CORINTHIANS, LETTERS TO THE

The First and Second Letters to the Corinthians were written by the apostle Paul in about AD 56–57. The letters are addressed to the Christian church in the city of Corinth. This church was founded by the apostle Paul during his second missionary journey. The two letters are among the longest and most important letters of the New Testament.

From the letters to the Corinthians we learn about the difficulties that the young Christian churches had to struggle with. The letters show, too, how the apostle Paul always took an interest in and cared about all that happened in these churches, and how he tried to help them with instructions and advice.

Outline of the contents	Chapter
Conditions in the church, with words of discipline and advice	1 Corinthians 1–7
Answers to questions about eating the meat from pagan sacrifices	1 Corinthians 8–10
Advice about the celebration of the Christian worship	1 Corinthians 11
The gifts of the Spirit and how they are to be used in the Church	1 Corinthians 12, 14
Christian love	1 Corinthians 13
The resurrection of the dead	1 Corinthians 15
Collection of gifts for the suffering church at Jerusalem	1 Corinthians 16
Paul speaks of the importance of being an apostle	2 Corinthians 1–7
The collection for the suffering church in Jerusalem	2 Corinthians 8–9
Paul defends himself against his opponents	2 Corinthians 10–13

CORNERSTONE

When houses were built in Palestine, a large block of stone was placed in the four corners to provide a foundation. The builder used these four cornerstones as reference points for building the rest of the house straight, level and accurate in its dimensions. Another cornerstone was placed on top to hold all together. In the Bible, Christ is pictured as the cornerstone in prophecy (Psalm 118:22; quoted by Christ of himself in Mark 12:10).

Paul and Peter both use the Psalmist's prophecy to show how Christ is the cornerstone of the church (Acts 4:11; Ephesians 2:20; 1 Peter 2:7).

COUNCIL SEE SANHEDRIN

COURT OF LAW

In ancient Israel the elders, who gathered in the city gate, formed the city's court of law (Ruth 4:1, 11; Job 29:7; Proverbs 22:22). Those who had a complaint to make, or a conflict that needed resolving, would turn to the elders. Testimonies before the court were very important. In the case of a death sentence the testimony of at least two or three witnesses was required (Deuteronomy 17:6). It was very common for people to be asked to swear an oath in order to solve their legal conflicts (Exodus 22:10–13).

The priests were also able to judge in conflicts among the people (Deuteronomy 19:17). It was possible, also, to go directly to the king (1 Kings 3:16–22; Proverbs 29:14). The court of law which had sat in judgement, also saw that the punishment was carried out immediately (1 Kings 21:13).

In Jesus' day the Sanhedrin, with the High Priest, was the Supreme Court of Israel. Above the Sanhedrin was the Emperor of Rome, and those who ruled Palestine on his behalf. In addition, there were courts in each city, each with about 20 members.

See also: Sanhedrin

COW SEE DOMESTIC ANIMALS

CRAFTS AND CRAFTSMEN

Tubal-cain is the first craftsman mentioned in the Bible (Genesis 4:22). From a very early period, there were highly skilled craftsmen in Egypt and Babylonia-Assyria. The Israelites learned a number of crafts in Egypt. Later, when they had settled in Canaan, they themselves gradually took up various crafts for a living.

Initially, everything that was needed for the household was manufactured by members of the family: tools, clothes, tent cloth, household utensils, houses and furniture. However, from the time of king Solomon, the Israelites began to work as professional craftsmen.

The craftsmen settled in the towns and cities (1 Kings 20:34). Those who worked in the same trade had their workshops and businesses in the same block or area in the city. Sometimes a town became known as the centre of one particular trade or craft.

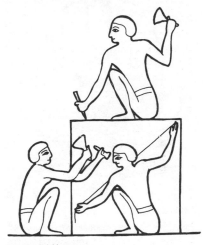

Egyptian bricklayers

Bricklayer. Palestine was short of timber, and therefore the houses were built of sun-dried brick or of stone and cement. The bricklayer was both stonemason, brick manufacturer and builder. It was very important to lay the foundations properly. The walls were built with the aid of a measuring rod and rope, and a plummet.

Archaeologists have found a particular kind of hammer with an indented edge. They were probably used to smooth the surface of the blocks of stone. During excavations in Egypt small baskets were found, with ropes attached. These were used in lifting up and emptying the soil when digging the foundations of a house.

See also: Brick, Plummet

Carpenter. When the bricklayer had finished, the carpenter continued the work on the house. The carpenter's job was to put the roof up, make doors,

43

Potter at work

Carpenter with a drill

window shutters, wooden partitions and screens. Tables, chairs and several pieces of household equipment were made by the carpenter. He also manufactured agricultural implements, such as ploughs and threshing carts. The tools which he used were saw, axe, hammer, square rule, drills and a glue-pot.

Joseph, the husband of Mary, was called a carpenter (Matthew 13:55). The Greek word used in connection with Joseph can also be taken to mean 'builder', in a wider sense. Jesus was trained in the same trade (Mark 6:3).
See also: Furniture, Dwelling

Fisherman See Fishing

Fuller. A fuller cleaned or bleached the cloth to make it as white as possible, before it was dyed.

Merchants See Trade

Potter. Metal vessels were very expensive in Palestine in Jesus' day. Clay pots were cheaper and were, therefore, used by most people for everyday needs. The

potter trod the clay with his feet until it was soft and workable. He placed a lump of suitable size in the centre of the potter's wheel. While he kept the wheel turning with his feet, he shaped the clay with his hands into a pot, a bowl, a dish, a lamp or something of that kind. While the clay was still soft, the potter would

Israelite clay vessels

make patterns on the pot, often by pressing a pointed stick into the clay. Afterwards, the pots were fired in an oven to make them hard and durable (Isaiah 41:25; Jeremiah 18:2-4).

Smith. In the Bible, 'smith' is the name of a craftsman who worked with various metals by various methods. He would,

An Egyptian metal foundry

for instance, cast metals and make axes, knives, arrow and spear points as well as different kinds of jewellery. During the 12th and 11th centuries BC iron came into use in Palestine. The ironsmith manufactured sickles, axes, picks, ploughs, nails and tools for joinery and bricklaying.

A melting pot

Specialist gold and silversmiths made jewellery and ornaments. The tools used by all smiths were tongs, hammers, anvil and bellows made either of goat-skin or leather (Isaiah 44:12-15).
See also: Gold, Iron, Silver, Ornaments

Tanner. The tanner's work was the preparation of leather from animal skins. Many useful objects were made from the leather: belts, sandals, wine and water skins, and coverings for shields.

The tanner was forced to live a little way outside the city, because of the stench which resulted from his work with the dead animal carcasses and the untreated skins. He also needed access to large amounts of water.

The Jews despised the tanner's profession. They believed that he became unclean, or ritually impure, when he touched the bodies of the dead animals. The house of Simon the tanner (Acts 10:6) was probably on the shore south of Joppa, where the tanneries are today.

Tent-makers. From the black goat's wool the tent-maker wove the coarse cloth, pieces of which he then stitched together into a tent. In order to make the tent water-proof, the cloth had to be woven very closely. The apostle Paul was a tent-maker. It was quite a natural choice of profession for him because large flocks of black goats used to graze

45

on the hills near the city of Tarsus, where Paul grew up. They supplied the basic materials for the most important industry in Tarsus, the weaving of tent-cloth (Acts 18:3).

An upright loom

Weavers. Nearly all women in Palestine knew the craft of weaving. The wool was spun from goat's hair, camel's hair or sheep's wool. The goat's hair cloth was a coarse black fabric, which was used for

A horizontal loom

sacks and tents. The camel's hair cloth was softer and more pliable. The cloth made from sheep's wool was the softest and most expensive material. The looms were of a very simple construction.

CRETE

An island in the Mediterranean. In the Old Testament the island was called Caphtor, and was one of the original homes of the Philistines (Amos 9:7). It is mentioned in connection with the apostle Paul's journey to Rome (Acts 27:7–13).
See also: Rome, map

CROSS

A simple pole or stake, hammered into

the ground, was used to hang up and execute criminals and prisoners of war.

The Romans also used a pole with a horizontal piece to execute people who had committed serious crimes, and the earliest traditions say that this was the type of cross on which Christ died. The

cross is a symbol of Christ's death, and an empty cross also reminds of Christ's resurrection. The cross which was a sign of shame and defeat has become a symbol of glory and victory.
See also: Atonement, Bronze Serpent, Golgotha, Jesus Christ, Passion of Christ, Punishment.

CROWN

Traditionally, a crown or a wreath has been the sign of royal or imperial rank and power.

The kings of Israel and the adjacent countries wore crowns (2 Samuel 12:30; 2 Kings 11:12; Jeremiah 13:18). Jesus was mocked with a crown of thorns (Matthew 27:29). In the Book of Revelation the angel speaks of 'the crown of life' as a prize given to the martyrs and other faithful followers of Christ. Just as the runner after the race received the wreath of victory, the man who had finished well the course of his life would receive the crown of life (Revelation 2:10).

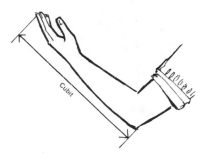

CUBIT

The Jewish cubit was a measure of 17½ inches (45 cm). It was the length of a man's arm from the elbow to the tip of the middle finger. Ezekiel's cubit was a span (9 inches) longer (Ezekiel 40:5).
See also: Measures

CUMMIN SEE HERBS AND SPICES

CUPBEARER

At the court of a king or prince there were one or several cupbearers, who looked after the supplies of wine and other drink. The task of the cupbearer could also be that of tasting the drink before passing it to his lord, in case it had been poisoned (Genesis 40:1–15; 1 Kings 10:5; Nehemiah 1:11).

CUSTOMS, CUSTOMS OFFICIALS SEE TAX, TAX-COLLECTORS

CYMBAL SEE MUSIC

CYPRESS SEE TREES

CYPRUS

An island in the eastern Mediterranean. In the days of the Old Testament, it was called Kittim (Ezekiel 27:6). Cyprus conducted a lively trade with Egypt and Palestine. The Cypriots sold copper ore and pottery. Many Jews lived on the island. Paul's fellow worker Barnabas came from Cyprus (Acts 4:36). Together they visited the island during the first missionary journey (Acts 13:4).

CYRENE

was an important city on the coast of the Mediterranean in North Africa. In Cyrene there were many Jews (Acts 2:10). Simon, who was forced to carry the cross of Jesus, came from Cyrene (Matthew 27:32).

CYRUS

was the king who founded the Persian Empire. He ruled during the years 550–528 BC. He was an instrument of God used to rescue Israel from Babylon where they had been in exile (Isaiah 44:28). In 539 BC, Cyrus captured Babylon and gave orders for the Temple to be rebuilt and restored (Ezra 1). He was sympathetic to Israel and in his first three years as King of Babylon, Daniel prospered. (See Persia).

The tomb of Cyrus

47

D

In the time of Paul, Damascus was under the control of Aretas IV (2 Corinthians 11:32). Paul's conversion occurred on his way there. As a new

DAGON

was one of the gods of the Philistines. Probably a corn god, although some think a fish god. His chief temples were in Gaza and Ashdod. Samson, one of the Judges of Israel, was kept captive at Gaza. Samson's last exploit took place at a celebration in the temple of Dagon, when he forced apart the two central pillars and made the whole temple fall to the ground (Judges 16:23-30; 1 Samuel 5:2-5; 1 Chronicles 10:10).

Entrance to 'The Street called Straight' at Damascus

DAMASCUS

The capital of Syria, Damascus is situated 2,300 ft above sea level and west of the Syrian–Arabian desert. Important caravan trading routes passed through the city from the Mediterranean to Egypt, Babylon and south to Arabia. The city has a long history of occupation, including that by David (2 Samuel 8:5, 6), but was lost during Solomon's reign (1 Kings 11:23-25). A Damascan noble called Hazael was anointed by Elisha on Elijah's behalf as a future King of Syria (1 Kings 19:15; 2 Kings 8:7-15), probably when he was invited to the city by Hazael. In 853 BC Hazael's predecessor, Benhadad I, joined Ahab of Israel and other rulers, and defeated the Assyrians at the battle of Qarqar (not mentioned in the Bible).

In 732 BC the Assyrians eventually captured Damascus (2 Kings 16:9), as predicted by Isaiah (Isaiah 17:1) and Amos (Amos 1:4). Gradually Damascus lost all political importance but continued to be an economic centre. From 64

Christian he preached in the synagogue there and stayed in the house of Judas in Straight Street where a disciple named Ananias visited him (Acts 9:10-19). Paul was forced to escape from the city in a hurry by being smuggled out in a basket lowered over the city wall (Acts 9:19-27). He returned to the city after a period in Arabia (Galatians 1:17). For centuries to come, Antioch remained more important than Damascus both economically and politically in Syria. But in AD 634, the Arab conquest put Damascus back into the political map of Syria, where it has remained to this day.

DAN

was one of the twelve sons of Jacob, the elder of two sons born to Jacob by Rachel's maidservant Bilhah (Genesis 30:1-6). He was the ancestor of the tribe of Dan who first settled between the territories of Ephraim, Benjamin and Judah (Joshua 19:40). In this region the stories of Samson, a famous Danite, took place (Judges 13). It is this settlement which Deborah's song describes in Judges 5:17. This part of the tribe was

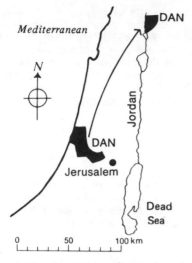

probably absorbed into Judah, but the majority migrated north to a new home near the source of the Jordan much earlier (Joshua 19:47). In the northern Danite settlement, a city called Laish (Judges 18:29) or Leshem (Joshua 19:47) was re-named Dan by the settlers. It was the most northerly city in Israel, hence the phrase 'from Dan to Beersheba' (Judges 20:1). Many Danites were taken captive by Tiglathpileser of Assyria in 721 BC (1 Chronicles 5:26). Today the city of Dan is called Tell El-Qadi.

Egyptian musicians and dancers, as shown on an Egyptian tomb painting

DANCE

was common in Israel, and often formed part of acts of worship.

The dance round the golden calf (Exodus 32:19).

Singing and dancing to the glory of God

after the crossing of the Red Sea (Exodus 15:20).

Dancing at the festival at Shiloh (Judges 21:19–21).

Dancing in the Temple (Psalms 149:2–3; 150:4).

Dance of David before the Ark of the Covenant (2 Samuel 6:12–14).

Dancing took place at wine and harvest festivals, at weddings and other feasts. Dancing was not two by two, men and women, but in groups, accompanied by the clapping of hands, singing and other music.

In the New Testament, there was dancing to celebrate the return of the lost son (Luke 15:25). Children danced (Matthew 11:17). And individual dancers performed at feasts in the Greek custom (Salome for example, Mark 6:22).

DANIEL, BOOK OF

The book of Daniel is partly narrative with Daniel speaking of himself in the third person (chapters 1–6), and partly prophetic with dreams, visions and references to events surrounding the Last Days (chapters 7–12).

The story of Daniel himself has given great comfort to Christians in times of crisis and oppression. Daniel was faithful to God, with a regular prayer life which he maintained despite threats to his life (chapter 6). His political involvement and responsibility were seen as an example of godly rule. The book was much read during the Maccabean period from about 167 BC. The dying Mattathias who led the Maccabee rebellion, reminded his sons of Daniel's example in the den of lions and urged them to continue the battle (1 Maccabees 2:60).

DAY OF ATONEMENT SEE FESTIVALS

DAY OF PREPARATION

This describes the day before the weekly

Sabbath (i.e. Thursday 6 pm to Friday 6 pm), when food was cooked for the Sabbath which began at 6 o'clock on Friday night (Mark 15:42; Luke 23:54; John 19:31, 42). It also refers to the day which prepared for the annual Jewish Passover Festival (John 19:14).

DAY OF THE LORD

This expression is used in the Bible to refer to the Last Days. Although the Day of the Lord is the day of God's intervention and vindication, Amos 5:18-20 warns Israel against presuming on God's favouritism.

Other prophets speak of individual nations receiving their time of punishment, which will be their Day of the Lord (Isaiah 13:6, 9; Jeremiah 46:10; Obadiah 15, etc) and also of visitations such as a locust invasion of guilty Judah (Joel 1:15; 2:1, 2). The climax of all God's judgements on man and nations in the context of world history is the Day of the Lord when Jesus Christ shall come.

New Testament writers use the phrase 'the day of Jesus Christ'. (1 Corinthians 1:8; 5:5; Philippians 1:6, 10; 2:16; 2 Thessalonians 2:2).

See Judgement

DEACONS

are mentioned in the New Testament. The word is taken from the Greek word *diakonos*, which means servant. The deacon helped the elder in various ways, in the worship and in the care of the members of the Christian congregation. Both men (Philippians 1:1) and women (Romans 16:1) could be deacons. Traditionally the Seven in Acts 6 are referred to as deacons, although they are not so called in the New Testament. (1 Timothy 3:8-13 gives the qualifications of a deacon.)

DEAD SEA SCROLLS

This is a popular name given to a collection of manuscripts found in caves above the Dead Sea area in 1947 and the following years. The most important Dead Sea Scrolls are those discovered in eleven caves around the Wadi Qumran, to the north-west of the Dead Sea. These scrolls formed the library of a Jewish community which had a desert headquarters at Khirbet Qumran. They occupied this area for 200 years before the whole community was destroyed in AD 70. They were almost certainly a splinter group of strict Jews called the Essenes. Under a leader they called 'The

Clay jar for storing scrolls

Teacher of Righteousness' they withdrew to Qumran and a life of strict isolation in about 150 BC. They expected God to judge Judaism and awaited a new age.

The library contained at least 500 books, most of which remain mere fragments, of mixed composition, although there are several complete books. Many of the remains are from Old Testament books in Hebrew, all being represented except Esther. These manuscripts are enormously important because they close the gap between the time of writing and the oldest surviving manuscripts by as much as 1,000 years. One scroll contained all 66 chapters of the book of Isaiah intact.

Non-biblical manuscript scrolls tell us about the life of this small and isolated community. They were strict on Jewish discipline, even more so than the Pharisees whom they rejected. They expected the End of Time to come in their own age and believed that their leader, the Teacher of Righteousness, had special revelation about how events would work out at the Last Days. They had fellowship meals together, which some have taken to be the pattern for the Christian fellowship meal of communion. This is not even the case, because there is no evidence that the first disciples and the apostles had any contact with this desert community. Some have suggested that John the Baptist visited them, but this is unproven. Also their meal had no significance such as the Christian communion meal has.

The New Testament also sees Jesus as Prophet, Priest and King of the House of David where the Qumran sect saw three different people fulfilling these prophecies. There is no suggestion in Qumran teaching that the Teacher of Righteousness would rise again. Therefore theories that early Christian writers borrowed from Qumran writings do not stand up to the evidence. The Qumran sect deserted their community base probably during the war AD 66-73 which destroyed them. Before they were wiped out, they stored their library of scrolls in jars hidden in caves.

See also Qumran, Essenes

Plan of the monastery at Qumran

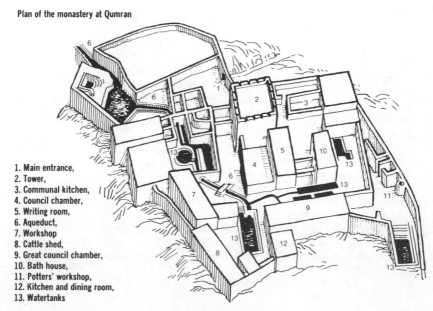

1. Main entrance,
2. Tower,
3. Communal kitchen,
4. Council chamber,
5. Writing room,
6. Aqueduct,
7. Workshop
8. Cattle shed,
9. Great council chamber,
10. Bath house,
11. Potters' workshop,
12. Kitchen and dining room,
13. Watertanks

Appis, the sacred bull, as worshipped in Egypt

DECAPOLIS

was the name of a league which originally consisted of ten cities east of the River Jordan. This league was probably formed in the decade between 70 and 60 BC largely by Greek settlers. The ten cities were: Damascus, Raphana, Kanatha, Dion, Hippos, Gadara, Pella, Gerasa, Philadelphia (now Amman) and Scythopolis, which was west of the Jordan. Deca means 'ten' and polis means 'city' in Greek (Matthew 4:25; Mark 5:20; 7:31).

DEITIES

To the Israelites all gods and deities other than Israel's own God were false gods (Exodus 20:3; Psalm 96:5). However, the Israelites still involved themselves in worshipping the different gods to whom other peoples in the area offered prayers and sacrifices (Psalm 106:36, 38), neither could they resist making images of the God of Israel. Thus, when the Israelites had left Egypt

and Moses spent some time away from them on Mount Sinai, they made a calf of metal, which was supposed to represent Israel's God (Exodus 32:8). The Israelites had seen in Egypt how the Egyptians prayed to images and statues of bulls.

When the Israelites conquered Canaan, there were many temples and high places of sacrifice, where the Canaanites worshipped their various gods. The Israelites soon learnt to pray to the gods of Canaan, and made more high places of their own (1 Kings 13:32; Psalm 78:58; Jeremiah 17:2). They believed that the Canaanite gods were able to give good weather and rich harvests to the farmers (Hosea 2:5).
See High Place

Baal was the most important god of the Canaanites besides El. He was lord of the earth and controlled the weather. The thunder was his voice and he gave rain and life to the earth. Images of Baal have been found in which Baal wields a fork of lightning.

Baal's consort (wife) was Baalat or

52

A coin depicting
the Temple of Diana
in Ephesus

Canaanite goddess from the 14th century BC found in Phoenicia

Zeus, as shown on a classical statue

Astarte. She was the mother goddess, the goddess of fertility. She looked after the propagation of human beings, animals and vegetation.

See Baal

El was the god of the sky and of creation. Since the name means 'God', it is regularly used of the God of Israel.

Asherah was another form of the mother goddess Astarte. One object which was linked with her was the holy tree, the tree of life. By the altar built in the 'high place' there was usually a pole, which represented this tree of life. The pole itself was also called asherah (Deuteronomy 16:21; 1 Kings 18:19). There was usually a stone pillar beside it, representing Baal (Deuteronomy 12:13; 2 Kings 17:10).

In the New Testament the apostle Paul found himself in opposition to certain people in the city of Ephesus in Asia Minor. They were worshippers of the goddess Artemis, called Diana by the Romans.

She was the goddess of the forests, the wild animals and hunting. At the same time she was the great mother goddess. In Ephesus there was a famous temple where she was worshipped. This temple was one of the seven wonders of the ancient world (Acts 19:23; 20:1).

Zeus was another of the Graeco–Roman gods. The Romans called him Jupiter. He was regarded as the highest ranking among the gods, as the father of gods and men. There were many temples dedicated to him throughout the Graeco–Roman world.

At Lystra Barnabas was thought by the people to be Zeus, and the priest of the temple tried to offer sacrifice to him (Acts 14:8–18).

Hermes was also a Graeco–Roman god. His Roman name was Mercury. He was the patron particularly of trade and of roads. Paul was identified as Hermes by the people of Lystra because of his facility in speaking (Acts 14:12). They wanted to offer sacrifices to him and Barnabas but Paul turned their attention from Zeus to the living God (Acts 14:8–18).

See also Dagon.

DERBE

A city in Asia Minor, which was visited by the Apostle Paul and his companion Barnabas (Acts 14:6), and later by Paul and Silas on their westward journey through Asia Minor (Acts 16:1). Paul's friend Gaius came from Derbe (Acts 20:4).

Derbe was situated in the Lycaonian region of Roman Galatia.

DEUTERONOMY SEE PENTATEUCH

DILL SEE HERBS AND SPICES

DISCIPLE

The Greek word means a learner, and hence one who follows his teacher.

The prophets in the Old Testament collected disciples, sometimes referred to as 'sons of prophets' (2 Kings 4:38).

In the New Testament the rabbis, the teachers of law, had disciples (Matthew 22:15, 16).

In the same way particular disciples gathered around John the Baptist and Jesus (Matthew 9:14).

When the gospels speak of 'the disciples' the word often refers to the twelve apostles (Matthew 10:1).

The word 'disciples' is also used about a larger group of people who were followers of Jesus (John 4:1).

Even after Christ's death and resurrection, those who had come to believe in Jesus were called disciples (Acts 6:1).

The word disciples is, however, most commonly used about those who had seen and listened to Jesus.

See also Apostle.

DISEASE

In Old Testament times, people believed that disease was often the work of evil powers (Job 2:7). Disease was also a consequence of sins which a person had committed, and therefore a punishment which the individual had justly deserved (Deuteronomy 28:58–61).

Thus, if a person was ill, he had sinned against God. And in doing so, he had broken his fellowship with God. Some diseases, such as leprosy, disqualified a person from the common worship and people avoided all contact with him (Leviticus 13:45, 46; Job 30:9, 10).

A priest with certain diseases or defects was not allowed to minister (Leviticus 21:16–24).

A really sick man would not only suffer from the disease itself, but he also felt deserted and rejected both by God and men (Psalm 102:1–11).

Jesus healed the sick. He did not sanction the popular belief that disease was always a punishment for the sufferer's own particular sins (John 9:2). The illness was not necessarily the sick person's own fault. When Jesus healed the sick, illness could even become a means of demonstrating the power of God to the people (John 9:3).

Jesus affirmed that the Jews were right when they said that disease could be the work of evil spiritual forces. When Jesus healed a Jewish boy he used the words: 'You dumb and deaf spirit, I command you, come out of him, and never enter him again' (Mark 9:25).

Various diseases are mentioned in the Bible. It is often difficult to determine exactly which illness is meant, in terms of modern diagnosis.

DOG SEE ANIMALS

DOMESTIC ANIMALS

The Israelites had a number of different domestic animals. Some were used by farmers as beasts of burden. Others were kept in large flocks or herds, and they provided the people with meat, milk and skins, as well as sacrificial animals for the service of the temple. Also travelling merchants needed animals on which to carry their wares.

The animals were often looked after by the sons or the daughters of the house, or by slaves or paid servants. To be a shepherd or herdsman was a very responsible job in an agricultural society. See also Shepherd

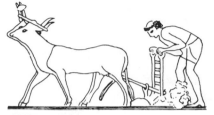

Ploughing with oxen

Oxen and Cows were used as beasts of burden. They pulled ploughs and simple wagons. They were led around the threshing floor to trample the corn out of the ears of corn at harvest time (Deuteronomy 25:4). The cows also provided the people with milk. Calves were often slaughtered and used as food. Oxen and cows were common sacrificial animals in the temple service (Job 1:14; Isaiah 1:3; Matthew 22:4; Luke 13:15; 14:19; 15:23).

The Ass or Donkey was one of the commonest domestic animals in Palestine. It was bigger, quicker, stronger and had more stamina than the donkeys now used in the south of Europe. It was reddish-brown in colour, and was quite happy in warm and dry conditions. It ate grass, hay, thistle and thorn-twigs. It was used to pull carts, for riding, carrying loads and also in time of war (Exodus 20:17; Isaiah 1:3; Matthew 21:5; Luke 10:34; 14:5).

Sheep and goats were kept together in large flocks, watched over by shepherds

with dogs. During the night the shepherd would shut the sheep in a special enclosure, made of large blocks of stone and with only one entrance. Often the top of the wall would be crowned with a low hedge of thorns.

The sheep provided the wool out of which were made most of people's clothes. The sheep were sheared once a year, after which there would be a celebration (1 Samuel 25). The flesh of the sheep was also used as food, and it was a very common sacrificial animal in the temple.

The goats provided meat and milk. The long black goat's hair could be woven into tent fabric. Goatskin was also used to make containers for water and wine. The goat, like the sheep, was a very common sacrificial animal (Genesis 22:7f; Leviticus 3:12; Psalms 23; 79:13; Isaiah 53:6f; Proverbs 27:27; Matthew 10:16; 25:32; Luke 15:6; John 10:27).

Shepherd and sheep are frequent pictures of the Lord and his people (Psalm 23; Isaiah 53:6; John 10:7–18; 1 Peter 2:25). See also Shepherd

Camel The camel mentioned in the Bible is that with only one hump, called the Dromedary. It can grow to over 6 ft high and 9 ft long, and is the colour of sand. It has wide feet, with special soft pads for walking on soft sand. The camel can live without water and with very little food for up to three weeks at a time.

It is used in the desert for both riding and carrying burdens. A good riding camel has been known to cover over a hundred miles a day, and a loaded camel normally covers about thirty miles. It can carry a load of up to 400 lbs.

Camel's milk is used as a beverage, and camel's hair is used for the weaving of clothes and tents (Genesis 24:14; 1 Chronicles 5:21; Isaiah 60:6; Matthew 3:4; 19:24; Mark 1:6).

Horse. The horse was used in war, but not as a domestic working animal. King Solomon equipped his army with horses. They were used to carry riders and to pull chariots (Exodus 15:1; 1 Kings

Horses pulling an Assyrian chariot

9:19; 20:25; 2 Chronicles 1:14; Psalm 33:17; Revelation 9:9; 19:14).

Pig. The Jews were not allowed to eat pork. The law of Moses said that the pig was an unclean animal, and experience in the east shows that pork easily becomes infected. Therefore the Israelites did not keep pigs as domestic animals (Leviticus 11:6–8; Deuteronomy 14:8; Luke 15:15).

Dove and Pigeon were used by poor people as sacrificial animals (Leviticus 5:7; 12:8; Luke 2:24). They were often kept in dovecotes or pigeon houses (Isaiah 60:8).

Hens were among the common domestic animals in Palestine during the time of Jesus (Matthew 23:37; 26:34, 74). It is unlikely that there were hens in the country in Old Testament times, although 1 Kings 4:23 may refer to imports from India for Solomon's table. Originally they came from India.

DRACHMA SEE MONEY

DRESS

Originally, the dress of the Israelite men was probably only a loin-cloth reaching to the knee.

But this soon gave place to a long shirt or coat-shaped garment with sleeves, which was called a *tunic*. It was made of white linen and fastened at the waist with a belt or a girdle. The belt

Wool twist

Headgear

Mantle

Belt-girdle

Tunic

Sandals with straps

might be a piece of rope, a leather strap or a pice of linen tape.

To *gird one's loins* was to lift up and fasten the hem of one's tunic under one's belt. It was done before starting work, or before setting out on a long, brisk walk (Exodus 12:11; Luke 12:35; Acts 7:58).

The *mantle* was the outer garment, usually consisting of a large piece of coarser cloth. It was either worn as a coat or draped round the body in such a way that it left the right arm free. The mantle was comfortable in rainy or cold weather, but was taken off during work (Matthew 24:18). During the night, while sleeping, people used their mantles for blankets (Exodus 22:26, 27).

The Bible does not describe what men wore on their heads, but inscriptions show easterners with brimless caps. Women's head-dress might consist of a headband or a turban (Isaiah 3:23), or a veil (Genesis 24:65).

The sandals were really only wooden or leather soles, tied to the feet with straps. A spare pair was often carried on a journey (Luke 10:4), or worn out sandals could be patched (Joshua 9:5).

In general the women's clothing was similar to the men's, but it was longer. They usually wore different kinds of veil. But they did not veil their faces. The Israelite women also wore various pieces of jewellery and ornaments (Isaiah 3:18–24).

See also Ornaments

DRINK SEE FOOD AND DRINK

DUNG GATE

The Dung Gate was one of the gates in the wall surrounding the city of Jerusalem (Nehemiah 3:13; 12:31). In all likelihood it was the gate in the southeastern corner of the wall, remnants of which have been found during excavations. It led to the rubbish dump in the Valley of Hinnom.

An early tent, such as the Israelites might have used

DWELLING

Abraham, Isaac and Jacob lived in tents, as did the Israelites during the wanderings in the desert. In such a hot climate, the greater part of the day was spent out of doors, and tents were used only for undisturbed rest and sleep. Some Israelites continued to live in tents after they entered Canaan, when the period in the wilderness was over.

Abraham came from the city of Ur, on the Persian Gulf, and probably lived in a real house when he was a child. Excavations at Ur have uncovered the remains of two-storey houses from the 3rd millennium BC. Many of these had

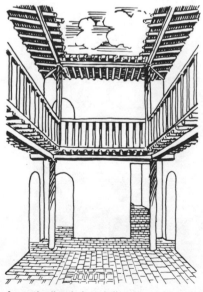
A reconstruction of a house in Ur

up to fifteen rooms, and were certainly very comfortable to live in. The rooms in these houses were arranged around an open courtyard.

Occasionally a cave provided a home, and a door was made for the entrance. But it was usual to erect supports to prevent the roof from caving in. A terrace could be built inside the cave, and this became the family's living space. The rest of the cave was used for the domestic animals. There were no windows.

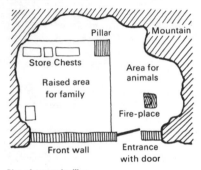

Plan of a cave dwelling

In Jesus' day, ordinary people lived in simple houses made of sun-dried brick.

In the hilly areas houses would be made of limestone. For the most part these houses had only one room, about half of which was built as a raised terrace,

An Israelite house

58

where the family lived. The domestic animals occupied the rest of the room. There were mangers, and containers for corn, fruit, water and oil.

In the family's part of the house there were various items of furniture. The windows were very small, and had no glass. The floors were of hard-trodden clay. On the outside of the house, a staircase led up to the flat roof. Around

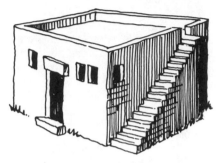

the edge of the roof, a low wall prevented accidents (Deuteronomy 22:8). This wall was a continuation of the house-wall upwards.

The roof was made of beams or planks of wood. Over them, twigs and branches were laid, after which they were covered over with clay and soil, which was then pressed down to give a smooth surface (Mark 2:4). An extra room might sometimes be built on the roof.

Up on the roof the family would gather during the cool evenings. House-work or handicrafts could be done, or they could talk to their neighbours on the roof next door.

Rich people could build bigger houses, sometimes of stone. Inside, the walls could be covered with expensive wood, with ivory ornaments and carved panels (Haggai 1:4). Such houses as these might be several storeys high, and were very comfortable to live in. Often they would consist of a number of rooms around a square courtyard.

See also Caves, Home, Brick, Tent

E

EDOM

EARTHQUAKES

Palestine has always been in an earthquake zone. In the Bible, earthquakes occurred on Sinai when Moses received the Law (Exodus 19:18), in the days of Saul (1 Samuel 14:15), Elijah (1 Kings 19:11), Uzziah (Amos 1:1) and Paul and Silas (Acts 16:26). When Jesus died, the earthquake which took place had supernatural significance (Matthew 27:51). The Bible foretells that earthquakes will accompany the winding up of this age when Christ returns (Matthew 24:7). Probably an earthquake caused the damming of the Jordan so that the Israelites could cross (Joshua 3:16). A similar event happened as recently as 1906 and 1927.

EBAL SEE GERIZIM

ECCLESIASTES

The writer calls himself 'The Preacher' in this unique Old Testament book which describes a man's search for the meaning of life. The early chapters look at the 'vanity' of life and the failure of the world to satisfy man's deepest longings. These can only be found in tune with God: 'Fear God and keep his commandments, for this is the whole duty of man' (Ecclesiastes 12:13). The word 'vanity' occurs over 30 times in the book. Chapter 3 begins with a famous meditation on time which has found its way into western folk culture: 'For everything there is a season, a time for every matter under heaven ...'. A book which once caused some people to ask

why it was in the Bible at all is today recognized for its great insight into man's search for reality and the ultimate reality that is God. Chapter 1:1 points to Solomon as the author, but his name is not actually mentioned so it cannot be certain.

ECCLESIASTICUS

(alternatively called The Wisdom of Jesus, the Son of Sirach) is one of the apocryphal books. It resembles closely the book of Proverbs in the Old Testament, contains a catalogue of famous men of Israel's past, and was probably written in about 190 BC.

See also Apocrypha

EDEN GARDEN OF EDEN

In the Old Testament we are told about Eden, where the first man and woman, Adam and Eve, lived. Genesis 2:10–14 locates it in the east, near the source of the rivers Euphrates and Tigris. When Adam and Eve ate of the forbidden fruit of 'the tree of knowledge' they were driven out of Eden (Genesis 3:24). The prophets refer to it as a place of beauty and fertility (Isaiah 51:3; Ezekiel 28:13; 36:35; Joel 2:3).

EDOM

was the name of a country and a people south of the Dead Sea. The people was of the family of Esau (Genesis 36). The largest part of Edom is desert and rocky mountain plateaux. In Edom there were rich iron and copper mines. In the city of Punon (Numbers 33:42, 43) large smelting-furnaces have been found, where the ore was melted down. The Edomites refused to allow the Israelites to pass through their territory on their way to Palestine (Numbers 20:14–21). King David conquered Edom (2 Samuel 8:13, 14) but it was lost in about 850 BC by King Joram (2 Kings 8:20–22). During the Babylonian capture of Jeru-

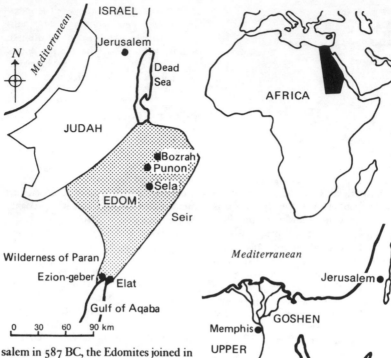

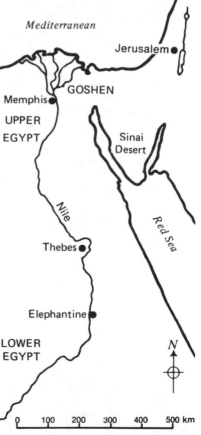

salem in 587 BC, the Edomites joined in the sack of the city and murder of Jewish refugees (Obadiah 10–14; Ezekiel 25:12–14). They remained in the land after the return of the Jews from captivity, and settled especially around Hebron, forming the Kingdom of Idumaea. The Idumaeans (Edomites) were conquered by John Hyrcanus in 120 BC and absorbed into Israel. The Herods were Idumaeans.

EDUCATION SEE SCHOOL

EGYPT (HEBREW *MIZRAIM*)

A very long time ago, Egypt consisted of small kingdoms along the Nile, which were gradually united. The ruler of Egypt was called Pharaoh. Beyond the Nile valley were deserts and infertile mountain regions. The climate was dry, but the yearly flooding of the Nile and numerous irrigation channels neverthe-

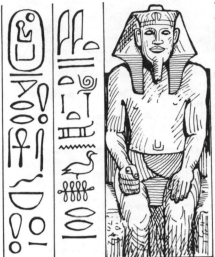

Egyptian hieroglyphics. Egyptian Pharaoh from an ancient statue

The special messenger of the god Osiris was Apis, the sacred bull, which one might compare with Israel's golden calf in the desert.

It was necessary for the life of the soul after death that the dead body should not deteriorate. This is why the body was embalmed, and the deceased put into a grave chamber with food, drink and other necessities.

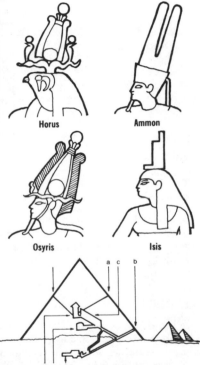

Horus   Ammon

Osyris   Isis

Pyramids showing, a. Air ducts, b. Entrance, c. The great hall, d. The large burial chamber, e. The royal burial chamber, f. Subterranean burial chamber

less made possible rich harvests of grain in the Nile Valley.

The oldest form of writing in Egypt is called hieroglyphic script. In the beginning this was pictorial, but later on the pictures evolved into simpler forms which still represented words rather than letters of the alphabet.

Various gods were worshipped in Egypt during different periods: Horus, the sun god, depicted with a falcon's head; the sun god Ra (or Re); the gods Amun and Osiris and the goddess Isis. The Pharaoh was believed to be divine, and the son of the god Ra or of Horus.

Old Kingdom	2740 BC	Royal graves with the earliest hieroglyphs. The time of the pyramids. The pyramid of Cheops was built 475 ft (145 m) high, and 705 ft (245 m) square at the base. Memphis is the capital city. Period of success.
	2560 BC	Grave temples with important murals.
	2420 BC	The power and influence of the king weakens. The princes of Egypt seize power.
	2270 BC	Period of decay and dissolution

Middle Kingdom	2000 BC	The period of most brilliant achievements in Egypt in the areas of agriculture, industry, mining, crafts, commerce, language, literature and architecture.
Empire of the Hyksos	1730 BC	Peoples of Asiatic origin and their kings, the Hyksos, seize power in Egypt. Horses and carts begin to be used. Joseph arrives in Egypt.
New Kingdom	1580 BC	The Hyksos lose power. The Egyptians themselves regain the rule.
	13th century BC	Egypt becomes a nation of warriors and conquers the countries as far as the Euphrates. The Amarna letters come into being. The Israelites in slavery to the Egyptians. A suggested date for the exodus is soon after 1200 BC but others suggest two centuries earlier.
Later history of Egypt	1085 BC	A time of decline begins for Egypt.
	670–660 BC	Egypt comes under Assyria.
	525 BC	Egypt comes under Persia.
	322 BC	Egypt comes under Greece (Alexander the Great). Many Jews settled in Alexandria.
	30 BC	Egypt becomes a Roman dominion. In the first 6 centuries of the Christian era, Egypt (especially Alexandria) became a strong centre of Christianity, developing eventually as the Coptic Church.
	AD 650 to today	Islamic era.

EKRON

was one of the five cities of the Philistines. It was situated about 24 miles (40 km) west of Jerusalem (Joshua 13:3; 1 Samuel 5:10; 2 Kings 1:2; Amos 1:8).
See also Philistia

ELDERS

In the village or city the elders were a group of men who would meet together to discuss and decide matters of common concern (Deuteronomy 25:7–10; Ruth 4:4; Jeremiah 26:17). It was often the most senior of the elders who made the decision and to whom the others would listen (Job 29:7–10). Younger people could also belong to the group of elders. A group of seventy elders received a special gift of the Spirit in order to help Moses (Numbers 11:16–30). In New Testament times one group among the 70 members of the Sanhedrin was called 'the elders' (Matthew 16:21; Acts 4:5–

8), and each synagogue was supervised by a local group of elders. In the Christian churches the leaders were called elders. The apostle Paul appointed elders who were to take responsibility for the leadership of the congregations (Acts 14:23; 15:4; 1 Timothy 4:14). *The tradition of the elders* (Matthew 15:2) or the oral law, were those explanations of the Law which gradually accumulated through the rabbis' study and discussions of the Torah, or Law. Later on, all this material was collected and arranged in the writings known as the Mishnah. These were later included in the Talmud.
See also Talmud

ELI, ELI, LAMA SABACH-THANI

were some of the words of Jesus on the cross (Matthew 27:46; Mark 15:34). They are in the Aramaic language and mean: 'My God, my God, why hast thou forsaken me?' (or in modern English,

'Why have you abandoned me?'). This question or explanation is a quotation from Psalm 22:1. Christians have linked the words to Jesus Christ's bearing of our sins on the cross (2 Corinthians 5:21; Galatians 3:13).

ELIM

was the site of one of the Israelite camps during the wandering in the desert. Elim was situated on the west coast of the Sinai peninsula. In this oasis there were 12 springs and 70 palm trees (Exodus 15:27; 16:1; Numbers 33:9–10).
See also Wandering in the Wilderness map.

EMBALMING

was a method of preserving the dead body from decay. One of the substances used was balm. In Egypt persons of high rank were usually embalmed.

Jacob and Joseph, both of whom died in Egypt, were embalmed, too. It was

Egyptian embalmers at work

not common among the Jews to do this to their dead (Genesis 50:2–3; 50:26).
See also Balm.

EMMANUEL

or Immanuel is a name of the Messiah, who according to the Christian faith came in the person of Jesus Christ. The prophet Isaiah uses this name in his prophecy, Isaiah 7:14. This was a sign for the future that in the birth of a child the presence of God is to be found. God is with his people and in Immanuel shall be hope and salvation. Emmanuel means 'God with us' (Isaiah 7:14; Matthew 1:23).

EMMAUS

was a village about 7 miles (in the Greek text 'sixty stadia'), i.e. 11 km, from Jerusalem. During a walk there Jesus joined two of his disciples after the Resurrection, and made himself known at supper in their house (Luke 24:13–32). The exact location of the village is not known.

EN-GEDI

was an oasis in the Desert of Judah, on the western shore of the Dead Sea. During his flight from Saul, David went into hiding for a period of time in the neighbourhood of En-Gedi (1 Samuel 24:1–3).

Pliny, a Roman governor, mentions in his *Natural History* that the Jewish community of the Essenes had taken up residence north of En-Gedi, and that the town was 'second only to Jerusalem in the fertility of its land and in its groves of palm-trees' (Song of Solomon 1:14).

EPHAH SEE MEASURES

EPHESIANS, LETTER TO THE

The Letter to the Ephesians in the New Testament was written by the apostle Paul. He is thought to have written it during the years AD 59 to 61, when he was captive in Rome, although some date it during his imprisonment in Caesarea (Acts 24:27). For references to imprisonment see Ephesians 3:1; 4:1; 6:20. The letter was addressed to Christians not only in the city of Ephesus, but probably to several Christian congregations in Asia Minor. The words 'at Ephesus' which occur in some Bible translations in Ephesians 1:1 are missing in some old manuscripts of the Greek text.

The letter speaks of the great importance of the Christian congregation. Paul wants to emphasize particularly that the congregation exists both for Jews and Gentiles. It is very important that there should be unity in the congregation.

The main theme is of God at work in his Church through Jesus Christ and the practical implications for all members of the Church, encouraged by the author to put on the armour of God against the enemy, described in chapter 6.

EPHESUS

was the largest city in Asia Minor at the time of the apostle Paul. The most important route of communication in Asia Minor, both on land and at sea, met at Ephesus. It was also the provincial capital of Ionia, with about 200,000 inhabitants.

In the city there was a famous temple consecrated to the worship of the goddess Artemis or Diana. The apostle Paul visited Ephesus several times. On one such visit he stayed for two or three years. Because of Paul's preaching and other work, riots broke out in the city (Acts 19).

See also Deities

The possible appearance of the ephod

EPHOD

The ephod was part of a priest's clothing in Israel. The high priest's ephod was elaborate and beautiful (Exodus 28:25–35). In 1 Samuel 2:18; 22:18 a linen ephod is mentioned as worn by priests and by Samuel, and David wore one when bringing in the ark (2 Samuel 6:14). It was probably a sleeveless coat, open at the sides, like an apron, put on over the shoulders and covering both front and back. The word 'ephod' occasionally seems to refer to an object connected with the image of a deity (Judges 8:26–27; 18:14–20).

The Temple of Diana at Ephesus

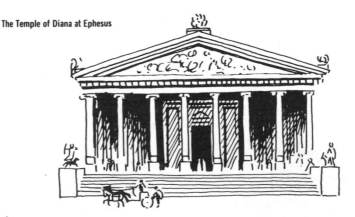

EPHPHATHA

A word in Aramaic, which means 'be opened'. The word was used by Jesus in healing a man who was deaf and dumb (Mark 7:34). This indicates that Jesus normally used the Aramaic language which had become the national speech. The Scriptures were still read in the Hebrew in which they were written.

EPHRAIM

was one of the sons of Joseph. It soon became the name of one of the twelve tribes of Israel. The area in which the tribe lived was also called Ephraim. This tribe held the central part of Canaan. Several of the important cities of Canaan were situated within this area, e.g. Bethel, Gilgal, Samaria, Shechem and Shiloh.

After the death of King Solomon, when Israel was divided, Ephraim became the leading tribe of the Northern Kingdom. Samaria was later built as the capital city (1 Kings 16:24). Many of the kings of the Northern Kingdom were of the tribe of Ephraim (Genesis 41:50-52; 48; Psalm 78:9; Isaiah 7:5).

EPICUREANS

were the followers of a Greek philosopher by the name of Epicurus (341–270 BC). He taught that it is unnecessary to believe in God or in any higher power capable of rewarding or punishing men. The highest goal of life was the quest for the good life—philosophy and art particularly. The Epicureans did not believe in a life after death. They were amongst the apostle Paul's audience in Athens (Acts 17:18).

ESSENES

The Essenes were members of a Jewish religious sect, which existed in Palestine during the early years of Christianity. The sect was similar to a monastic order and also possessed a monastery at Qumran by the Dead Sea. The buildings have been excavated. It is believed that about 4,000 people belonged to the sect in Palestine.
See also Dead Sea Scrolls, Qumran

ESTHER, BOOK OF

The Book of Esther in the Old Testament tells us about the Jewish girl Esther, who became the wife of Xerxes the King of Persia. By following the advice of the Jew Mordecai, her cousin, Esther saved the Jews from extermination in Persia. The Jews celebrate the feast of Purim in memory of this event.

The Apocrypha contains a Greek version of the book with six additional passages. These are traditionally printed together at the end of the book, following Jerome (the author of the Vulgate translation) who removed them because they had no Hebrew equivalents. The Jerusalem Bible now prints them in the text but does so in italics.
See also Apocrypha

ETHIOPIA

or Cush was the name of the country

south of Egypt. In Acts we are told that the evangelist Philip baptized a courtier of Queen Candace of Ethiopia (Acts 8:26-40). Present-day Ethiopia is farther to the south-east.

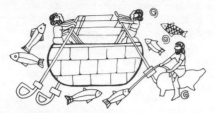

An Assyrian relief showing a boat on the river Tigris

EUPHRATES

The Euphrates is mentioned as one of the rivers flowing out of the Garden of Eden, or Paradise (Genesis 2:10-14). It flows through Mesopotamia. About 75 miles (120 km) from its outlet in the Persian Gulf it merges with the river Tigris. The two rivers Euphrates and Tigris flowed through the ancient kingdoms of Assyria and Babylonia. It is sometimes referred to simply as The River (Joshua 24:14, 15; Isaiah 7:20).
See also Jeremiah 2:18; Revelation 9:14; 16:12

EXODUS

is the name of the Second Book of Moses. The word means 'going out', and tells of Israel's deliverance from slavery in Egypt and of the giving of the Law to Moses on Mount Sinai.

EZEKIEL, BOOK OF

The Book of Ezekiel contains the message of the prophet Ezekiel who was one of the exiles in Babylonia. It is generally considered to have been written before 516 BC.

Outline of Contents	Chapter
Ezekiel's call through a vision of God	1, 2
Speak of judgement over the kingdom of Judah	3-24
Speak of judgement over the different Gentile nations	25-32 and 35
God will save His people, ('valley of bones' vision, 37)	34, and 36-39
The new Temple and worship there	40-48

EZION-GEBER

Ezion-Geber was situated at the northern end of the Gulf of Aqaba. It was a place where the Israelites camped during their wandering in the wilderness (Numbers 33:35, 36). Solomon used it as a port for imports and exports (1 Kings 9:26-28).

EZRA, BOOK OF

The Book of Ezra in the Old Testament is a direct continuation of the Second Book of Chronicles, and deals with the return from the captivity in Babylon and with the scribe Ezra. Two sections of the book have been preserved in Aramaic which was the diplomatic language of the day, suitable for letters between Palestine and Persia.

1 Esdras in the Apocrypha is a Greek version of Ezra and a portion of Nehemiah with certain variations.

F

tatiously: Matthew 6:16–18; Mark 2:18; Luke 18:12.
Acts, church leaders fasted before making big decisions: Acts 13:2, 3; 14:23.

FATHOM SEE MEASURES

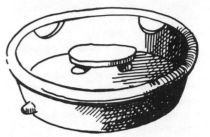

FALCON SEE BIRDS

FALL, THE SEE EDEN, TREE OF LIFE

FAMILY SEE HOME

FAMINE

A bowl for foot washing

was not uncommon in Palestine, often due to droughts in which the harvest withered away. The vegetation in the fields could also be destroyed by large swarms of locusts or be burnt by enemies.

Sometimes a famine might have spiritual significance linked with disobedience of man to God. The curse of God on nature was one of the results of the Fall, to be reversed only when Christ returns (Romans 8:22–23).
For examples see Genesis 12:10; 26:1; Ruth 1:1; 1 Kings 17:1; 2 Kings 6:25; 8:1.
See also Climate

FAST

To fast means to go without food for one or more days. Fasting could be a sign of sorrow or mourning. During a fast people often dressed in coarse sackcloth and sprinkled ashes on their heads. Fasting was also an aid for people who wanted to devote themselves entirely to prayer and sacrifices during a period of time.

Some Bible fasts
Moses: Exodus 34:28
Jesus in the wilderness: Matthew 4:2, Luke 4:2
The Pharisees fasted, often osten-

FEAST

A feast was arranged in someone's honour (2 Samuel 3:20; 2 Samuel 12:4; Luke 5:29; John 12:2.)

There were feasts at weddings (Genesis 29:22; Matthew 22:2; John 2:1–10), birthdays (Genesis 40:20; Hosea 7:5; Matthew 14:6), funerals (Jeremiah 16:7), sheep-shearing (2 Samuel 13:23), and grape harvest (Judges 9:27).

The Day of Atonement was a day of fasting rather than feasting (Numbers 29:7–11), but there was feasting at other annual festivals (see Festivals). For private feasts the guests were usually invited by special messenger (Proverbs 9:3; Matthew 22:3–4). They were greeted with a kiss of welcome. Their feet would be rinsed in water and

The places of honour

sometimes rubbed with oil (Genesis 18:4; Luke 7:38, 44–46; John 12:3; 13:5). The most important guests were given the places of honour at the table

(Genesis 43:33; 1 Samuel 9:22; Mark 12:39; Luke 14:8–9).

Everyday living, including food, was in simple style. At the feasts, however, there was an abundance of food and drink. Meat and wine were the most important parts of the meal (Genesis 18:7; Matthew 22:4; Luke 15:23). The guests were entertained with singing, music and dancing (Amos 5:23; Mark 6:22; Luke 15:25).

In Jesus' day, people would eat reclining on low sofas alongside low tables (see under Furniture). They would lean on their left arms and lift food and drink to their mouths with their right hands (John 13:23–25).

See also Wedding, Funeral, Food

FESTIVALS

Passover The Passover is the most important festival of the Jews. According to the Pentateuch it was celebrated in memory of the rescue and exodus of the Israelites out of Egypt (Exodus 12:1–51).

On the 14th day of the month Nisan (March–April) the head of the family would kill a young and perfect lamb, 'without blemish'. On the original occasion in Egypt he collected the blood and brushed it with a sprig of hyssop on the doorposts of the house where the Passover meal was to take place, and the Lord spared the first-born sons in the houses where blood was on the

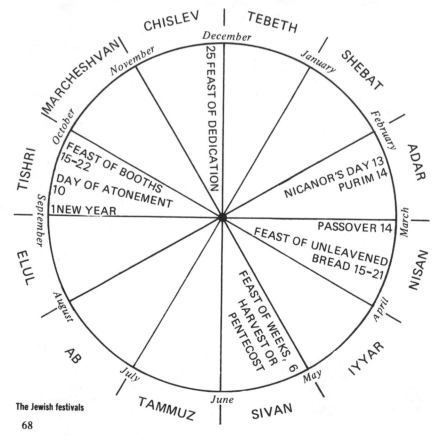

The Jewish festivals

Jewish family sharing the Passover

door-posts and lintels.

During the night they ate the lamb, which had been prepared in advance. At the same time bitter herbs and unleavened bread were eaten. These were also prepared quickly. The bitter herbs were a reminder of Israel's sufferings in Egypt. In Egypt the meal was eaten in haste, and the people held their staffs and were dressed ready for a sudden departure (Exodus 12:39).

The Passover was a festival which families enjoyed celebrating in their homes. There was a careful plan to be followed during the meal itself. The readings of psalms and passages from Exodus 12–15 were interrupted by breaking bread, eating the Passover lamb and drinking the prescribed four cups of wine.

Later in Israel's history large numbers of Jews congregated in Jerusalem during the Passover in order to attend the large services in the Temple, since Passover lamb could be slaughtered only in the Temple at Jerusalem. During the next seven days the Jews celebrated the Feast of Unleavened Bread (Leviticus 23:6).

At the Passover during which Jesus was crucified in Jerusalem, he ate the Passover meal together with his disciples. But he gave this meal, which has since been called 'the Last Supper', a completely new content and significance. Therefore, when Easter is celebrated in the Christian Church, it is not in memory of Israel's exodus from Egypt, but recalls the passion of Christ, his death and, above all, his resurrection (1 Corinthians 5: 7, 8).

Pentecost Pentecost is the Greek name of the Jewish festival which was celebrated 50 days after the beginning of the Passover, on the 6th day of the month Sivan (May–June). It was also called the Feast of Weeks and the Feast of Harvest. It was a festival of thanksgiving to God for the first-fruits of the harvest. Later, the Feasts of Weeks came to be celebrated in memory of the Lord giving Israel the ten commandments on Mount Sinai (Exodus 23:16; Deuteronomy 16:10).

In the Christian Church, Pentecost received a new content. Ten days after Christ's ascension, during Pentecost, the disciples were given the gift which Jesus had promised them: the gift of the Holy Spirit (Acts 2). This is the reason why the Christian Church celebrates Pentecost or Whitsunday (Whitesunday: so called because in the early Church it was a favourite day for white-robed candidates to be baptized).

Feast of Booths (Tabernacles) The Feast of Booths, in Hebrew *Succoth* ('booths'), was a harvest and thanksgiving festival in connection with the fruit harvest in the autumn. It was also celebrated as a reminder of God's help during Israel's time in the desert, when the people lived in tents (Leviticus 23:43). During the Feast of Booths people moved out of their homes into simple huts built from leafy branches and ornamented with fruits. They rejoiced in the new harvest.

In Jerusalem, people carried torches and palm branches in a festive procession. A very solemn part of the celebra-

Building a booth for the Feast of Tabernacles

tions took place on the first day, when the priests fetched water from the Pool of Siloam. This water was then used in the Temple services during the following six days of the festival. It was on this occasion that Jesus spoke of himself as giving the living water (John 7:2, 37–39). After the return from the Babylonian exile the Feast of Booths was divided into three holy days: New Year's Day, on 1st Tishri (September–October); the Day of Atonement, 10th Tishri; and the Feast of Booths, 15th-22nd Tishri.

New Year (Trumpets) (in Hebrew *Rosh Hashanah*, 'the head of the year'). The celebrations of the Jewish New Year began on 1 Tishri (September–October). The first two days of this festival were called the Feast of Trumpets. The Festival continued up to the great day of Atonement, ten days later.

Day of Atonement (called in Hebrew *Yom Kippur*) was celebrated on the tenth day of Tishri (September–October), and it was the peak of the New Year festival and the New Year's day proper.

The Day of Atonement was a general day of penitence, when all Jews observed the Sabbath laws and a strict fast. In the

Temple two goats were brought forward. By casting lots, one of them was chosen to be sacrificed for the sins of the people and for the purification (cleansing) of the Temple. The High Priest entered the Holy of Holies, sprinkled blood from the sacrifice on the Ark and secured God's forgiveness 'for himself, his house and for all the assembly of Israel'. Then the High Priest laid his hands on the head of the second goat and confessed the sins of the people, on their behalf. Their sins were 'transferred' to the scapegoat, and it was chased out into the desert (Leviticus 16). Five days later began the Feast of Booths (see above).

Purim (an obscure loan-word, according to Esther 3:7 and 9:24 meaning 'lots'). The Purim-festival took place on 14 and 15 Adar (February–March). It was celebrated in memory of the Jewish girl Esther, who became Queen of Persia, as the wife of King Ahasuerus. She managed to prevent the extermination of the Jews in Persia on 14th and 15th Adar.

Purim was a festival of joy, when people sent one another gifts. The word 'purim' is connected with the lots which were cast in order to decide on the date of the extermination of the Jews (Esther 9:19–26).
See also Esther, Book of

Feast of Dedication (in Hebrew *Hanukkah*, 'dedication'). During the Wars of the Maccabees the Temple was for some time in the hands of the King of Syria, Antiochus Epiphanes. The Jews succeeded in driving out the enemy and recapturing the Temple. In memory of the purification and rededication of the Temple, the Jews celebrated Hanukkah. It began on the 25th Kislev (December) and continued for eight days. People carried palm branches and lit candles both in the home, outside, and in the Temple. Sometimes they called this the Festival of Lights (John 10:22).

Nicanor's Day In about 160 BC, Judas Maccabeus, a successful general during the Maccabean revolt, defeated the Syrian enemy forces under the command of Nicanor. This famous Jewish victory during the time of the Maccabees was commemorated every year on 13 Adar (February–March), up to AD 70. In the Apocrypha, see 2 Maccabees 15:36.

Festivals at sheep-shearing and vine-harvest were celebrated annually within the family, or with all the relatives together (1 Samuel 25:7, 11, 18, 36). Festivals of the New Moon and the Sabbath recurred regularly (1 Samuel 20:5; Hosea 2:11; Mark 1:21).

Christian festivals The first Jewish Christians continued to observe the Sabbath (Colossians 2:16), but the weekly celebration was soon changed to the First Day of the week, the day of Christ's resurrection (Acts 20:7; 1 Corinthians 16:2). This soon became known as the Lord's Day, and is so called in Revelation 1:10.

All Christians celebrate Christmas, Good Friday, Easter, and Whitsun, and many observe other festivals, such as Trinity, Advent, Saints' Days and local anniversaries.

Christmas The exact date of Christ's birth is not known, but from about AD 330 December 25 was being observed in Rome. The date was probably selected as an answer to the Roman Saturnalia and Festival of the Unconquered Sun, which were held at this period. It is indeed a suitable date for celebrating the coming of the Light of the world into the darkness of midwinter (at least in the Northern Hemisphere where the idea originated). The Eastern Orthodox celebrate Christ's birth on January 6, which the Westerns keep as Epiphany, the visit of the wise men.

Good Friday and Easter The Council of Nicaea (AD 325) decided that Easter should be kept on the Sunday after the spring full moon. Ascension Day then falls on the Thursday forty days after Easter (Acts 1:3), followed by Pentecost (meaning fiftieth) on the next Sunday but one. Whitsun (Whitesun), the Christian name for Pentecost, was a great day for baptisms, with the candidates wearing white.

FIELD OF BLOOD

The Field of Blood, or the Potter's Field, was the name of a plot of ground which Judas Iscariot bought, according to Acts 1:18–19, with the money received after his betrayal of Jesus. In Matthew 27:6–7, we are told that after Judas' death the high priests bought the Potter's Field for the 30 pieces of silver. The field was to be used as a burial-ground for non-Jews. The Field of Blood was probably situated south of Jerusalem in the Valley of Hinnom.

There were two reasons for the name. 1. It was the place where Judas fell (probably after he had hanged himself) and 'burst open' (Acts 1:18, 19). 2. The sale was actually concluded by the chief priests with the 'blood money' that Judas returned to them (Matthew 27:6–8).

FIG TREE SEE TREES

FIRST-FRUITS

The very first part of the gathered harvest was called the first-fruits. It was to be left in the Temple. Here the gift was consecrated by being placed in front of the altar, while special prayers of thanksgiving to God were recited (Leviticus 23:10–11; Numbers 15:20–21; Deuteronomy 18:4; 26:2).

In the New Testament, Christ is called the first-fruits of them that slept, meaning the first to be raised out of death (1 Corinthians 15:20). Romans 8:23 describes Christians as having the first-fruits of the Spirit.

Egyptians fishing on the Nile, a drawing from the 15th century BC

FISH

The Bible does not enumerate different species of fish by name. Instead, the animals of the sea and the lakes were divided into clean and unclean. The clean animals could be eaten, but the Jews were forbidden to use the unclean

A stone from the catacombs in Rome showing a fish symbol

ones for food. Those fishes which had fins and scales were regarded as clean (Leviticus 11:9–12). Josephus, the Jewish historian who lived in the time of the New Testament, wrote that there were species of fish in Lake Gennesaret that differed in taste and appearance from those found in other lakes. At the present time, about 35 different kinds of fish are found in this lake. It is common for certain of these species to form very large shoals in the lake (Luke 5:6). Fish was a common and cheap source of food for the people, who were often poor.

The fish is often used as a Christian symbol. It is one of the oldest symbols of the name of Christ. The initial letters of the expression Iēseous CHristos THeou Yios Sōtēr (= Jesus Christ, God's Son, the Saviour) form the word ICHTHYS. ICHTHYS is the Greek word for 'fish'.

FISH GATE

The Fish Gate was one of the gates in the city wall surrounding Jerusalem. It was probably situated in the northern part of the wall, and it has been assumed that a fish market was held somewhere near the Fish Gate (2 Chronicles 33:14; Nehemiah 3:3; Zephaniah 1:10).

FISHING

Fishing in the Mediterranean is not mentioned in the Bible. In the New Testament we are told a certain amount about the fishing in Lake Gennesaret. Many of Jesus' apostles were fishermen and lived near the lake.

A Jewish historian, Josephus, who lived in the time of the New Testament, tells us that during the Jewish war of liberation he collected all available boats on Lake Gennesaret, and they numbered altogether 330. Each boat had a crew of at least four. On the shores of Gennesaret there were several cities where people earned their living chiefly by fishing: Chorazin, Capernaum, Magdala and Bethsaida, which means 'house of fishermen'. The apostles Philip, Peter and Andrew came from Bethsaida (John

about 4 m

An old form of fishing boat which is still used on Lake Galilee

A fisherman with a throw net

1:44). Several of the apostles of Jesus were fishermen.

The fishing was done with hooks, small nets or large dragnets. The throw-net was a circular, cone-shaped net. The

Egyptians using hooks

fisherman threw the net over the shoal of fish which he could spot from where he stood, a little way out in the water. Round the edge of the net there were weights, which pulled the net down over and around the shoal. The throw-net was used by those who could not afford larger pieces of fishing-tackle (Matthew 4:18; Mark 1:16).

The dragnet was a large net, about 220 yards (200 m) long. It was lowered into the water from one or more boats, some distance from the shore. The fishermen then dragged the net towards the shore, while the net collected all the fish that happened to be in its way. When the net had been pulled ashore the catch was sorted (Matthew 13:47).

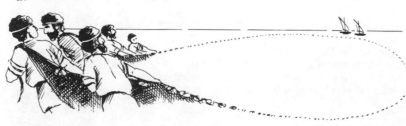

Drag net being pulled ashore

73

FLOOD THE SEE NOAH

FLOWERS

The flowering-time of most species of flowers in Palestine is the month of February, March and April. In May there are searing hot easterly winds, which burn the vegetation. Numerous plants flower shortly before the autumn rains, too. During the winter rains the plants are green but very few have their period of flowering at that time.

Wild anemones

In Palestine there are numerous species of wild flowers e.g. anemones, tulips, hyacinths, crocus, narcissi, cyclamens, irises, orchids, violets and carnations.
See Isaiah 35:1, 2.

The lilies, which Jesus spoke of in Matthew 6:28–29, may have been anemones, which flowered during the spring in their thousands and in many different colours. The lily that is mentioned in Song of Solomon 2:16 (and frequently thereafter) is probably the scarlet *Lilium chalcedonicum* although some think it is a hyacinth.

FLUTE SEE MUSIC

FOOD AND DRINK

The most important food in Palestine was bread. Bread was made from barley (2 Kings 4:42; John 6:9), but wheat was also used (1 Kings 5:11).

People ate the meat of sheep, goats, calves and oxen, boiled or fried over the glowing embers of the fire. With the meat they served different kinds of vegetables. The meat of birds and other game was also used for food. The meat of animals which were unclean according

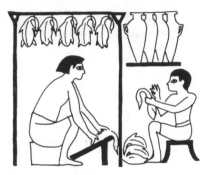

Egyptians preparing birds for food as shown on an ancient tomb painting

to the Law of Moses was not eaten (Leviticus 11). The pig was one such unclean animal and could therefore not be used for food by the Israelites. Salted locusts were quite frequently served (Matthew 3:4). The locusts were also ground into a powder, and people made a certain kind of bread from this flour-like substance.

Fish was a cheap source of food. In the Mediterranean and in Lake Gennesaret there was plenty of fish. There was one gate in Jerusalem which was called the Fish Gate. It is thought that there the fishermen sold their catches to the inhabitants of the city.

Different kinds of fresh fruit were on the daily menu during part of the year, such as figs, dates, olives, grapes and apples. Dried fruit was eaten all the year round. Figs and raisin cakes are mentioned (1 Samuel 25:18; 2 Samuel 6:19).

People used different kinds of spices in cooking (see Herbs and Spices). Salt was needed both in order to prevent food from going bad and to give it taste (Matthew 5:13). Wild honey was used as a sweetener (Exodus 3:8; Matthew 3:4) as it was in most countries before sugar was generally known. The most common drink was water. Besides water people drank milk from sheep, goats and cows (Judges 4:19; Proverbs 27:27; Isaiah 7:21, 22). Although butter was sometimes churned by squeezing or shaking the milk in a skin bottle (Proverbs 30:33), the so-called butter was generally soured milk or curds, like the Indian ghee. Cheese was curdled milk with the whey drained off (Job 10:10).

After the settlement of the Israelites in Canaan, when they had become farmers, wine became more and more important as a drink with meals. People normally drank the wine undiluted, and wine mixed with water is a symbol of moral deterioration (Isaiah 1:22).

Usually people had two meals a day, one early in the morning before going to work, and the other in the evening, when the day's work was done. Many people had a very simple and light morning meal. While people took a break in their work at noon, they usually ate a packed lunch (Ruth 2:14).

King Asshurbanipal of Assyria at the banquet

The Israelites enjoyed arranging banquets and feasts. While people ate sparingly and simply at everyday meals, nothing, on the other hand, was missing from these banquets.

See also Birds, Bread, Feast, Fish, Herbs and spices, Salt, Skins, Trees, Winemaking.

FOOL

The words fool, foolish and foolishness are often used as opposites to words like competent, circumspect, wise. But in the biblical text 'foolish' often has the meaning of 'godless'. 'It is the fool who says there is no God' (Psalm 14:1).

FOUNTAIN GATE

The Fountain Gate was one of the city gates in the south-eastern wall which surrounded Jerusalem (Nehemiah 2:14; 3:15; 12:37).

FOX SEE ANIMALS

FRONTLETS

(in Hebrew *totaphoth*).
See Prayer

FULLER

A fuller was a man who cleaned or bleached cloth to make it as white as possible before it was dyed. The fuller depended on a rich supply of water for his work. Therefore he was often obliged to work outside the city wall at some stream or spring. The fuller also needed a large open field in order to be able to spread the fabrics out to dry in the sun (Malachi 3:2; Mark 9:3).

FUNERAL

When a member of a Jewish household died, the funeral took place almost immediately. The body of the deceased was washed, anointed with oil and wrapped in a linen shroud. His hands and feet were bound with bandages. His

75

Mourners at a Egyptian funeral

face was covered with a cloth. Often myrrh and aloes were placed in the shroud in order to give a pleasant and fresh smell. Embalming was not common in Israel.

The deceased was carried to the grave on a bier or in an open coffin. The mourners walked behind the bier. Music, weeping and lamenting were part of the funeral. Women were sent for, who were professional mourners, and who took part in the family's expressions of sorrow.

Certain other customs were connected with the bereavement. The relatives would fast, tear their clothes (i.e. tear

Cross section of a cave tomb, showing 1. Circular stone door, 2. Narrow entrance, 3. Ante-chamber, 4. Burial chamber, 5. Hollow in wall in which the body was placed.

open their mantles at the neck), strew ashes on their heads, dress in coarse sack-cloth, shave off their hair and beards and tear themselves with their nails until blood showed in the scratches.

The graves were sometimes in the yard of the family's house, but most often they were in a separate grave mound. Only the rich could afford to have tombs made in the soft limestone rock (Isaiah 22:16). Poor people used natural caves in the hills for tombs, as well as graves dug into the soil.

The usual practice among Christians was burial in common graveyards.

See Matthew 23:27; Mark 5:38; Luke 7:11–16; John 11:38–44; 12:3, 7; 19:38–42; Acts 5:5–6; 9:37. See also Aloe, Myrrh

FURLONG SEE MEASURES

FURNITURE

As a rule, the furniture in an Israelite home was very simple. Since the climate was warm, the people could spend the greater part of the day outdoors.

Before people used tables, they simply spread out a cloth on the ground. At the end of the meal, the edges of the cloth could simply be gathered together for convenience. Low tables were used in wealthier homes, but the people seemingly sat on rugs (Isaiah 21:5). Tables are mentioned in 2 Kings 4:10; Psalm 23:5; Acts 6:2. Tables were often

Relief showing a Roman banquet

Bed found in Egyptian grave

Banquet shown on a carving found in a Syrian grave

higher in New Testament times, and the pet dogs sat underneath waiting for scraps (Mark 7:28).

It was a Roman and Greek custom to recline, rather than to sit, at table; the custom spread in those parts of the world to which the Greeks and Romans came. This included Palestine (John 13:23).

In ancient times people often sat on backless stools, though the rich would also have chairs with back and arm-rests, often richly carved (Psalm 122:5; Matthew 23:2).

The rich also had settees in their homes. They would be used to recline on at mealtimes (though later especially low settees were used for this purpose); or as beds, together with a coverlet and pillow (1 Samuel 28:23; Amos 6:4).

Poorer people had no beds; they slept wrapped in a cloak or a blanket, either on the floor or on the bare earth, perhaps on a mat, perhaps not. They slept fully clothed. During the warm season people would often sleep on the roof of their house (Exodus 22:26, 27; Deuteronomy 24:10–13; 2 Samuel 11:2).

Chests and cupboards for clothes were kept in a corner of the family's single room. The other part of the room, on a lower level, might be kept for the domestic animals. Heating in the cold season was by means of charcoal braziers and ovens.

See also Brazier, Crafts and Craftsmen, Feast.

G

GABBATHA SEE PRAETORIUM

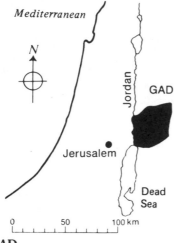

GAD

meaning *Good fortune*, was one of the sons of the patriarch Jacob (Genesis 30:9–11) and the father of the tribe of Gad, one of the twelve tribes of Israel. Gad is described as a warlike people (Genesis 49:19). The mountainous region where the tribe lived was east of the river Jordan (Numbers 32; Deuteronomy 33:20, 21; 1 Samuel 13:7). They were eventually taken into captivity by Tiglath–pileser III in 732 BC (1 Chronicles 5:26).

GALATIA

was a province in Asia Minor. The apostle Paul preached and founded several churches there (Acts 16:6; 18:23; 1 Corinthians 16:1; Galatians 1:2; 2 Timothy 4:10).

78

GALATIANS, LETTER TO THE

The Letter to the Galatians was written by the apostle Paul. The dating would be about AD 49 if the 'second visit' refers to Acts 11:30, but if Galatians 2:1 refers to Acts 15 then the date would be about AD 55. This is a matter of dispute – most theologians prefer the later dating.

The letter is addressed to Christian

congregations in the province of Galatia. Some Jewish teachers of the Law had been trying to persuade the Christians in Galatia to keep parts of the Jewish law, on the ground that faith in Jesus Christ was not enough. In his letter the apostle Paul emphasizes that men are saved only by believing in Christ. He who wants to keep to the many commandments of the Jewish Law becomes removed from Christ, and is again enslaved under the Law and under sin.

Galatians is the great letter about freedom in Christ.

GALILEE

was the name of the northernmost of the three provinces of Palestine. It was in Galilee that Jesus grew up and began his work, as prophesied in Isaiah 9:1, 2. In Jesus' day Galilee was a province of the Roman empire.

Galilee was a fertile country, rich in springs and rivers, and therefore produced large harvests. The Jewish historian Josephus calls Galilee one large

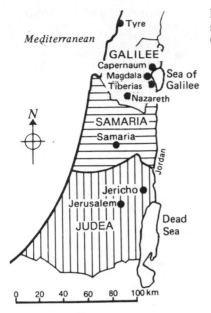

Israel. But most Jews did not participate in the competitions of the Greeks. The Greeks competed in: running, long

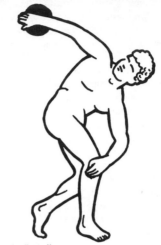

Statue of a discus thrower

garden. He also tells us that there were about 3 million inhabitants in Galilee, but this is probably too generous an estimate. When the Romans destroyed Jerusalem in AD 70, there were many Jews who fled to Galilee. The province then became a centre for the Jewish Scribes and teachers of the Law.

See Matthew 2:22; 4:23; 17:22; 26:32; 28:16; Luke 2:4; 3:1; John 2:1; 7:1.

GAMES AND SPORTS

The Bible does not tell us a great deal about the games of the Israelites. Naturally children loved to play (Zechariah 8:5), and their games included imitating adults, e.g. in playing weddings and funerals (Matthew 11:16–17). They played with a ball (Isaiah 22:18). They held races (Jeremiah 12:5). They shot at marks with bows and arrows (1 Samuel 20:20). They practised weight-lifting (Zechariah 12:3). They guessed riddles (Judges 14:12).

The athletic games and sports of the *Greeks* later became common also in

jumping, discus-throwing, javelin-throwing, wrestling, boxing, pentathlon, horse racing, races with horse-drawn chariots.

The Greeks used to build a special stadium for their competitions. Along the track, places for the spectators were arranged in terraces.

The Romans arranged fights between gladiators who would fight each other to

Fight between Roman gladiators

79

the death. Chariot races and fights with wild animals were common (1 Corinthians 15:32). Special amphitheatres and circuses were built for these competitions.

The amphitheatre was a round or oval building built around a stage or arena. Around this arena there were rows of seats rising in terraces and open to the sky (see the picture under Colosseum). The apostle Paul often uses images and expressions from sports competitions in his letters: running (1 Corinthians 9:24–27; Hebrews 12:1–2), boxing (1 Corinthians 9:26, 27), wrestling (2 Timothy 2:5).

Doubtless, as in Egypt and elsewhere, toys and board games were used in Israel, but dolls may have been frowned on as a breach of the second commandment on images.

The Golden Gate at Jerusalem, now bricked up

GATE

In the time of the Old Testament most cities were surrounded by a wall, which had one or more gates. The gate could be an impressive piece of architecture, also containing rooms for the men of the city guard. It was closed during the night and locked with a bar on the inside (2 Samuel 18:24; Nehemiah 7:3; Psalm 147:13).

The men used to gather in the evening in the open space inside the city gate (Genesis 19:1; Psalm 69:12). This is where buying and selling took place (2 Kings 7:1). The elders used to gather there to decide about the common concerns of the people in the city (Job 29:7–25) and to form the city's court (Deuteronomy 21:18–21; Ruth 4:1–10; Isaiah 29:21; Amos 5:12).

GATH

was one of the five cities of the Philistines. It was situated about 15 miles (20 km) from the coast of the Mediterranean, south-west of Jerusalem. The champion warrior, Goliath, whom David vanquished, came from Gath. When the Philistines had taken the Ark of the Covenant from Israel, it was sent from Ashdod to Gath.

See Joshua 13:3; 1 Samuel 5:8–10; 17:4.

GAZA

was the most important of the five cities of the Philistines. It was situated about three miles (just under 5 km) from the Mediterranean coast south-west of Jerusalem. It was at Gaza that Samson spectacularly died (Judges 16).

See Joshua 13:3; Judges 16:1–3, 21; 1 Kings 4:24; Jeremiah 47:1; Acts 8:26.

GEHENNA

A name formed from the Valley of Hinnom, where rubbish was continually burning. Except for James 3:6 the word is used only in the Gospels of hell, God's place for burning rubbish after the final judgement (e.g. Matthew 5:22; Mark 9:47, 48).

See Hinnom, Molech, Kingdom of the Dead

GENESIS

is the name of the First Book of Moses. It is a Greek word meaning 'origin' (beginning).

See Pentateuch

GENTILE

In the Bible all those peoples who are not Jews are called Gentiles. The Israelites regarded foreign peoples as enemies of their God, because they worshipped other gods. The words which in our Bible have been translated with the word 'Gentiles' originally and properly mean peoples, nations, races.

In the Christian church from the 4th century it gradually became common usage to refer to all those who were not Christians as pagans (lit. country folk outside the cities), which would be a Christian equivalent of Gentiles. The writings of Luke (Gospel and Acts) focus on God's love for all men, Gentiles as well as Jews.

GENTILE CHRISTIANS

Those Gentiles (i.e. non-Jews) who had become Christians were called Gentile Christians. Often they had first become Jewish proselytes, and attended the synagogue services (e.g. Acts 13:42–48). The oldest congregation consisting mainly of Gentile Christians was the one at Antioch in Syria (Acts 11:20, 21). Jews who joined the Christian congregations were called Jewish Christians (or Judaeo-Christians).

GERIZIM

is a mountain about 31 miles (50 km) north of Jerusalem. It is about 2850 ft (870 m) high.

Mount Gerizim was the mountain on which the blessings of the Law were read while the curses were read on Mount Ebal (Deuteronomy 11:29; 27:12; Joshua 8:33). Gerizim was in the beginning Israel's holy place of worship in Canaan. Later, the inhabitants of Samaria built a temple at Gerizim, and this formed the subject of discussion between Jesus Christ and the Samaritan woman (John 4:20–22).

GETHSEMANE

was a garden near the Mount of Olives east of Jerusalem (Luke 22:39). The name means 'oil press', and it may have been an orchard of olive trees surrounded by a wall. Jesus went to Gethsemane together with the apostles after their last supper, as he had often done before (John 18:1, 2). Here he prayed before Judas Iscariot came with the Jewish soldiers to arrest him.

GIHON SPRING

was a spring south-east of Jerusalem in the Kidron Valley. It is now called the Well of Mary. It was the place where Solomon was anointed king (1 Kings 1:33, 45). In about 700 BC King Hezekiah had a tunnel built, about 1,750 ft (537 m) long, through solid rock, which carried the water from the Gihon Spring to the Pool of Siloam inside Jerusalem. (2 Kings 20:20; 2 Chronicles 32:30). In this way Jerusalem would have a supply of fresh water even during an enemy siege.

In 1880 the following inscription, in old Hebrew characters, was found where the tunnel opens out into the Pool of Siloam:

'This is the story of the boring through: whilst the miners lifted the pick each towards his fellow and whilst three cubits yet remained to be bored through, there was heard the voice of a man calling his fellow, for there was a split (or overlap) in the rock on the right hand and on the left hand. And on the day of the boring through the miners struck, each in the direction of his fellow, pick against pick. And the water started flowing from the source to the pool, twelve hundred cubits. A hundred cubits was the height of the rock above the head of the miners.'

GILBOA

Mount Gilboa in northern Palestine was the scene of a battle between King Saul and the Philistines. Saul and his son Jonathan were killed and Israel lost the battle (1 Samuel 28:4; 31:1–8).

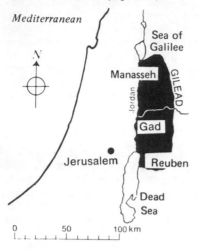

Mediterranean

Sea of Galilee

Manasseh

GILEAD

Jordan

Gad

Jerusalem

Reuben

Dead Sea

0   50   100 km

GILEAD

was the name of the area east of the river Jordan. The tribes of Reuben, Gad and half the tribe of Manasseh lived there (Joshua 12:6). Several battles were fought in Gilead. Foreign peoples trying to invade Israel from the east first had to penetrate into Gilead. It was there that Jephthah (Judges 11) and Saul (1 Samuel 11) defeated the Ammonites, and David overcame his own son Absalom (2 Samuel 17:24, 18). Ahab and Jehoshaphat made an unsuccessful attempt to retake Ramoth-gilead after the Syrians had occupied it (1 Kings 22).

During the time of the Romans ten cities in Gilead formed a league, Decapolis. Elijah came from Gilead (1 Kings 17:1). The area was noted for the sweet scented and curative balm (Genesis 37:25; Jeremiah 8:22; 46:11; 51:8).

GILGAL

was a place near the city of Jericho where the leaders of Israel put up twelve stones, one for each tribe, to commemorate the

crossing of the River Jordan. Gilgal was Israel's first camp in the land of Canaan. At Gilgal Saul was crowned King of Israel.

See Joshua 4:19–20; 5:10; 9:6; 10:6; 14:6; 1 Samuel 7:16; 10:8; 11:15.

GOAD

A stick with a sharp point at one end, which was used to make the oxen move faster. There was often a spade at the other end for clearing mud from the plough (Judges 3:31; 1 Samuel 13:21; Acts 26:14).

GOAT SEE DOMESTIC ANIMALS

GOD

The Old Testament uses several names for God, the main ones being

1. *Elohim.* The -im indicates a plural of majesty, and this is the first name used in the Bible (Genesis 1:1) and thereafter frequently.
2. *El, elah, eloah,* are general terms which can be used of any god, although in the Old Testament almost entirely of the true God.
3. *Yahweh* (Jehovah), is the covenant name whose significance was revealed to Moses as I AM (Exodus 3:14). Translations often print it as LORD in capitals.
4. *Adonai.* Translated as Lord. A general term of respect. It corresponds to the Greek *kyrios.*

The Old Testament stresses the oneness of God, since the people were continually going after the deities around them (see Deities). The coming of Jesus Christ and the Holy Spirit showed that God is more than a bare mathematical unity, and the Church gradually realized, by comparing one Scripture with another, that God is Trinity or Triune, three Persons and yet one God.

GODS SEE DEITIES

GOLD

was often used in the lands of the Bible. People used gold in ornaments, in the

Golden arm band

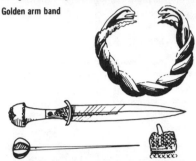

Gold dagger from Ur. Ornamental pin and ear-ring of gold from Asia Minor

Egyptian goldsmiths at work about 2000 BC

temple, in drinking-vessels. Gold became common in Israel during the reign of King Solomon. Archaeologists have found numerous objects made of gold in the countries of the Bible.

See Genesis 13:2; Exodus 25:11; 32:24; 1 Kings 6:22; 10:14; 10:21; 2 Chronicles 1:15; Matthew 2:11.

Small statue of a bull found in a temple north of Galilee

GOLDEN CALF

On Mount Sinai Moses received the Ten Commandments from the Lord. While Moses was on the mountain the people asked Aaron to make a visible image of their God, which they could worship. Aaron collected the Israelites' gold ornaments, melted them down and made the calf in cast metal. He built an altar, and sacrifices were offered to the calf, and there was feasting and licentious dancing. When Moses came down from the mountain, he was angry, destroyed the calf and punished the people (Exodus 32). When the kingdoms were divided, Jeroboam set up two golden calves, one at each end of his territory (1 Kings 12:28–30; Hosea 8:5; 13:2).

GOLDEN GATE

The Golden Gate is the name usually given to one of the gates in the city wall of Jerusalem. It was situated in the eastern part of the wall, and opened from the Temple area (i.e. Herod's Temple) into the Kidron Valley. It is believed that it was through this particular gate that Jesus entered Jerusalem. The gate is now bricked up (Matthew 21:1-11).

GOMORRAH SEE SODOM

GOSHEN

was the name of that area in Egypt where the patriarch Jacob and his sons settled. Goshen was east of the Nile delta. It was regarded as the very best part of Egypt, because there was excellent pasture land (Genesis 47:1–6), and plenty of vegetables and fish (Numbers 11:5).

GOSPELS

Gospel means simply 'good news', Old English *gōd* (good) *spel* (tidings). The Greek is *euangelion*. Evangelism is proclaiming 'good news' of Christ's coming and the salvation that he has brought. The first three gospels in the New Testament (Matthew, Mark and Luke) are very similar to each other as regards

83

the contents and the order of events. These three gospels as a group are usually called the *synoptic* gospels. The Greek word *syn-opto* means 'view to-gether'. The fourth gospel, the gospel of John, is in many ways different from the other three.

GOURD SEE CASTOR OIL PLANT

GOVERNOR

A governor was the official whom a king would appoint to rule an area or province on his behalf. According to the impor-tance of a province the official title might vary.

See Nehemiah 2:7; 5:14; Matthew 27:2. See also Satrap

GRACE (GREEK *CHARIS*)

The word grace in the Old Testament is a term which describes the good gifts which God has given and still gives to his people Israel.

The fact that God chose Israel to be his own people is a proof of his grace (Exodus 33:16). Israel thought that God showed grace only to his chosen people.

In the New Testament all men and peoples are objects of God's grace (Titus 2:11) but this grace must be received in order to be enjoyed (Romans 5:2; 2 Corinthians 6:1). By this grace of God, there is forgiveness of sins and fellowship with God through Jesus Christ. Grace is God's love-gift to us in Christ, unde-served by us. None of the other apostles speaks as often about God's grace as does the apostle Paul. In John 1:14 Jesus is described as full of grace and truth – a perfectly balanced personality.

GRACE, GIFTS OF

Gifts of grace, or spiritual gifts, are certain abilities which God may give to particular individuals in the Christian

church. The apostle Paul speaks of these gifts in 1 Corinthians 12–14. They are charismatic gifts because *charis* means grace. They range from healing to administration.

GRAIN

The most widely cultivated varieties of grain in Palestine were wheat and barley. Spelt was also grown.

See also Agriculture

GRASS

The word 'grass' in the Bible includes flowers as well as grass. During February and March the vegetation comes to life again, but withers and dies in April and May. Since the plants only last such a short time, the Bible uses the grass as a picture of everything that quickly per-ishes (Psalm 90:5–6; 103:15–16; Isaiah 40:6–8; 1 Peter 1:24).

GRASSHOPPER SEE ANIMALS

GRAVE SEE FUNERAL

GREAT SEA

The Israelites called the Mediterranean the Great Sea (Numbers 34:6, 7).

GREECE

consisted of a number of small disunited states. In 338 BC one of these, Mace-donia, seized power through its ruler, Alexander the Great. He quickly made Greece into a world power. He invaded Asia Minor and conquered Jerusalem in 333 BC.

When Alexander died in 323 BC his empire was divided between his generals. One of them, Ptolemy, claimed Egypt, and another, Seleucus, made Antioch in Syria his headquarters. During the pe-riod 300–200 BC these two and their successors fought over Palestine. Greece

Ancient Greek vase

itself was conquered by the Romans in about 150 BC, but meanwhile many Jews adopted Greek customs and habits. Greek became the common language throughout the Mediterranean area. Therefore it was quite natural for the New Testament to be written in Greek. During his second and third missionary journeys the apostle Paul visited Macedonia and Greece and founded Christian congregations there. He then wrote letters to some of these congregations or individual members of them: to the Christians in Corinth, Philippi and Thessalonica.

The Greek culture was very strong and its philosophers – particularly Plato and Aristotle – have had a profound influence on the whole of western society, especially as a result of the Renaissance.

GREEK SEE LANGUAGES

GUILT OFFERING SEE SACRIFICE

85

H

HABAKKUK

Nothing is known about the author of the Book of Habakkuk. His book was probably written in about 600 BC. In the first chapter the prophet laments the wickedness of his people. He speaks of how God's punishment will come over Israel through the Chaldaean people. In the second chapter the prophet has a vision of how the Chaldaeans themselves will be destroyed. Chapter 3 contains a psalm of prayer and praise.

HADES SEE KINGDOM OF THE DEAD

HAGGAI

The book of Haggai was written about 520 BC, after the prophet's return to Jerusalem from the captivity in Babylon. The prophet was saddened when he saw the Temple in ruins when the people had been given permission to rebuild it (Ezra 1:2–6). He exhorts the people to rebuild the Temple before starting to reconstruct their own houses. He was supported by a contemporary prophet, Zechariah (Ezra 5:1).
See also Prophets

HALLELUJAH

means 'praise the LORD' (Psalms 104:35; 135:1; Revelation 19:1).

HAMMURABI

was the first king who ruled over the united kingdom of Babylonia in about 1700 BC. Babylon became the capital city, and the borders of the kingdom were extended. The king built canals, fortifications, temples and cities. He is best known for his legal code, 'The law of Hammurabi', which was carved in a stone pillar, nearly 7 ft. (2 m) high. At the top of the pillar there is a picture of the king receiving the law from the sun god. Scholars think that originally there were 282 separate laws on it. The inscription was made in cuneiform script.
See also Babylonia, Writing

HARAN

was an important market town on the caravan route between Asia Minor and the rich countries by the rivers Euphrates and Tigris. Abraham's father, whose name was Terah, moved to Haran from the city of Ur (Genesis 11:31). From Haran, Abraham continued with his wife Sarah and his nephew Lot to the land of Canaan (Genesis 12:4). Abraham sent to the family home for a wife for Isaac (Genesis 24). Jacob also took refuge there and married Laban's daughters, Leah and Rachel (Genesis 29). Early on, Haran was the centre of worship of the moon-god Sin.
See also Abraham

HARVEST SEE AGRICULTURE

HARP SEE MUSIC

HEALING

The fact of disease and illness as a part of normal human experience means that the Bible frequently refers to sickness and healing, just as it includes other areas of life. But the Bible also gives a spiritual explanation of the cause of disease – suffering is common to man and a result of sin and rejection of God. So when we look at healing, the spiritual reality behind disease and the physical reality are often inseparable. Hence

Jesus' words to the woman with a haemorrhage, 'your faith has made you well' (Matthew 9:22). Here there is no suggestion that her physical trouble resulted from sin. In the case of the paralytic man, Jesus forgave his sins and told him to rise up and walk (Mark 2:11). We may conclude that illness might result from individual sin, but perhaps in the majority of cases it is a symptom of mankind's fall from perfect communion with God. The physical sickness always has a spiritual reality somewhere behind it. Looking at the example of Jesus, his practices of healing varied. Normally he used a word of command (Mark 2:11; 5:41) but on two occasions he used saliva as part of his cure of blindness (Mark 8:23; John 9:6). Healings such as the raising of Lazarus from the dead have no natural explanation; they are supernatural, though in the presence of Christ what is miraculous is also normal in the Kingdom of God. Jesus said to followers of John the Baptist: 'Go and tell John what you have seen and heard: the blind receive their sight, the lame walk, lepers are cleansed, the deaf hear, the dead are raised up, the poor have good news preached to them' (Luke 7:22). Healing is an integral part of the good news – Jesus heals our relationship to God and healing in the physical realm is a continuing part of the work of redemption.

It should be noted that demon possession is clearly distinguished from disease (Mark 1:32–34) and the ministry of exorcism is distinct from healing (Matthew 10:8). In the Gospels, some people are healed by Jesus at a distance (the nobleman's son for example in John 4:46–53), some close up, some without physical contact; others Jesus touched (e.g. Jairus' daughter in Mark 5:41) or they touched Jesus (Mark 5:27). Healing is immediate and often linked with faith. In John's Gospel, healings are not only mighty works but also signs, which means that they have significance as pointers to the arrival of God's Kingdom in Christ. Matthew links miraculous healings of Jesus with the prophecy of Isaiah 53:4 (Matthew 8:17). They show that Jesus was the promised Messiah (Luke 7:22) and in Acts 2:22 they are classified as mighty works, wonders and signs. Jesus promised his disciples that greater works would follow (John 14:12), namely that Jesus' power would spread through them to a wider waiting world. The Acts includes several healing miracles involving the disciples themselves, e.g. Paul's snake-bite (Acts 28:3–6). James 5:13–20, speaking of healing through prayer and anointing by the elders is not an instant-healing formula, but more an encouragement to pray to God for healing of an individual and for the whole church to be involved. It urges men to pray. It does not invalidate doctors or medicine – Jesus used natural means to heal (clay and spittle in Mark 8:23; John 9:6). Prayer and medical aid should go together. In some cases where medicine cannot help, the prayer of faith has brought healing.

To conclude, healing in the Bible is always a physical demonstration of a spiritual reality that the sin of man, which first brought death and disease into the world, has been dealt with by Christ and man redeemed. Therefore the work of redemption restores a man to God and healing is a part of this redemptive work. Healing points to the power and glory of God's kingdom, and is never done for its own sake. It has significance whether the means be miraculous, natural, medicinal or linked with faith and prayer. All disease is a matter for prayer.

Ecclesiasticus 38 (in the Apocrypha) expresses a sensible attitude: 'My son, if you have an illness, do not neglect it, but pray to the Lord, and he will heal you. Renounce your faults, amend your ways

.... Then call in the doctor, for the Lord created him ....'
See Disease

HEAVEN, KINGDOM OF, SEE KINGDOM OF GOD

HEBREW SEE LANGUAGES

HEBREWS

is another name for the Israelites, possibly connected with Eber (Genesis 10:21–25; Genesis 40:15; 1 Samuel 4:6; Jonah 1:9; Acts 6:1; 2 Corinthians 11:22; Philippians 3:5).

HEBREWS, LETTER TO THE

The letter was written either before the Fall of Jerusalem (which is not mentioned), in AD 60–70 or after AD 80 if the author used Paul's epistles. The author is unknown. Certain scholars believe that the letter was written in Italy, because at the end of the letter 'those who come from Italy' send a greeting (Hebrews 13:24). The letter is addressed to one particular group of Jewish Christians, but it is not known where these lived.

The author of the Letter to the Hebrews is concerned to show how the Jewish Old Testament is fulfilled and transcended by Christ.

Outline of Contents	Chapter
Christ, the Son of God, is greater than the prophets	(Hebrews 1:1–2)
Christ is superior to the angels	(Hebrews 1:4–9)
Christ is greater than Moses	(Hebrews 3:3)
Christ is the high priest above others	(Hebrews 7:26–28)
Christ's sacrifice once for all is greater than the daily sacrifices of the priests	(Hebrews 9:26; 10:11–14)
The new covenant with God through Christ is a better one than the old covenant through Moses	(Hebrews 7:22)

Chapter 1 contains a famous hymn or meditation on the divinity of Jesus Christ which is followed up by examination of his relation to Old Testament promises. He is Prophet, Priest and King. Chapter 11 is the New Testament 'Who's who' with a definition of faith and a list of the great men and women of faith in God, from Abel, through David and the prophets, culminating in 12:2 'looking to Jesus, the pioneer and perfecter of our faith ... Consider him'.

HEBRON

which was probably built about 1720 BC (Numbers 13:22), was a Canaanite city in the beginning, called Kiriath-Arba (Genesis 23:2). Abraham lived in the vicinity of Hebron for a period of time (Genesis 13:18). The cave of Machpelah was near Hebron. Abraham bought this as a grave for Sarah and himself (Genesis 23) and Isaac, Rebekah, Jacob and Leah were also buried there (Genesis 49:31; 50:13). At Hebron David was anointed King of Israel, and during the first years he resided there (2 Samuel 5:1–5).

In present-day Hebron there is a mosque (a Muslim place of worship) which is said to have been built above Abraham's grave in the cave of Machpelah.

HELL SEE GEHENNA, KINGDOM OF THE DEAD

HEN SEE BIRDS, DOMESTIC ANIMALS

HERBS AND SPICES

The peoples of the Bible used herbs and spices in food, for medicine, perfumes and incense. Devout Pharisees paid tithes even on these small plants as well as on the main crops (Matthew 23:23; Luke 11:42).

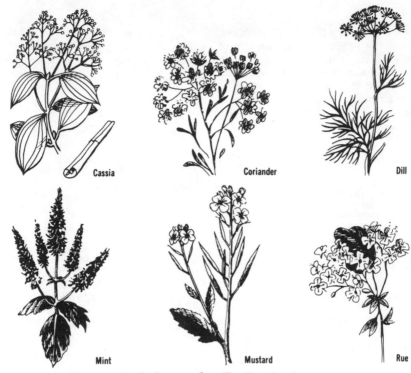

Cassia   Coriander   Dill

Mint   Mustard   Rue

Cummin (Caraway) is a herb, 1 to 2 ft tall (30–69 cm), of the carrot family, with a thin stalk and many branches. It has long thin seeds with a strong smell and bitter flavour. It is well liked as a flavouring in bread (Isaiah 28:24–27).

Cassia is the inner bark from the cassia tree, less valuable than cinnamon (Exodus 30:24; Psalm 45:8).

Cinnamon. The cinnamon tree is a medium-size tree which grows in parts of Asia. The cinnamon is the orange-coloured inner bark which is peeled off the tree and is sold in bundles. It is a valuable commodity (Exodus 30:23; Song of Solomon 4:13–14).

Coriander is a plant which has white or reddish, strongly scented flowers. Its seeds are used as a spice in cooking and for medicinal purposes. The leaves are also used for spicing soups and wine

(Exodus 16:31).

Dill is a culinary herb which grows in the countries around the Mediterranean.

Mint is a plant with a strong, fresh smell. It contains large amounts of scented oil, and has violet flowers. The Jews used mint as a herb with food.

Mustard. The herb which Jesus mentions in the parable of the mustard seed (Luke 13:19) is the black mustard. It exists in both wild and cultivated state in Palestine. The seed is very small, about 1 mm in diameter. The seeds are used as a spice, in preserving foodstuffs and as medicine. The mustard plant can grow up to 6 ft high.

Rue is used as a culinary as well as a medicinal herb. It is a 3 ft (just under 1 m) high plant, with yellow flowers and an unpleasant odour (Luke 11:42).

See also Balm, Myrrh, Nard, Wormwood

HERMON

is a mountain in Syria, at the northern border of Israel. It reaches a height of 9,065 ft (2,760 m) and is visible from a great distance. The snow-covered peaks of Mount Hermon can be seen even in the far south of Israel. The river Jordan has its sources on the slopes of this mountain. It was also called Sirion, or Senir.

See Deuteronomy 3:8, 9; Joshua 11:17; Psalm 89:12; 133:3.

HERODIANS

The Herodians were probably a political group of Jews who were favourably disposed towards Herod and the Romans. They were among Jesus' enemies.

See Matthew 22:16; Mark 3:6; 12:13.

HERODOTUS

was a Greek writer, who was born about 500 BC. He travelled widely in Europe, Asia and Africa. Herodotus collected into a large book of history all that he observed and was told during his travels. Large parts of this work deal with the lands and peoples of the Bible.

HIEROGLYPHS

Egyptian script.
See also Egypt, Writing

HIGH PLACE

In the Old Testament this word is mostly used as a name for the Canaanites' open places of worship and sacrifice.

These were often situated on hilltops or mountains. In the high place there would be a pole, called the *asherah*, which symbolized the tree of life, and a stone pillar or *matsebah* (e.g. Deuteronomy 7:5. N.B. The *asherah* was cut down i.e. wooden, and the pillar was broken in pieces i.e. stone). For many years the

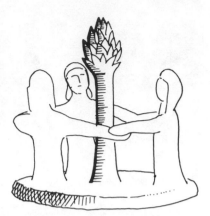

Model of Asherah found in the Island of Cyprus

Israelites followed Canaanite religious practices and sacrificed and worshipped in the high places throughout Palestine (1 Kings 15:14; Hosea 10:8). Later on the Temple in Jerusalem became the only place where sacrifices were to be offered (Deuteronomy 12:10–14).

See also Deities, Asherah

HIGH PRIEST

The High Priest was the leader and the head of the priesthood in Israel. He was responsible for the services in the temple and for the temple building itself. He had to see to the proper use of the temple taxes. Certain special sacrifices had to be offered by the High Priest, and he alone could enter the Holy of Holies (Leviticus 16; Hebrews 9:7). He presided at the meetings of the Sanhedrin.

The first High Priest in Israel was Aaron. His robes are described in Exodus 28. He was consecrated by Moses. From then onwards the office was handed on to the eldest son, who remained in office for the rest of his life. However, when the Romans had seized power in Palestine, they deposed and appointed High Priests fairly frequently. Consequently there were several people who could call

The High Priest's clothing, 1 & 2 Precious stones, 3. Ephod, 4. Waistband, 5. White tunic, 6. Pomegranates, 7. Golden bells, 8. Woven breastpiece with twelve precious stones symbolizing the twelve tribes of Israel, 9. White headband, 10. Gold Plate with inscription 'Holy to the Lord'

The High Priest's vestments are described in Exodus 28.

See Exodus 28:1; Leviticus 21:10; Matthew 2:4; 26:3; Mark 14:54; Luke 3:2; John 11:49; Acts 22:30.

See also Sanhedrin, Urim and Thummim

HINNOM

The Hinnom Valley was situated on the south side of Jerusalem. During the reigns of King Ahaz and King Manasseh, children were sacrificed here to the god Moloch. In the Hinnom Valley all the rubbish from the whole of Jerusalem was dumped and burnt, and the fires were always burning there.

The Hinnom Valley was also called Gehenna, and this name was later used for the place of the lost souls in the Kingdom of the dead.

See 2 Kings 23:10; Jeremiah 32:35; Matthew 5:22; Mark 9:43; James 3:6.

See also Gehenna, Molech

HITTITES

The Hittites were one of the peoples who lived in Canaan when Abraham

themselves High Priests at one and the same time: the High Priest who was in office, plus one or more high priests who had been dismissed but who still lived in Jerusalem.

During the Passover, when Jesus was crucified, it was Caiaphas who was High Priest. He was the son-in-law of one of the earlier High Priests, Annas, but Annas still had considerable influence (John 18:13). Caiaphas remained in the high-priestly office during the years AD 18–36.

came and settled there (Genesis 15:20; 23:3, 5, 7; 26:34). They were a part of the large Hittite kingdom with its centre in Asia Minor.

The capital of the Hittite kingdom

Hittite king as shown on a relief

has been found in excavations. It is now called Boğhazköy. There archaeologists found large amounts of clay tablets in cuneiform writing and some tablets with a form of pictorial script.

When the Israelites penetrated into Canaan, after their wandering in the desert, during the 1250's BC, the main Hittite kingdom was in the process of dissolution, but the Hittites of Syria continued until about 700 BC (Judges 3:5, 6; 2 Samuel 11:3; 2 Kings 7:6).

HOLY, HOLINESS

The word *holy* means someone or something that is separate, divine, pure, elevated. In the Bible the word is used:

About God	(Isaiah 6:3; John 17:11; Revelation 4:8),
About Christ	(Mark 1:24; Luke 1:35),
About the Holy Spirit	(Luke 1:15; 2:25; 3:16),
About particular places	(Genesis 28:17; Exodus 3:5; 26:33; Acts 6:13),
About individuals	(Leviticus 11:44; Ezra 9:2; Mark 6:20),
About Christians and the Church	(Acts 26:10; Romans 15:25; 2 Corinthians 1:1; Ephesians 2:19; Philippians 4:22).

To be holy is to be set apart for God. This does not mean living away from the world, an isolated, individual holy-unit. But one should be totally involved and at the same time uncontaminated. The whole thrust of the Sermon of the Mount is that a Christian is different because he can love when others can only hate. Jesus' holiness enabled him to cut every class barrier, and be friends with tax-collectors and prostitutes, yet be perfect, complete and always loving. He told his followers to be holy as he is holy – set apart yet totally integrated into real life, pouring out God's love for men.

HOLY OF HOLIES SEE TEMPLE

HOLY SPIRIT SEE SPIRIT

HOME/FAMILY

The institution of the family was very important to the Israelites. In times of joy and happiness for any member of the family, all would rejoice together. And in times of sorrow and misfortune for any member, the whole family would share in that sorrow.

The family was like a little kingdom, the king of which was the father of the family. He expected everyone to obey him, and he was responsible for seeing that every member did his or her proper work. The family assembled in the home,

A small oil lamp

which as well as being a place of security, gave shade and coolness during the heat of the day. In the evenings the family would gather on the roof of the house to rest and work.

During the day it was rather dark inside the house, since the little windows – although they shut out the heat – shut out the light as well. In the evening, wooden shutters were placed over the windows, which had no glass in them. In the centre of the room, there was a pillar of wood or stone, which held up the roof; half way up the pillar there was a niche in which stood an oil lamp.

The flat roof was used in a number of different ways. It was a place of assembly for the family, where the festivals could be kept; at the Feast of Tabernacles, the tabernacles themselves could be built on the housetop. It was also a place where grain, fruit and wood could be dried in the sun. Sometimes an extra room might be built on the roof.

In Jesus' day, the furniture in the house was very simple in style. Elaborate furniture was not needed, since most of the day was spent outdoors. Household utensils were also kept in the family's part of the house, together with cupboards and trunks for the family's other belongings. During the day, bedclothes were kept rolled up either in a box or in a niche in a wall.

The poorer family's accommodation in the house was a level higher than the part of the house in which the domestic animals were kept. As well as the animals, the lowest level of the house contained mangers and a hearth. The oven for baking was sometimes out in the yard. Early in the morning the women of the house would also grind corn there with a hand-mill for the needs of the day.

Pots, cups and other utensils were made of baked clay, which was cheap. Milk, wine and water might also be kept in leather bottles.

In many homes the women themselves spun and wove the wool of sheep and goats. In the towns, however, there were craftsmen to do much of the work which women had previously had to do at home. In an Israelite home it could be clearly seen that Israel was the chosen people of God. The most important day of the week was the Sabbath, which lasted from Friday evening until Saturday evening. During the earlier part of Friday, the home was prepared for the Sabbath, which began at 6 p.m. with the lighting of lamps. On Saturday morning, which was the Sabbath proper, everyone went to worship in the synagogue.

The most important events during the year were the major and minor festivals. If people were unable to travel to Jerusalem, they would celebrate the holy days at home (see Festivals).

The children in the family received their upbringing and early education from their parents. The mother looked after the education of the girls, and the father would take care of the boys' schooling. At the age of five or six, the boys were sent to school in the synagogue. The girls continued their education at home, learning all the different skills involved in housekeeping.

See also Brazier, Bread, Crafts and Craftsmen, Dwelling, Food, Furniture, Herbs and spices, Lamp, Marriage, Sabbath, School, Tent, Wedding, Well, Wineskins.

HOMER SEE MEASURES

HOREB SEE SINAI

HORN

The horn was a wind instrument, made of a ram's horn. In Hebrew it is called *shofar*. It was mostly used for giving signals in war, in the worship and during certain festivals (Joshua 6:5).

The extensions at the corners of the altar are called horns (Exodus 19:12) and could be grasped by people seeking sanctuary (1 Kings 1:50).

The horns of animals are used as symbols of strength (Psalm 75:10) and in visions of kings and empires (Daniel 7:20–24; Revelation 13).

HORSE SEE DOMESTIC ANIMALS

HOSANNA

was a Jewish cry, used in prayer or greeting, which means 'help us' or 'save us'. In the Old Testament a form of the word occurs in Psalm 118:25 and this is quoted, with v. 26, in Matthew 21:9; Mark 11:9, 10; John 12:13.

HOSEA

Hosea came from the Northern Kingdom and was possibly a baker (7:4–8). The book of Hosea has been described as a love story that went wrong. He was a married man whose wife deserted him, and he describes the loss of his wife as a picture of Israel's desertion from God (chs. 1–3). Judgement will follow continued rebellion (chs. 11–13). Hosea complains that Israel is like a dove fluttering between Assyria and Egypt, instead of turning to God (7:11). In 721 BC, Samaria fell to Sargon II of Assyria. 27,000 Israelites were deported as captives and the Northern Kingdom effectively destroyed. Hosea proved to be right (e.g. 5:8–14). But in a beautiful final chapter God promises restoration in response to genuine repentance (ch. 14).

HOSPITALITY

The Israelites enjoyed entertaining visitors. Not to show hospitality was regarded as a serious breach of the rules of common courtesy (e.g. Genesis 18; Leviticus 19:33,34; 2 Kings 4:8–10). In the New Testament the Christians are asked to be hospitable: by the apostle Paul in Romans 12:13, by the apostle Peter in 1 Peter 4:9, in Hebrews 13:2, by John in 3 John 10. When persecutions scattered Christians it was all the more important that no Christian refused hospitality to his brother in need.

HOUSE SEE DWELLING, HOME

HOUSEHOLD GODS OR TERAPHIM

were probably small statues of deities or of ancestors which were kept in the home. In the Old Testament we are told about people who owned them. Rachel, Jacob's wife, stole her father's teraphim (Genesis 31:19, 34). Archaeology shows that possession of the family gods went with the right of inheritance and Rachel may have wished to secure this for her husband. The man Micah had a shrine in his house (Judges 17:5; 18:14). Michal, Saul's daughter, put the teraphim in David's bed to deceive Saul's messengers (1 Samuel 19:13) (see note on Rachel above). King Josiah put away the teraphim in the land of Judah (2 Kings 23:24).

It is not known what the teraphim signified, but, if the word is connected with *rephaim* (the dead) they may have represented the ancestors of the family. Later they were used for divination (Ezekiel 21:21; Zechariah 10:2).

HYSSOP

was a plant which was used at the first Passover in Egypt. A branch of hyssop was dipped in blood, and this was brushed on the doorposts and lintel of the house (Exodus 12:22). Since this was to avert the angel of death in Egypt, there is no mention of it in subsequent Passovers. Hyssop was convenient for dipping in blood or in water to sprinkle on lepers or on objects and people who were ritually unclean (Leviticus 14:4, 6, 51, 52; Numbers 19:6, 18; Psalm 51:7). Hyssop belongs to the same botanical family as the herb marjoram, and has been used both for cooking and medicinal purposes. It can grow up to 3ft (1m) tall. Some think that the hyssop of John 19:29 was the tall sorghum cane.

I

ICONIUM

A city of Asia Minor visited by Paul and Barnabas in Acts 14. Paul remembered it as a place of special suffering (2 Timothy 3:11). Timothy also came from this area (Acts 16:2.). It was a productive and wealthy town in the Roman province of Galatia.

IDUMEA SEE EDOM

IMMANUEL SEE EMMANUEL

INCENSE

The peoples of the Orient are as a rule fond of scents of different kinds. They burn substances which spread a highly fragrant smoke, in their homes, at parties and in connection with their worship (Proverbs 27:9 where 'perfume' is literally 'incense'). In the time of both the Old and New Testaments they burnt herbs, the wood or bark of certain trees, seeds and various resins. Most of these substances came from Arabia. Incense could be made from myrrh, cassia, spikenard, saffron, cinnamon, balm, certain species of cedar, stacte, onycha galbanum (a resin). The mixture of incense used in worship might not be reproduced for secular use (Exodus 30:34–38).

In the Temple at Jerusalem there was a special altar, the altar of incense, where the daily incense offering took place (Luke 1:9). One of the gifts which the Magi brought to the child Jesus at Bethlehem was frankincense (Matthew 2:10, 11). This was a resin-like sub-

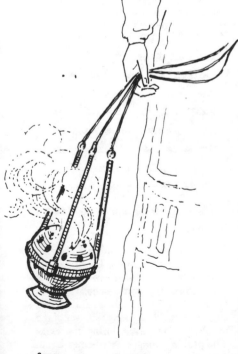

Censer

stance, derived from a shrub or small tree in the desert areas of Arabia.

Ephesians 5:2, 'Christ gave himself up for us, a fragrant offering and sacrifice to God,' possibly carries an allusion to incense. Its smell was supposed to be pleasing to God, and the smoke it produced was a picture of the cloud which surrounded Sinai and of the holiness and mystery of God.

Incense is also used as a symbol of prayer (Psalm 141:2; Revelation 8:3, 4).

INHERITANCE

Among the Israelites the eldest son inherited twice the amount of each younger son (Deuteronomy 21:17). Widows received no part of the inheritance whatever. If there were sons, daughters did not inherit, but, if there were no sons, daughters inherited, but had to marry within the tribe (Numbers 36). The eldest of the sons was obliged to care for his unmarried sisters.

See also Birthright

INN

The inns in Palestine offered travellers shelter for the night. They were situated along caravan routes and close to a spring or well, from which the traveller could draw water for himself and his camels or donkeys.

The camping place was often very simple, but might consist of a yard surrounded by high walls to protect the animals and the luggage against robbers (Jeremiah 9:2). Adjoining the yard there were rooms, where the travellers slept. They had to provide their own food. The inn of the Good Samaritan was of this kind. The Greek word here means roughly 'open to all' (Luke 10:34). It is thought that the inn at Bethlehem, where there was no place for Joseph and Mary (Luke 2:7), was a smaller lodging-house. The Greek here means 'a place to

96

loosen one's burdens'.

INSECTS SEE ANIMALS

INTERTESTAMENTAL PERIOD SEE MACCABEES

IRON

Tubal-cain is described as 'the forger of all instruments of bronze and iron' (Genesis 4:22). His date is not known, but occasional iron objects have been found dating from about 3000 BC. From the 12th century BC iron began to be regularly used in weapons and tools in Palestine. There is no iron in the hills of Palestine, but it was imported from the mines in the adjoining countries: the Taurus Mountains, Lebanon, the country east of Jordan and Arabah, south of the Dead Sea.

The Philistines at one time had a monopoly of the iron trade.

See Joshua 6:19; Judges 1:19; 4:3; 1 Samuel 13:19–22; 1 Kings 6:7; 2 Kings 6:6; Ezekiel 27:12.

Dead Sea scroll containing part of the book of Isaiah

ISAIAH

The traditional view of the book of Isaiah is that it was written by one man. However there is disagreement over the authorship, and some scholars see a division at chapter 40 and a second author, probably a young follower of the prophet, taking over during the exile. The problem hinges on whether Isaiah himself foresaw the exile (39:6) and also foresaw the deliverance from Babylon in chapters 40–66. Chapters 55–66 have also been divided into the work of a third author by some scholars. The discussion is complex and a commentary should be consulted for further information. Evangelical scholarship usually supports the traditional view of one author, the 8th Century BC prophet Isaiah. He was called to be a prophet (6:1) in 740 BC, was married (8:3) with at least two sons (8:18). Though prosperous under Uzziah, Judah under Ahaz came under dangerous Assyrian influence. Like his contemporary Micah, Isaiah warned Judah and Jerusalem in prophecy.

Conclusion : The debate over authorship only relates to history and the age in which the author lived. Regardless of dating, the prophecies still stand out as a wonderful promise of God's intervention for his people, which was fulfilled with Jesus Christ. Chapters 9, 11, and 53 stand out especially.

ISRAEL

was the new name, meaning 'He strives with God', given to the patriarch Jacob after wrestling with God during the night, at the ford of Jabbok (Genesis 32:22–28). Later the name Israel is used:

1. of the whole people; Israel, the children of Israel, the people Israel, the Israelites (Genesis 34:7; 2 Samuel 7:23–24; Psalm 14:7).

2. of the ten tribes of the Northern Kingdom. After the death of Solomon the country was divided into the Northern Kingdom – Israel, and the Southern Kingdom – Judah (1 Kings 12:19, 20, 28).

3. of the people after the captivity in Babylon (Matthew 8:10; Mark 15:32; Luke 1:68; Acts 13:16; Philippians 3:5).

Israel, History of

Approximate date	
1900 BC	Through the patriarchs Abraham, Isaac and Jacob God began to create and choose one particular people for his own, Israel.
1700 BC	Joseph came as a slave to Egypt, and rose to become Pharaoh's closest adviser. Joseph's family moved to Egypt.
1600 BC	Under successive Pharaohs the Israelites became slaves. They took part in the building of pyramids, walls, fortifications and cities.
1300 BC	The Israelites left Egypt under Moses' leadership. The period of wandering in the desert began.
1250 BC	The Israelites began to penetrate into Canaan and settle there.
1100 BC	The time of the Judges, those special leaders of the people, who emerged when Israel was threatened by warlike neighbouring nations. The last of the Judges was Samuel.
1030–1015 BC	Saul became the first king of Israel.
1015–975 BC	David king of Israel. The boundaries of the kingdom were extended. The Ark of the Covenant was moved to Jerusalem.

975–936 BC   Solomon king of Israel. The kingdom reached the boundaries promised to Abraham (1 Kings 4:24; 10:28, 29; Genesis 15:18–21). Solomon built a temple and other great buildings in Jerusalem. Trade with other countries increased. The people were taxed heavily.

936 BC   Solomon's kingdom was divided into the Northern Kingdom – Israel, and the Southern Kingdom – Judah. Solomon's son Rehoboam became king of Judah, with Jerusalem as his capital city. Jeroboam became king of Israel, with Shechem as his capital city (1 Kings 12:2).

Judah		Israel	
936–919 BC	Rehoboam king. Attempted to regain the kingdom of Israel, but failed.	936–919 BC	Jeroboam king.
930 BC	The Pharaoh of Egypt conquered Jerusalem, plundered the Temple and the royal palace.	886–874 BC	Omri king. He made Samaria the capital, and recaptured lost areas.
875–850 BC	Jehoshaphat king of Judah. Judah weaker than Israel.	874–852 BC	Omri's son, Ahab, king of Israel. The kingdom of Judah a vassal kingdom under Israel. Through Ahab's queen Jezebel, from Phoenicia, a special form of Baal worship entered Israel. The prophet Elijah defeated the prophets of Baal on Mt. Carmel.
850–842 BC	Jehoram king. Period of weakness. Philistines and other peoples raided and plundered.	853 BC	Together with several other kings Ahab fought Shalmaneser, king of Assyria, in a battle at Qarqar. Victory went to the Assyrian king.
		841–821 BC	Jehu ruled the Northern Kingdom. Several areas were lost. Elisha prophet until c. 800 BC.
		841 BC	Jehu sought help from Assyria against his enemies. He had to pay dearly for this to the king of Assyria. Nonetheless Jehu lost.
795–786 BC	Amaziah king. Judah defeated by king Joash of Israel. Jerusalem plundered. Amaziah taken captive.	804–788 BC	Joash king. The Northern Kingdom strengthened, and the lost areas regained. Joash defeated King Amaziah of Judah, conquered Jerusalem and plundered the city.
		788–747 BC	Jeroboam II king. Israel's period of greatness. The prophets Amos and Hosea appeared.
741–727 BC	Ahaz reigned. Attacked by the kings of Israel and Damascus, who wanted Ahaz to join their alliance against Assyria. But Ahaz sought Assyria's assistance.	735–732 BC	Pekah reigned. Together with the king of Damascus he attempted to defeat the king of Assyria.
732 BC	Help arrived. Damascus was captured. Israel was attacked and had to surrender to Assyria. Isaiah and Micah began to proclaim their prophecies.	732 BC	Tiglath-Pileser III, king of Assyria, deported part of the people of Israel. Hoshea became tributary king of Israel under Assyria.

| 727–696 BC | Hezekiah king. Broke the alliance with Assyria. Built the tunnel from Gihon to Siloam in order to provide Jerusalem with water. | 722 BC | King Hoshea tried to liberate Israel. The Assyrians besieged the capital, Samaria, and the city fell to the Assyrians 3 years later. The greater part of the people taken away into captivity. |
| | | 720 BC | Revolt in Israel among those Israelites who had been left in the country. This revolt was unsuccessful. The kingdom of Israel ceased to exist, and foreigners were settled in their territory. |

The kingdom of Judah

701 BC	King Sennacherib of Assyria laid siege to Jerusalem. The siege was interrupted, and the city was saved.
639–609 BC	Reign of Josiah. The Assyrian kingdom fell apart, and the kingdom of Judah was liberated. Josiah died in a battle against the Egyptians, and then Judah became a vassal kingdom under Egypt. Jeremiah appeared as a prophet in Judah until 586 BC.
608–597 BC	Reign of Jehoiakim.
605 BC	King Nebuchadnezzar of Babylonia defeated the Egyptians. Thus Judah became a tributary kingdom under Babylon.
597 BC	Jehoiakim revolted. Nebuchadnezzar captured Jerusalem. He carried away the treasures and riches of the city, and part of its inhabitants were taken into captivity, including Ezekiel.
597–586 BC	Zedekiah king. He rebelled against Babylonia.
586 BC	Jerusalem was conquered once more, the Temple was destroyed and the walls of the city were pulled down. All the inhabitants were taken prisoners and exiled to Babylon. The time after the exile (the post-exilic period). The Jews subject to various world powers.
539 BC	The Persian king Cyrus captured Babylon.
538 BC	The Jews began to return to their own country. They rebuilt the Temple under the inspiration of the prophets Haggai and Zechariah.
458 BC	Ezra led a fresh party of Jews from Babylon.
445 BC	Nehemiah rebuilt the walls of Jerusalem. The priest Ezra reformed the life of the Jews, so that they again followed the Law of Moses, the Torah.
333 BC	Alexander the Great captured Jerusalem. He was emperor of Greece. He spared the city from destruction.
323 BC	Alexander died.
300 BC	Alexander's successor in Egypt seized Palestine.
198 BC	One of Alexander's successors in Syria, Antiochus III, conquered Palestine.
167 BC	Antiochus' son, Antiochus IV Epiphanes, desecrated the temple and tried to force the Jews to worship the Greek gods. The Jewish priest Mattathias of the family of Maccabees became the leader of a Jewish war of liberation.
167–63 BC	Various members of the Maccabean family were leaders and commanders of the Jews.
63 BC	The Jewish leaders became disunited. Some of them sought help from the Roman commander Pompey, who conquered Jerusalem and subjected the country to Rome.
37–4 BC	Herod the Great feudal king of the Jews.
20 BC	The construction of Herod's temple at Jerusalem began.
5 BC (approx.)	The birth of Christ.
4BC – AD 6	Archelaus, son of Herod, ruled Judea. After him, Judea was ruled by Roman governors, for example Pilate.
4 BC – AD 39	Herod's son Herod Antipas governed Galilee and Perea.
AD 30 (approx.)	The death of Jesus.
AD 41–44	Herod Agrippa I ruled the whole of Palestine.

AD 47	The apostle Paul began his missionary journeys.
AD 54–100	Herod Agrippa II ruled part of Palestine.
AD 66	The Jews rebelled against the Romans.
AD 70	Jerusalem was totally destroyed by the Roman general Titus. The Jews were forbidden to remain in Jerusalem, and were scattered throughout the Roman empire.

ISSACHAR

was one of the sons of the patriarch Jacob and his wife Leah. Issachar became father of the tribe of Issachar, one of the twelve tribes of Israel. The area where this tribe lived was given the same name, and was situated just south of Lake Gennesaret.

It was a fertile area, but one of the smaller tribal areas in Israel. When the kingdom had been divided after King Solomon, the tribe of Issachar came to belong to the northern kingdom.

See: Genesis 30:18; 49:14–15; Joshua 19:17–23; Judges 5:15; 1 Kings 15:27–34

first century BC Ituraea became a kingdom, but it was divided in AD 34. The name of the country is connected with that of the tribe of Arabs who originally settled in the area. It formed part of the kingdom of Philip, brother of King Herod (Luke 3:1).

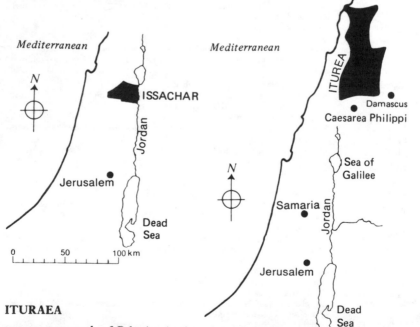

ITURAEA

was an area north of Palestine in the vicinity of Mount Lebanon. During the

J

JABBOK

is the name of a tributary of the River Jordan. It flows from the east into the Jordan. It is rich in water, but fairly shallow, with many fords where people are able to cross it.

The patriarch Jacob wrestled with God on the shore of the River Jabbok, before he went to meet his brother Esau (Genesis 32:22–32).

JACKAL SEE ANIMALS

JACOB'S WELL

was probably on the piece of land which the patriarch Jacob bought near Shechem, when he had returned to Canaan (Genesis 33:18, 19). Joseph's bones were interred here (Joshua 24:32). It was by Jacob's Well between the cities of Shechem and Sychar in Samaria that Jesus spoke to the Samaritan woman (John 4:5–30). A certain well near Shechem, which is 105 ft (32 m) deep and carefully constructed, has traditionally been identified as Jacob's Well. As early as at the end of the fourth century a church was built over this well.

JAMES, LETTER OF

The Letter of James in the New Testament contains only five chapters. In the Early Church it was thought that the letter had been written by James, brother of Jesus (Matthew 13:55; Galatians 1:19). If so it would date from about AD 60. The letter is addressed 'to the twelve tribes in the Dispersion'. The author means the Jewish Christians throughout the Roman Empire. 'Faith without works is dead' is the very practical message of this important letter.

Outline of Contents	Chapter
Resist temptation!	James 1:12–15
Do not only hear the word of God – do what it says!	James 1:22–25
Treat both rich and poor alike!	James 2:1–9
Faith which does not result in good deeds is a dead faith.	James 2:14–26
Be careful what you say!	James 3:1–12
Resist evil! Draw near to God!	James 4:1–8
The judgement of God will fall upon the unrighteous rich man. The poor and suffering should wait patiently. Christ's coming is near.	James 5:1–9
If you suffer, pray!	James 5:13
If you are ill, pray!	James 5:14, 15
Pray, as the prophet Elijah did!	James 5:17, 18

JEREMIAH, BOOK OF

The Book of Jeremiah in the Old Testament contains the speeches and prophecies of the prophet Jeremiah. In chapter 36 it is said that Jeremiah's friend Baruch wrote down, on the prophet's dictation, 'all the words of the Lord which he had spoken to him'.

Outline of Contents	Chapter
Prophecies and events before the destruction of Jerusalem by King Nebuchadnezzar of Babylon, and before he took the people away into captivity.	Jeremiah 1–39
What happened to Jeremiah and his fellow countrymen at home and in Egypt after the fall of Jerusalem.	Jeremiah 40–45
Prophecies about foreign peoples.	Jeremiah 46–51

JERICHO

is regarded as one of the oldest cities in the world. It is known to have been in existence as far back as the year 7000 BC, and perhaps even earlier. People

Pottery vase found at Jericho dating from the 17th century BC

lived in stone houses grouped around open courtyards. The site of ancient Jericho is about 11 miles (16 km) northwest of the point where the River Jordan runs into the Dead Sea.

Present-day Jericho is about 1 mile (1½ km) away. Jericho is situated in the Jordan Valley 820 ft (250 m) below sea-level, at the foot of the mountains of Judaea. There it is hot and humid all the year round, and the climate and vegetation is tropical. People grew date palms, balm and myrrh here. The Old Testament sometimes calls it the city of palm trees (Deuteronomy 34:3; Judges 1:16).

Jericho was the first city that the Israelites conquered, when, under Joshua as their military commander, they penetrated into Canaan in about 1200 BC. The walls of Jericho fell, and the city was occupied by the Israelites (Joshua 2–4).

The city of Jericho is in an area where earthquakes have been quite frequent, and it could be that the walls which surrounded Jericho were pushed outwards by an earthquake shock.

Jericho was the home of Zaccheus, the tax-collector (Luke 19:1–10), and also that of the blind man called Bartimaeus (Mark 10:46).

JERUSALEM

is situated on a high plateau in the mountains of Judea, about 2,675 ft (800 m) above sea level. One of the hills on which the city is built is called Mount Zion, and Jerusalem is sometimes called the city of Zion (e.g. Psalm 48:12; Jeremiah 3:14; Joel 2:1). The highest point is the Mount of Olives, east of the city, at 2,684 ft (818 m) above sea level.

Jerusalem was easily defended against enemies, since there were precipices on three sides, to the east, south and west of the city. There were a number of springs near Jerusalem. The Gihon spring was an especially important water supply for the city.

Jerusalem was in existence as early as at the time of Abraham. At that time the city was called Salem (Genesis 14:18). When the Israelites crossed into Canaan after wandering in the desert, Jerusalem was called 'Jebus', because it was the home of a tribe known as the Jebusites (Joshua 15:63; Judges 19:10; 1 Chronicles 11:4). Even in those early days the city was surrounded by a defence wall.

The city was conquered by King David, who made it the capital of Israel (2 Samuel 5:7; 1 Chronicles 11:7). David brought the Ark containing the two tablets of the Law to Jerusalem (2 Samuel 6:1–19). Jerusalem became a centre of worship of the God of Israel. David built an altar of burnt offering in a place which was called Araunah's (or Ornan's) threshing-floor (2 Samuel 24:18–25; 1 Chronicles 21:18–27). It was probably on this site that the Temple was built some years later.

Traditionally Mount Moriah, where Abraham was prepared to sacrifice his son Isaac, has been identified with the Temple hill in Jerusalem (2 Chronicles 3:1), although other scholars suppose

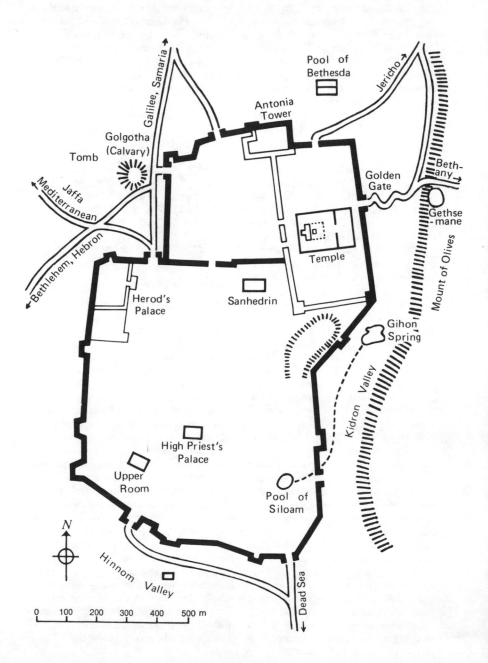

Pool of Bethesda

Jericho

Antonia Tower

Galilee, Samaria

Golgotha (Calvary)

Tomb

Beth-any →

Golden Gate

Jaffa

Mediterranean

Gethse-mane

Temple

Bethlehem, Hebron

Sanhedrin

Herod's Palace

Mount of Olives

Gihon Spring

High Priest's Palace

Kidron Valley

Upper Room

Pool of Siloam

N

Hinnom Valley

Dead Sea

0   100   200   300   400   500 m

that the description in Genesis 22 suggests another mountain with the same name. King Solomon built the first Temple in Jerusalem (1 Kings chs. 6 and 7). He also constructed a new wall around the city (1 Kings 9:15). King Hezekiah continued the fortification of the city walls, and also built the long tunnel (about 1,750 ft or 537 m), which brought water from the Gihon Spring into Jerusalem (2 Kings 20:20, see Gihon).

During Hezekiah's reign Jerusalem was besieged by the king of Assyria, Sennacherib, but the siege was lifted and Jerusalem was saved (2 Kings 18:13–19:36). In 597 BC Jerusalem was conquered by Nebuchadnezzar, king of Babylonia, who plundered the temple treasures and took the leading figures into captivity to Babylon (2 Kings 24:10–16). Nebuchadnezzar appointed Zedekiah king of Judah, but after a few years Zedekiah rose in revolt. Nebuchadnezzar now had all cities and fortifications in Judah burnt to the ground. He then besieged Jerusalem, which fell in 586 BC. The walls of Jerusalem were torn down, and the Temple was burnt. The greater part of the citizens were taken to Babylon as prisoners (2 Kings 25).

In about 539 BC the first party of Jews returned from Babylon to Jerusalem (Ezra 1). The Temple and some private houses were rebuilt. The prophets Haggai and Zechariah encouraged the people in their work (Ezra 5:1). Nehemiah returned as governor in 445 BC, and urged the inhabitants of Jerusalem to reconstruct the wall which had surrounded the city and build ten city gates. Approximately 100 years later Alexander the Great invaded Asia Minor and captured Jerusalem, but refrained from destroying it.

In the year 37 BC Jerusalem was occupied by the Roman tributary king Herod. He rebuilt large parts of Jerusalem, expanded the city and strengthened its walls. Herod rebuilt and enlarged the Temple over many years (John 2:20) adding to the Temple area large courtyards, terraces and colonnades. The palace of Herod and the fortress of Antonia were built during this period.

The Jews revolted against the Romans in AD 66. The Roman military com-

Titus's victory arch at Jerusalem

mander Titus besieged Jerusalem with 80,000 soldiers. The city was stormed and totally destroyed. Of the original buildings only a few of the gates, part of the west wall and three towers were left. The historian Josephus tells us that the bodies of about 600,000 Jews who had been killed in the battle were lying in the streets of Jerusalem. Most survivors were sold as slaves. All this happened in AD 70.

In Rome, on the Arch of Titus which was erected in memory of the Roman victory over the Jews, there are pictures of the seven branched lampstand (candlestick) and the table of the Bread of the Presence which the Romans took away with them from the Temple in Jerusalem. After this, the Jews were prohibited from living in Jerusalem. This ban was in existence for several hundred years. The city was gradually rebuilt. In AD 637 the Muslim ruler Omar conquered Jerusalem. On this site of the Temple the so-called Dome of the Rock was built, and this mosque is still there today.

A detail from Titus's Arch showing the seven armed candlestick from the Temple in Jerusalem

In 1917 Palestine and Jerusalem were conquered by British troops. The Jews began to return to Palestine. 1948 saw the foundation of the new State of Israel. Jerusalem was divided between Jews and Arabs, and became the capital of Israel. In 1967 the Israeli forces occupied the whole of Jerusalem.

JERUSALEM, COUNCIL OF

The Council of Jerusalem is the commonly used name for one particular meeting in Jerusalem during the earliest years of the Christian Church, about AD 48–49 (Acts 15). In this council, under the presidency of James, the Lord's brother, the apostles and other Christian leaders agreed that Gentiles who had become Christians were not obliged to be circumcised and to keep the Law of Moses. It was not the Law which gave men salvation, but faith in Jesus Christ.

JESUS CHRIST, LIFE OF

The most important writings from which we may learn about the Jesus of

history are the gospels by Evangelists Matthew, Mark, Luke and John and the letters of Paul. Jesus Christ is also mentioned by the non-Christian historians Josephus and Tacitus, among others. There is overwhelming support in historical writings for the existence of Jesus, and it is simply not possible to claim that he never existed.

The name 'Jesus' means 'God is salvation', and the title 'Christ' means 'the anointed one', that is, the Messiah.

The New Testament calls Jesus	
The Messiah – the anointed one	Matthew 16:16; Luke 4:41; John 20:31
The Son of God	Luke 1:35; John 11:27
The Lamb of God	John 1:29, 36; Revelation 5:6, 12
The Son of Man	Matthew 9:6; Mark 2:28; Luke 12:40
The Saviour of the World	Luke 2:11; John 4:42; 1 John 4:14
The Son of Mary	Matthew 13:55; Galatians 4:4

Important events in the Life of Jesus	
Jesus is born	Matthew 1–2
Jesus at the age of twelve in the Temple	Luke 2:41–52
Jesus is baptized by John the Baptist	Matthew 3:13–17
Jesus is tempted in the desert	Matthew 4:1–11
Jesus begins his ministry	Matthew 4:12–17
Jesus calls his first disciples	Matthew 4:18–22
Jesus heals the sick	Matthew 8:16–17
Jesus feeds the five thousand	Matthew 14:13–21
Jesus is recognized by Peter to be the Messiah	Matthew 16:13–20
Jesus talks to Moses and Elijah on the Mount of Transfiguration	Matthew 17:1–8
Jesus blesses the children	Matthew 19:13–15
Jesus rides into Jerusalem	Matthew 21:1–11
Jesus cleanses the Temple	Matthew 21:12–17

Jesus speaks of his second coming	Matthew 24:4-8
Jesus institutes the Lord's supper (Holy Communion, Eucharist)	Matthew 26:26-29; I Corinthians 11:23-26
Jesus is betrayed by Judas and arrested in Gethsemane	Matthew 26:36-56
Jesus is tried by the Jews and sentenced by Pontius Pilate	Matthew 27:15-26
Jesus is crucified	Matthew 27:33-56
Jesus is laid in the tomb	Matthew 27:57-61
Jesus rises from the dead	Matthew 28:1-10
Jesus shows himself to his disciples	Matthew 28:16-17
Jesus gives his disciples 'the great commission'	Matthew 28:18-20
Jesus ascends into heaven	Acts 1:9-11

There are parallels to the above references in the other Gospels

See Passion of Christ, Gethsemane, Golgotha, Cross, Resurrection, Sermon on the Mount, Parables.

JEWELS SEE ORNAMENTS

JEWISH CHRISTIANS SEE JUDAEO-CHRISTIANS

JEWS

After the Babylonian captivity the Israelites were usually called Jews. It was only the inhabitants of the kingdom of Judah who returned to Palestine from the exile. The inhabitants of the Northern Kingdom, Israel, never came back *en masse* after having been removed to Assyria in 721 BC. Through the inhabitants of Judah, the Jews, the people of Israel lived on.

JEZREEL

was the name of a city and a plain in Palestine situated southwest of Lake Gennesaret. This plain, or valley of Jezreel (as it was also called), was a very fertile area. The Hebrew name means 'God sows' or 'May God make fruitful'.

Jezreel was the site of Ahab's palace and his seizure of Naboth's vineyard (I Kings 21) and here Jezebel and her son, Joram, were massacred (2 Kings 9).

JOB, BOOK OF

Job is the main character in the Book of Job in the Old Testament. It is difficult to say exactly how old the book is. Perhaps it dates back as far as the 9th century BC. Its theme is suffering. People regarded wealth and prosperity as God's reward for good behaviour. On the other hand they saw suffering as a punishment for sinful behaviour. The book of Job demonstrates that this is not always true and that the problem of suffering cannot be dismissed in this easy way.

Outline of Contents	Chapter
Job lived in the land of Uz near Arabia. He was a just man who feared God.	Job 1:1
He had seven sons and three daughters, and possessed great riches.	Job 1:2, 3
The Adversary, Satan, received God's permission to test Job and his faithfulness to God!	Job 1:9-12; 2:6
Job was now struck by several disasters. He lost his sons and daughters, and all his possessions were taken from him. Finally he suffered a serious illness.	Job 1:13-19; 2:7
In spite of illness and disaster Job tries to keep his faith in a just and merciful God.	Job 1:20-22; 2:10
Job's three friends, Eliphaz, Bildad and Zophar, come to comfort him.	Job 2:11
Job curses the day of his birth and wishes for death.	Job 3
The friends assume that Job must have sinned, and tell him to confess his sin. Each speaks in turn and Job answers him.	Job 4-31
A young man, Elihu, takes	

on when the friends are silenced.	Job 32–37
Finally God gives Job his answer. Before God's majesty and omnipotence Job stands quiet and humble. God is greater than man's understanding.	Job 38–41
Job humbles himself before God. His happiness and wealth are returned to him	Job 42

JOEL, BOOK OF

The author of the Book of Joel in the Old Testament is the prophet Joel, the son of Pethuel. The book probably dates back to the time before the Babylonian exile. The Book of Joel tells us that bad drought and swarms of locusts plagued the land. The prophet bewailed the disaster and exhorted the people to repentance. The words were a message to the prophet's contemporaries. But prophets also spoke about events far into the future. The day of the Lord will descend on Israel, if the people do not repent. But over those who repent (the 'remnant' of Israel) God will send his Spirit.

The apostle Peter quoted the Book of Joel 2:28–32 at the first Pentecost, in order to explain to his astonished listeners what was happening: 'And it shall come to pass afterward, that I will pour out my spirit on all flesh; your sons and your daughters shall prophesy, your old men shall dream dreams and your young men shall see visions.'

JOHN, GOSPEL OF

The Gospel of John is the Fourth Gospel in the New Testament. Traditionally the author has been identified with the apostle John, son of Zebedee and brother of James. He is referred to as the 'disciple whom Jesus loved' (John 21:20). It is likely that the letters and Gospel of John

are written by the same author. The Fourth Gospel is generally considered to be the latest of the Gospels, written after AD 90. However, recent archaeological discoveries and research have suggested that John contains material dating back as early as anything in the other Gospels. The language of John resembles the Palestinian thinking found in the Dead Sea Scrolls in 1947. Excavations completed in the 1930's actually dug up the Pool of Bethesda (John 5:1) and the Pavement where Pilate sat in judgement on Jesus (John 19:13). All this evidence has re-affirmed the historical basis of the Fourth Gospel. But it stands apart from the other three Gospels in its structure, with the seven 'I am' sayings and in its content, with its very few parables and independence from Mark's Gospel, which Luke and Matthew both made extensive use of.

Written in Greek, the purpose of the gospel writer is made clear in John 20:31; 'These things are written that you might believe that Jesus is the Christ, the Son of God; and that believing you might have life through his name.'

There are other differences from the other three gospels of Matthew, Mark and Luke. It lacks many of the events in the life of Christ, which are told in the first three Gospels. But the Gospel of John instead contains material that is not found in the others. This Gospel gives greater space than the others to Jesus' preaching, to what he said in his conversations with individuals, or when there were a number of listeners, especially on his visits to Jerusalem the other Gospels do not record.

The Gospel of John may be divided into different sections:

A solemn introduction introducing Jesus Christ as the eternal Word of God who is himself God (1:1–18).

Events during Christ's life on earth (Chapters 1–12).

Jesus tells his disciples about his death and his return (Chapters 13-17).

The passion, death and resurrection of Jesus Christ (Chapters 18-20).

JOHN, LETTERS OF

The Letters of John in the New Testament are probably written by the same John who is the author of the Gospel of John. There are three letters.

The First Letter lacks an address and the usual ending with greetings, but its opening is similar in theme to the opening of the Gospel. The letter contains teaching, exhortation and warning. Certain teachers had come into the Christian churches who taught that Jesus had never possessed complete and true human nature, or been a man among men. They said that he was a heavenly being, who perhaps borrowed a human body only during the time from his baptism to the crucifixion. John warns the Christians against believing such talk (1 John 2:22; 4:2; 5:1, 6). He also exhorts Christians to love each other. The well-known words 'God is love' are found in this letter (1 John 4:16).

The Second Letter is addressed to 'the elect lady and her children'. It is thought that the author means one particular Christian church and its members. The letter ends with greetings. In this letter John asks the Christians to love each other and to guard against those teachers mentioned already in the first letter.

The Third Letter is written to an individual, Gaius. John praises him as a faithful worker in the church. The letter is concluded with greetings and a wish for a meeting before long.

JOHN, REVELATION, SEE REVELATION TO JOHN

JONAH, BOOK OF

The Book of Jonah is one of the prophetic books of the Old Testament. It deals with Jonah, who was a prophet in the 8th century BC (2 Kings 14:25). He was commanded by God to preach judgement and punishment over the godless city of Nineveh, capital of Assyria.

Jonah did not obey the Lord, but sailed in a ship in the opposite direction. There was a storm, and during the storm the mariners reluctantly threw Jonah overboard, after he had admitted that he was the cause of it. The storm ceased immediately. Jonah was swallowed by a great fish, but after three days the fish threw him up on land, unharmed.

After that Jonah was willing to act on God's command, to go to Nineveh and warn the inhabitants about the imminent judgement. The people of the city repented their evil actions and turned to God. The city was spared from judgement and destruction.

Jonah was angry when he saw that God did not punish the city. At the end of the book, Jonah shelters from the hot sun under a plant (probably the castor oil plant, although the Authorized Version reads 'a gourd'), which then withers and dies. Jonah is upset over this, but God teaches him by this means that he is a loving and merciful God, not only towards Israel, but also to other nations.

JOPPA

In Jesus' day, Joppa was the name of a seaport on the coast of the Mediterranean north-west of Jerusalem.

The apostle Peter visited the city. There he brought the dead girl Tabitha back to life, and stayed with Simon the tanner (Acts 9:36-43). Here he saw the vision of the sheet of sail cloth (NEB) filled with all kinds of animals, many of them unclean according to the Jewish Law. It was from there that he was taken to the Roman centurion, Cornelius, at Caesarea, whom he might have rejected as an unclean Gentile if he had not had his vision (Acts 10:28, 29). King Solomon used the city as a port, when the materials for the building of the Temple were imported into the country (2 Chronicles 2:16).

The modern city is called Jaffa. Today Jaffa is one of the most important ports in the Republic of Israel. The main export through this port is oranges.

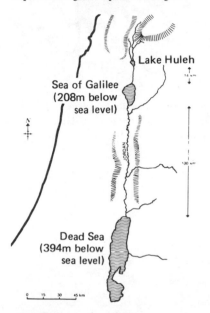

JORDAN

is the most frequently mentioned river in the Bible, ie some 200 times. The river itself is about 240 miles (380 km) long. Its course is meandering. It comes from sources at the foot of Mount Hermon. It flows in a valley through Lake Huleh and Lake Gennesaret to the Dead Sea. Dense shrub vegetation grows along its banks. In the past this offered protection and hiding places to lions and other wild animals. The amount of water in the river is greatest in April-May, when the snows on the Lebanon hills are melting.

Israel crossed the Jordan into Palestine under the leadership of Joshua (Joshua 3 and 4). Jordan was Israel's boundary against the different peoples who lived to the east. John the Baptist preached and baptized by the River Jordan. Jesus, too, was baptized by John in this river (Matthew 3).

In our day there are power stations by the river, and plants for irrigation (watering) of dry or desert areas.

Modern hymns and spirituals use the crossing of Jordan as a picture of passing from the wilderness of earth to the promised land of heaven.

JOSEPHUS

was a Jewish historian who lived in about AD 37 – 100. He came from a priestly family and he was a Pharisee. When the Jews rose in revolt against the Romans in the years after AD 60, Josephus was given the task of organizing the resistance against the Romans in Galilee. Josephus was taken prisoner, and thereafter was suspected as being an agent of Rome. Josephus has written about this war in his book *Wars of the Jews*.

In his other book, *Antiquities of the Jews*, he began with the creation and wrote the whole history of the Jewish people, retelling and supplementing the Old Testament.

JOSHUA, BOOK OF

After Moses' death it was Joshua who led God's people into the promised land of Canaan. The story is told in the book of Joshua. Joshua, the son of Nun, had been Moses' assistant during the time in the wilderness (Exodus 24:13; 33:11; Numbers 11:28). He had been one of the spies who entered the promised land (Numbers 13) and had battle experience before the conquest (Exodus 17:8-14; Numbers 27:18-21; Deuteronomy 3:38; 31:1-6; 34:9). After crossing the

Jordan, probably in the 13th century BC, Joshua led the people in their conquest of the land. He divided the land among the people and gave them a stirring reminder of all that God had hoped for them and all that he required of them, in his final address (Joshua 24).

JUDAEO-CHRISTIANS

or, more simply, Jewish Christians, is a convenient way of referring to those Jews who had become Christians. In the beginning most of the members of the Christian church were Jewish Christians. Some of them thought that the Christian faith was little more than a branch of Judaism. Later, when Gentiles were converted to Christianity, some Jewish Christians demanded that the Gentile Christians, too, should live according to the Jewish Law. Paul was one of the apostles who argued most strongly that the Christian was not bound by the laws and regulations of Judaism.

At a council in Jerusalem the apostles agreed on a number of rules concerning the Gentile Christians. They accepted that the Gentile Christians would not have to be circumcised and adopt Judaism. (Acts 15:1–33; Galatians 2:2–10). See: Jerusalem, Council of

JUDAH

was one of the sons of the patriarch Jacob. Judah became the father of the tribe of Judah. The area in which the tribe lived was also called Judah, and was in the southern part of Palestine (Joshua 15:1–12).

During the reign of king David, Judah became the most important of the twelve tribes of Israel. Judah is the tribe from which the future Messiah was to come (Genesis 49:8–12; Micah 5:2; Matthew 2:6). When the country was divided after king Solomon the southern part was called the Kingdom of Judah.

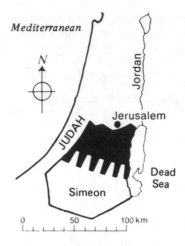

Jerusalem was in this kingdom, and since the Temple was in Jerusalem, Judah continued to be the centre of Jewish worship.

JUDAH, KINGDOM OF

When king Solomon died, Palestine was divided into two kingdoms, and the southern centred round Judah (see under Israel, History of).

The map shows the kingdoms of Judah and Israel when their borders were at their widest.

JUDE, LETTER OF

The letter of Jude, towards the end of the New Testament, warns against false Christian teachers who have come into the Christian churches. It is thought that the author is Jesus' own brother, Jude (Matthew 13:55). It is not known to whom the letter was addressed.

JUDEA

In the New Testament Judea is the name of the area around Jerusalem. The name began to be used after the Exile to describe the Jewish state. Under the Maccabees Judea became an important kingdom. Sometimes the name was taken to mean the whole of Palestine as, for instance, during the Roman occupation, when Herod the Great was titled king of Judea (Matthew 2:1; Luke 5:17). The Wilderness of Judea was the arid and mountainous region immediately west of the Dead Sea (Matthew 3:1).

An Egyptian relief showing captives from Palestine. The central figure is a Philistine. (The Philistines were some of the most bitter enemies of the Israelites during the time of the Judges)

JUDGES, BOOK OF

The Book of Judges was named after the 'judges' who, on various occasions during the 13th and 12th centuries BC, were raised up by God as leaders and princes of Israel. The Judges often came into power when Israel was threatened by the warlike peoples of its neighbour countries. The Judges could also call up one or more of Israel's tribes for expeditions of conquest or plunder.

Only on rare occasions would the Judges exercise a legal function, passing judgement in conflicts between individuals and distributing sentences.

The Book of Judges contains the history of Israel from the death of Joshua to the time of the Judge and Prophet Samuel.

Judges in Israel	Chapter
Othniel, of the tribe of Judah	Judges 3:9–11
Ehud, of the tribe of Benjamin	Judges 3:15–30
Shamgar	Judges 3:31
Deborah, of the tribe of Ephraim	Judges 5
Gideon, of the tribe of Manasseh	Judges 6–8
Tola, of the tribe of Issachar	Judges 10:1, 2
Jair	Judges 10:3–5
Jephthah	Judges 11:1–12:7
Ibzan	Judges 12:8–10
Elon of the tribe of Zebulon	Judges 12:11, 12
Abdon of the tribe of Ephraim	Judges 12:13–15
Samson of the tribe of Dan	Judges 13–16

In addition Abimelech set himself up as king (Judges 9). Many of the judges were in power at one and the same time in different areas. In 1 Samuel Eli and Samuel are mentioned as being the last Judges of Israel (1 Samuel 4:18; 7:15–17). Samuel's sons were unacceptable as Judges (1 Samuel 8:1–3).

K

KADESH

or Kadesh-Barnea was a place on the Sinai peninsula near the southern border of Palestine, but the exact site is not known. The Israelites stayed here on several occasions during their wanderings in the desert.

See Numbers 13:26, 27; 20:1, 2; Deuteronomy 1:19; Judges 11:16–17; Psalm 29:8

KEYS SEE LOCKS

KIDRON

was the name of a valley east of Jerusalem between the city and the Mount of Olives. This valley was also called the Valley of Jehoshaphat. At the bottom of the valley there was a brook, which was dry for the greater part of the year. Jesus crossed the Brook of Kidron in order to reach Gethsemane, on the night when he was seized by his enemies.

See 2 Chronicles 29:16; John 18:1.

KINGDOM OF GOD, OR KINGDOM OF HEAVEN

The rule of God inaugurated on earth by Christ, the Messiah (Isaiah 9:6, 7; Mark 1:15). It is now being worked out through Christ's people (Matthew 6:10; John 3:3, 5; 1 Thessalonians 2:12). Eventually it will be consummated through the Second Coming of Christ (Revelation 11:15). Commentators differ over whether Revelation 20:4–6 refers to a rule of Christ and his people on earth, or whether the description is symbolic of the whole Christian era.

See Day of the Lord

KINGDOM OF THE DEAD

The Old Testament speaks of the kingdom of the dead (Hebrew *Sheol*) as a life of shadows. The kingdom of the dead is spoken of as situated in the earth or under it. It was a silent dark and desolate country where oblivion reigned, and from which no one returned (Job 10:21, 22; Psalm 6:5; 30:9). Gradually the Jews began thinking that there were two areas in Sheol, one for the righteous and the other for the unrighteous. Eventually there would be a resurrection for bliss or judgement (Psalm 17:15; 49:15; Isaiah 26:19; Daniel 12:2).

In the New Testament, too, there is a division of good and evil after death, in Hades, which is the Greek equivalent of Sheol (Luke 16:19–31). But here the emphasis is on the good news: 'Christ is the conqueror of death' (1 Corinthians 15:12–19; 2 Timothy 1:10) although hell is still for the wicked.

See Gehenna

KINGS, BOOKS OF THE

The Books of the Kings in the Old Testament contain the history of Israel from the last years of David's reign to the end of the Babylonian captivity.

The Books of the Kings may be divided into different sections:

Contents	Chapter
Israel's period of greatness under king Solomon	1 Kings 1–11
The period after Solomon, when the kingdom was divided into the Northern Kingdom (Israel) and the Southern Kingdom (Judah), up to the destruction of Israel in 722 BC	1 Kings 12– 2 Kings 17
The history of the kingdom of Judah up to the fall of Jerusalem and the Babylonian captivity in 586 BC	2 Kings 18–25

L

LACHISH

Situated 30 miles south west of Jerusalem, Lachish was an important fortified city of Judah guarding the main road to Jerusalem. It was captured by Joshua (Joshua 10:32) in a two-day attack and was then burnt. Rehoboam rebuilt the city as one of 15 fortified cities to protect Judah from any attack from Egypt or the Philistines (2 Chronicles 11:5–12). There was a double-walled defence with massive stone masonry (2 Chronicles 14:6). Micah listed reliance on Lachish's strength as a sin of Israel (Micah 1:13). In 701 BC Sennacherib put the city under siege (2 Kings 18:13) to cut off Jerusalem from any Egyptian support. The siege can be seen pictured on the walls of his palace at Nineveh now preserved in part at the British Museum. Lachish fell and was taken over by the Assyrians. The rebuilt city was attacked again at a later period by Nebuchadnez-zar II in 597 BC (see Jeremiah 34:7), and the walls demolished.

Nebuchadnezzar's attack crushed the rebellion started by King Zedekiah. From 1932–1938 the city was excavated by the Wellcome-Marston Archaeological Expedition, and many important inscriptions found. These include remnants of letters written on pottery, which contain reports to the city army commanders showing the desperate situation of the city.

LAMENTATIONS

The Old Testament book of Lamentations focuses on grief, doom and hope. Although an anonymous book, some traditions point to Jeremiah as a possible author, on the basis of 2 Chronicles 35:25 where the prophet laments the death of Josiah. The first four chapters are poetic, the first three with 66 lines and the fourth with 44. They were written in an acrostic style to help memory of the poems. Each verse of chapters 1 and 2 begins with a fresh letter in alphabetical order. In chapter 3, three successive one-line verses use all 22 letters of the Hebrew alphabet. The repetitive dirge-like rhythm can be depressing to read and carries the feeling

The city of Lachish

of grief powerfully. Though the overall message is of God punishing and destroying Jerusalem for its sin, there are glimmers of hope (3:19–39). The author links suffering to the goodness of God in the midst of the disasters of the third chapter. The book was written as a poetic song for funerals and mourning, but the promise of God's mercy gives hope (5:19).

Ancient Israelite lamp for one of several wicks.

Oil lamp from the early Christian era with a spout handle and a hole for pouring in oil

LAMPS

Lamps could be found in every home in Palestine. They consisted of pottery bowls filled with olive oil. The lamp could have one or several wicks. During the night one lamp at least would be kept burning, so that fire and light were always available (Proverbs 31:18). Sometimes these oil lamps were put on a special lampstand or candelabrum so as to spread their light better (Matthew 5:15).

In the Temple at Jerusalem there was the seven-armed lampstand, called the Menorah. An oil-lamp was placed at the top of each of its arms (Exodus 25:31–39; 1 Kings 7:49). After the Exile there was a continually burning lamp in the Temple and in the synagogues. This

Seven armed lamp stand (The Menorah) from the Temple in Jerusalem

eternity lamp is found also in present-day synagogues, and is a reminder of the presence of God.

The lamp was not only a household article but was also carried to light the way (Matthew 25:1–10). Thus Psalm 119:105 likens the Word of God to a lamp; 'thy word is a lamp to my feet and a light to my path'.

LANGUAGES

In Genesis we are told about the great Flood, when Noah and his family were saved. The descendants of Noah and his sons, according to the biblical story, became the inhabitants of different parts of the earth, but were still one people speaking the same language. The story of the Tower of Babel is the Old Testament's explanation of the emergence of different languages as a punishment for man's evil (Genesis 11:1–9).

The Old Testament is written in the Hebrew language, with the exception of certain short passages, which are in Aramaic. Hebrew became the language of the Israelites after the settlement in Canaan. Hebrew is a Semitic language, and is, like the other Semitic languages, a 'consonant language', where vowels occupy a subordinate position.

In the Babylonian exile the Israelites came into contact with the Aramaic language, which was the internationally understood language of Asia Minor. In the 6th century BC Aramaic was generally spoken in Palestine, but Hebrew remained the language of worship, the sacred language.

Hebrew mixed with Aramaic was used in Jewish Scriptures after the biblical period. Modern Hebrew came from this mixed language. Yiddish, the language of many Jews in Europe and America, is basically German, with additions from Hebrew and other languages. It is written in Hebrew script. The name comes from the German *judisch*, Jewish.

The New Testament was written in Greek. When the books of the New Testament were compiled, Greek was the universal language of the Roman Empire. The language of New Testament Greek was the common language of the day, Greek as it was spoken in conversation, not literary Greek.

The Bible links the outburst of speaking in tongues at Pentecost (Acts 2) with the Tower of Babel story, and suggests that the confusion of languages at Babel was reversed at Pentecost. People from all over the world heard the good news preached and praised God in their own language.

LAODICEA

A commercial city in the Roman province of Asia, founded by Antiochus II in the mid-3rd century BC and named after his wife Laodice. It was so wealthy that even when an earthquake devastated it in AD 60, it was able to refuse financial help offered by the Romans (Revelation 3:17). It was on the cross-roads across Asia Minor between Syria and the ports of Ephesus and Miletus. There was no water supply in the city and so water had to be piped from hot springs some distance outside the city down into the city. The hot water was therefore luke-warm when it reached the town. The writer of the letter to the Church of Laodicea in Revelation 3 criticizes it for being luke-warm like its water supply (v.16) and refers to the eye salve for which it was famous (v.18). Colossians 4:16 refers to the 'letter from Laodicea' which was probably their copy of 'Ephesians' which was circulated in Asia Minor.

LAWYERS SEE SCRIBES

LAYING-ON OF HANDS

The New Testament records several incidents in which hands are laid on or the hands of one person are placed upon another for a variety of purposes. Jesus and later the apostles laid on hands for the purpose of healing (Matthew 9:18; Mark 7:32; 10:16; Acts 9:12; 28:8). Hands are also laid on for the giving of the Holy Spirit (Acts 8:17; 19:6) and for commissioning in Christian service (Acts 6:6; 13:3; 1 Timothy 4:14). We should bear in mind that healing also takes place, and the Holy Spirit is received, without the laying-on of hands.

It is important not to think of the laying-on of hands as a kind of magic formula for conveying power. It was a sign, used with prayer to authenticate God's action in an individual to prepare him for some special task, and used also to convey healing and preparation for Christian ministry.

LEAVEN SEE BREAD, FESTIVALS

LEBANON

is a mountain-range which extends from Syria to the northern border of Palestine. It is about 100 miles (160 km) long with several peaks of 9,840 ft (3,000 m), which are snow-covered for a large part of the year.

Parallel with and east of Lebanon is Anti-Lebanon, which is a mountain-range of about the same length and height. Mount Hermon is situated on the Anti-Lebanon. There is a fertile valley between the two mountain-ranges. At the time of the Bible the Lebanon was covered with large forests of cedar and cypress, and some groves of trees still remain.

See 1 Kings 5:6–14; 2 Kings 14:9; 19:23; Isaiah 40:16; 60:13

LEGION

was the name of a Roman army unit, consisting of about 5,000 soldiers. In the New Testament the word 'legion' is also used to signify a very large number.

See Matthew 26:53; Mark 5:9; Luke 8:30.

LEPROSY SEE DISEASE

LETTERS

were fairly common in the ancient Orient. Important finds of letters have been made at Lachish in Palestine. Letters which were sent to and from Palestine before Israel's settlement there have been found at Amarna in Egypt.

Papyrus letters dating from the time after the Exile have been found at Elephantine in Egypt.

Large parts of the New Testament are written in the form of letters (or 'epistles', from the Greek word meaning letter). The apostle Paul is the author of most of them. There was no regular postal service, so letters were sent by special messenger or with travellers.

The writing materials were tablets of wax, potsherds or papyrus strips. The latter could be rolled up and kept in a tube for protection.

If a person wanted to have a letter written, he or she could ask for help from professional scribes, who would write the letter, and who would be paid a sum of money for their services. Paul's reference in Galatians 6:11 shows that he dictated his letters, owing probably to poor eyesight, even though he added something in his own hand. Paul's letters tend to begin and end in the same way, which was in keeping with the pattern of his day where letter-writing was a definite art form.

LEVI

was one of the sons of the patriarch Jacob (Genesis 29:34). Levi became the father of the tribe of Levi. This tribe was not given an area of their own in Canaan, when the country was divided between the tribes of Israel, but the Levites were settled in forty-eight cities up and down the land (Numbers 35:1–8). They became assistants to the priestly family of Aaron. As a salary for this service they were given tithes by the people and became the priestly tribe (Numbers 18:2–7, 21–32). They were responsible for the music and singing in the Temple (1 Chronicles 6:31–48; 15:16–24).

LEVITICUS

This, the third book of Moses, deals mainly with matters of Jewish law and ritual. Hence it is often formal and legal in style like the rubrics and regulations in Prayer Books. This does not indicate different authorship from the narrative portions.

LIFE, BOOK OF SEE BOOK OF LIFE

LIFE, TREE OF SEE TREE OF LIFE

LILIES SEE FLOWERS

LINE

A line attached to a plummet was used when building houses to ensure that the walls were vertical (Zechariah 4:10). Also a measuring line was used as we use a measure today (Isaiah 34:17; 44:13; Zechariah 2:1, 2). See also Plummet.

LION SEE ANIMALS

LOCKS AND KEYS

were usually made of wood. The oldest device for locking a door was a bar or bolt. With these a door could be locked from the inside. Gradually people learnt to use locks which could be locked and unlocked from the outside with a key. See Judges 3:23-25; Isaiah 22:22; John 20:19; Revelation 1:18; 3:7; 20:1.

LOCUSTS SEE ANIMALS

LORD'S DAY SEE FESTIVALS

LUKE, GOSPEL OF

The third Gospel is normally regarded as the work of Luke, a doctor who accompanied Paul on some of his travels. It was written to one man, Theophilus, in order to give him accurate knowledge of the Christian faith. The author, Luke, wants Theophilus to know the truth of the events about Jesus Christ of which he has heard (1:1-4).

In chapter 3, where he tells us about John the Baptist, he mentions several contemporary and well-known people by name: the emperor Tiberius, the governor of Judea Pontius Pilate, the regional tetrarchs Herod, Philip and Lysanias, and the high priests Annas and Caiaphas. Luke shows that Jesus is Saviour not only of the Jews but of all mankind. He also likes to describe how Jesus meets tax-collectors, sinners and poor people.

The gospel of Luke may be divided into several parts:

Outline of Contents	Chapters
The birth and childhood of Christ.	Luke 1:5-2:52
The vocation and work of Jesus in Galilee.	Luke 3:4-9:50
The journey to Jerusalem.	Luke 9:51-19:27
The passion of Christ.	Luke 19:28-ch.23
The resurrection of Christ from the dead.	Luke 24

Luke has a particular interest in history (e.g. 3:1-2), in women, in the poor and in the non-Jew. Such stories as the Good Samaritan, the Prodigal Son, the Rich Man and Lazarus occur only in Luke, in the section chs. 9-18, which contains material not used by the other Gospel writers. It is believed that Luke may have discovered these recollections of Jesus' teaching in the district of Caesarea.

LYCAONIA

was the name of an area in Asia Minor, which the apostle Paul travelled through. He preached there in the cities of Lystra and Derbe.

LYSTRA

Situated in an obscure part of Asia Minor, Paul visited it on his first and second missionary journeys. Paul and Barnabas hoped to find refuge there after a stormy visit to Iconium, but their plan badly misfired. Superstitious practices brought hostility to Paul and he was stoned. His injuries were so severe that his persecutors abandoned his body outside the town thinking he must be dead (Acts 14:19). This was perhaps the closest Paul came to death on this journey. Nevertheless, the good news found its way to the people of Lystra and a church was established (Acts 14:20-23). From the town that nearly killed Paul emerged the young Timothy, one of the apostle's closest friends and most dedicated colleagues (Acts 16:1-5; Philippians 2:19-24).

M

MACCABEES, BOOKS OF THE

The Books of the Maccabees are four apocryphal books of the Old Testament (see Apocrypha).

1. The first of the four Books of the Maccabees tells the history of events in Israel during the years 175–135 BC. This book is an especially valuable source of information about this period.

The Syrian king, Antiochus IV Epiphanes, wished to prevent Jewish worship and built a pagan altar in the Temple at Jerusalem. Then the Jews, under the leadership of a priest called Mattathias of the Maccabean family, began a war of liberation. This war is described in the First Book of the Maccabees.

2. The Second book of the Maccabees describes the same period in Israel as the First, but scholars regard the First Book as a more accurate source of historical information.

3, 4. The Third and Fourth Books of the Maccabees treat of certain individual events from the history of Israel, partly from the Maccabean period.

MACCABEES, HISTORY OF

333 BC	Alexander the Great, ruler of the Greek empire, conquered Palestine.
323 BC	Alexander the Great died.
300 BC	Alexander's successor in Egypt (of the Ptolemaic Dynasty) conquered Palestine.
198 BC	Alexander's successor in Syria, Antiochus III (of the Seleucid dynasty) conquered Palestine.
167 BC	Antiochus' son, Antiochus IV Epiphanes, wanted to force the Jews to worship Greek gods. The image of a Greek god was set up in the Temple at Jerusalem. The Jewish priest Mattathias (of the Maccabean family) killed one Jew who had sacrificed to Greek gods, as well as the Syrian who had forced him to sacrifice. This event was the beginning of the Jewish war of liberation. Mattathias had to flee to the mountains with his five sons. He gathered large numbers of freedom fighters around him.
166 BC	Mattathias died and his son Judas Maccabeus became the leader of the Jewish revolutionaries. He continued the revolt.
165 BC	The Temple at Jerusalem was purified and rededicated (December). After this event the Feast of Dedication was celebrated every year (see under Festivals).
163 BC	The Jews won the right of worshipping their God as before.
161 BC	Judas Maccabeus was killed in battle and his youngest brother, Jonathan, continued the Jewish war successfully.
153 BC	Jonathan Maccabeus was appointed High Priest in Jerusalem.
144 BC	Jonathan was killed and his elder brother Simon Maccabeus became High Priest and leader of the Jews. The Jews no longer needed to pay tribute to Syria. Israel now became an independent country.
135 BC	Simon's son, Judas Maccabeus, was killed and was succeeded by his brother, John Hyrcanus (135–103 BC). The successors of the Maccabees fought one another for the power over Israel.
63 BC	Several groups from the Jews sought help from the Roman general, Pompey, who had conquered Syria. Pompey marched into Jerusalem with his army. This was the beginning of Israel's period as a vassal country under Rome.
37 BC	Herod became the Roman vassal king of Palestine (37–4 BC).

MACEDONIA

was a province north of Greece, from which came Alexander the Great. At the time of the New Testament Macedonia was a Roman province. The apostle Paul travelled through Macedonia on his second missionary journey, and founded Christian churches there, including Philippi (Acts 16), Thessalonica (17:1–9) and Beroea (17:10–15).

MACHAERUS

was a fort east of the Dead Sea. It was rebuilt by Herod the Great. The Jewish historian Josephus tells us that it was in this fort that John the Baptist was imprisoned and executed (Matthew 14:1–12). It was one of the last places of resistance in the rebellion against Rome in AD 70.

MAGDALA

was a city on the western shore of Lake Gennesaret. Mary Magdalene came from here (Luke 8:2). In Matthew 15:39 we are told that Jesus visited the city of Magdala = Magadan.

MALACHI

whose name means 'My messenger' was a post-exilic prophet. His book was probably written in the middle of the 5th century BC. The prophet exhorts the people not to forget the worship and the Law, even in the midst of difficulties and worries, and finally looks on to the day when the Lord vindicates the faithful and punishes the wicked.

MALTA

is an island in the Mediterranean, where the apostle Paul was shipwrecked (Acts 28:1–11).

MAMMON

The Aramaic word for riches. It is used by the rabbis to mean 'worldly concerns' such as property and money (Luke 16:9–11). Jesus says: 'You cannot serve God and mammon' (Matthew 6:24).

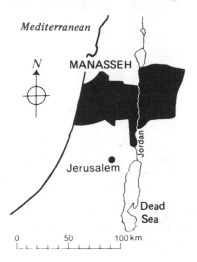

MANASSEH

was the eldest son of the patriarch Joseph (Genesis 41:51). Manasseh became the name of one of the tribes of Israel. The area in which this tribe lived was also called Manasseh, and was situated west and east of the river Jordan (Joshua 17:7–13). The successful Judges, Gideon, Jair and Jephthah, came from the tribe of Manasseh. Another Manasseh was the idolatrous king of Judah (2 Kings 21).

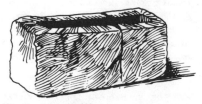

Stone trough from Megiddo

MANGER

The Old Testament mentions cribs (or mangers) where the animals were fed

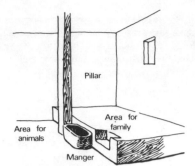

Layout of a Palestinian farmer's house

(Job 39:9; Isaiah 1:3). During the excavation of stables at Megiddo there were found special feeding troughs made of stone, for the horses to eat from.

In a farmer's house in Palestine there was one lower section where the animals were kept, and at the edge of the higher section, where the family lived, there was usually a manger or rack for hay (Luke 13:15). It was very likely in a manger of this kind in a cattle shed adjoining the inn that the infant Jesus was laid (Luke 2:7, 12, 16).

MANNA

This was the food given by God to the Israelites during their journey of 40 years through the wilderness desert. They pleaded for food and in the morning found 'bread from heaven', little drops of manna. These were little round grains which looked like hoarfrost on the ground. The grains had a sweet taste and could be ground and made into bread. When the sun rose, the manna melted. It could not be stored because it became decayed, maggoty and unuseable. The Israelites were able to collect about one small bowlful per day and two on the day before the Sabbath, when none was supplied (Exodus 16:14–30; Numbers 11:7–9).

Although it does not exactly fit the biblical description, it is widely thought that manna might have been the substance from the tamarisk shrub. A scaly plant lice is found on the shrub which produces drops of sweet and sticky liquid. These fall to the ground as grains. The Bible, however, implies that the manna came by a miracle; it was not seasonal, but continuous (Joshua 5:12).

Manna also had a spiritual significance. When other food ran out, God supplied manna to make the Israelites 'know that man does not live by bread alone but by every word that proceeds from the mouth of the Lord'. Jesus said this to Satan in the desert and Deuteronomy 8:3, 16 records the saying in its first context. The lack of manna on the seventh day was to teach obedience in keeping the Sabbath Day of rest. In John 6:49 Jesus refers to manna as bread from heaven (quoting Psalm 105:40) and himself as the Bread of Life (see Bread).

In Revelation 2:17 'hidden manna' means spiritual food given by the Spirit. Moses put a gold vessel containing a bowl of manna inside the Ark of the Covenant to remind Israel of God's provision in the desert (Exodus 16:32–36).

MANSLAUGHTER SEE MURDER

MARAH

was the first camp of the Israelites after leaving Egypt. At Marah there was a spring with water that was bitter (brackish). On God's command Moses threw a piece of wood into the water, and it became drinkable (Exodus 15:22–25).

MARANATHA

are two Aramaic words which mean: 'Our Lord, come!' The expression was probably used in the worship of the Christian church during its earliest days. It contains a wish and a prayer that Jesus

Christ, the Church's Lord, would soon return from heaven (1 Corinthians 16:22; Revelation 22:20; compare 1 Corinthians 11:26).

MARK, GOSPEL OF

The Gospel of Mark is the second Gospel in the New Testament. It is the shortest of the four Gospels. John Mark is believed to be the author (Acts 12:12). We are told that Mark later accompanied the apostle Peter on his journeys (1 Peter 5:13). It is thought that Mark has written down in his Gospel that which the apostle Peter had told about Jesus and the events of his life. This is first mentioned by Papias, whose date is about AD 60–130. Peter is mentioned in ten of the sixteen chapters of the gospel.

The Gospel of Mark was written in such a way as to give the gentile Christians knowledge of the life of Christ. There is not a great deal included in this Gospel of the speeches which Jesus made and of his sermons.

The Gospel of Mark was probably written between the years 60 and 70 in Greek, the first written account of Jesus' ministry.

It is thought that Matthew and Luke read Mark and took a significant part of their material from it. The last twelve verses of the Gospel are missing in the oldest manuscripts. They have probably been added later, as a conclusion.

The Gospel of Mark may be divided into the following parts:

Outline of Contents	Chapter
Introduction. John the Baptist. The baptism of Jesus and the temptations of Jesus.	Mark 1:1–13
Jesus' work in Galilee and surrounding areas.	Mark 1:14–9:50
Jesus' walk to Jerusalem, his death and resurrection.	Mark 10–16

MARKET-PLACE

In biblical times every city would have a large open space, where merchandise was sold and meetings were held (Nehemiah 13:15, 16). There were also streets of bazaars as in oriental towns today, with traders' stalls (1 Kings 20:34). In the open space children played (Matthew 11:16) and labourers waited to be hired (Matthew 20:3). Important people paraded there to attract attention (Matthew 23:7).

MARRIAGE

The most important event in Israelite family life was marriage. People married early in life in Israel. The father in the family decided whom his son or daughter was to marry (Genesis 38:6). When it had been decided who the young man's wife was to be, a period of preparation for their marriage began. It was called betrothal, and generally lasted for about one year (Matthew 1:18). At the betrothal the young man delivered a marriage present to the girl's father (Genesis 34:12; Exodus 22:16, 17). The young man would also give presents to his betrothed (Genesis 24:51–53).

A man could have several wives, but in Jesus' day most men probably had only one although Herod the Great had nine at one time. The patriarchs, the heads of the tribes and kings like David and Solomon might have many wives, although the story shows that this polygamy usually caused trouble and often sin (1 Kings 11:1–8).

The Law stipulated that the first wife's position should not be worsened if her husband took one or more additional wives (Genesis 25:1; 2 Samuel 5:13; 1 Kings 11:3).

A concubine was a woman who occupied a secondary position to a man's first wife, but with a position recognized by law. In the time of Abraham a wife who was unable to have a son could give her servant-girl as a concubine to her husband. The servant-girl might bear a child and in this way the wife would have the son whom she was longing for (Genesis 16; 30:3-13).

In the law of Israel there was a clause which said that a man should marry his brother's widow, if his dead brother did not have a son. The first son to be born in this marriage with the widow became the dead brother's heir. This is known as levirate marriage (from Latin *levir*, husband's brother) (Deuteronomy 25:5, 6; Matthew 22:23-28). The Israelites were forbidden by the Law to marry women from other peoples (Deuteronomy 7:1-5).

The basic ingredients of marriage from Genesis 2:18 to 1 Corinthians 11:9 are that a man should leave his parents' home, live in love with his wife and become one flesh with her. In Christian terms this involves them taking vows before God, setting up their own home, and enjoying physical, emotional and spiritual oneness.

See also Wedding

MARTYR

The Greek word has to be translated according to the context as either 'martyr' (Acts 22:20) or 'witness' (eg. Matthew 18:16). The word 'martyr' gradually came to mean one whose witness involved the shedding of blood, i.e. one who died for the sake of his beliefs. The Greek verb means simply to bear witness.

MATTHEW, GOSPEL OF

The Gospel of Matthew is the first gospel in the New Testament. It is the longest of the four. The apostle Matthew is traditionally the author. The Gospel was written some time after AD 70, perhaps in the eighties. The Gospel was written for Jews. Papias (soon after AD 100) and Irenaeus (about AD 180)

say that Matthew originally wrote a Gospel in Aramaic, but this may have been largely a collection of the teachings of Jesus, since Papias describes this Gospel as 'sayings'. This Gospel wants to show that Jesus is the Messiah whose coming was promised by the prophets. He is also the great teacher, who in sermons and parables instructs his followers about the kingdom of God and life in this kingdom. At important points in the life of Christ, Matthew often mentions that Scripture and the prophecies have been fulfilled.

The Gospel of Matthew, as well as that of Luke, is very similar to the Gospel of Mark in its contents and the order of events. Scholars believe that the authors of Matthew and Luke have taken part of their material from the Gospel of Mark.

The Gospel of Matthew may be divided into the following parts:

Outline of Contents	Chapter
Jesus' childhood and period of preparation	Matthew 1:4-4:11
His work in Galilee	Matthew 4:12-18:35
Work in other areas of Palestine	Matthew 19-20
Work in Jerusalem	Matthew 21-25
The passion, death and resurrection of Christ	Matthew 26-28

MEAL OFFERING SEE SACRIFICE

MEASURES

Measures of distance in Old Testament times

finger's breadth	about ¾ in. (2 cm)
handsbreadth	„ 3 in. (8 cm)
span	„ 8½ in. (21 cm)
cubit	„ 17½ in. (45 cm)
reed	„ 9¾ ft. (3 m)
day's journey	„ 19-22 miles (30-35 km)

In New Testament times

cubit	about 17½ in. (45 cm)
fathom	about 6 ft (185 cm)
stadion	„ 629 ft. (192 m)
mile (Roman)	just under 1 Eng. mile

In New Testament times

Measure	Approx. capacity in litres
'quart', choinix	1.01
'measure' = OT seah	12.148
bath = OT bath and ephah measures	36.44
great measure = approx. the OT ephah measure	36.44
'measure', koros = the OT cor measure	364.44

Measures of capacity in Old Testament times

There are some variations in estimates

Measure	Approx. capacity in litres	Liquid Measure	Dry Measure
log	0.506	×	×
kab = 4 log	2.024	×	×
omer	3.644		×
hin = 3 kab	6.074	×	
seah = 6 kab	12.148		×
ephah = 3 seah = 10 omer	36.44		×
cor or homer = 10 ephah	364.4		×
bath	36.44	×	

Measures of weight in Old Testament times

Unit of weight		Approx. number of grammes or kilograms
talent	60 minas – 3,600 shekels	60 kg
mina	60 shekels	1 kg
shekel	2 half shekels or 2 beka	17 g
shekel	4 quarter shekels or 4 reba	17 g
shekel	20 gerah	17 g

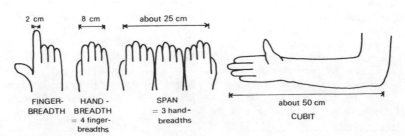

2 cm	8 cm	about 25 cm	
FINGER-BREADTH	HAND-BREADTH = 4 finger-breadths	SPAN = 3 hand-breadths	about 50 cm CUBIT

In New Testament times the units of
weight of the coins in use

Unit of weight	Approx. weight
denarius	8 g
drachma	8 g
minah	½ kg
talent	30 kg
libra (Roman pound) rendered as *litra* in John	325 g 12:3; 19:39

MEDIA

was a country south and south-west of
the Caspian Sea. During the 9th–7th
Century BC Assyria attempted to conquer Media.

Allied with the Babylonians the
Medes instead succeeded in defeating
the Assyrians in the year 612 BC. About
50 years later the Persian king Cyrus
conquered the kingdom of Media, and
united it with Persia before taking
Babylon (Isaiah 13:17,18; Daniel 5:28;
6:8; Acts 2:9).

MEDICAL CARE AND MEDICINE

In ancient Israel people knew very little
about the care of the sick and the cure of
various diseases. According to the Law
they were not allowed to touch dead
bodies, and consequently they learned
nothing about human anatomy.

In countries where embalming of the
dead was normal practice, people were
able to gain greater knowledge about the
human body. The Israelites did not as a
rule embalm their dead.

It was believed that disease was a
punishment for particular sins. What a
sick person would have to do was to
confess his sins and offer sacrifices.
Perhaps, then, God would forgive the
sin and remove the disease. As a universal

explanation this was refuted by the Book
of Job.

The priests had to be familiar with
certain diseases. They would have to be
able to decide, for instance, whether a
person suffered from leprosy or not
(Leviticus 13).

In Jeremiah 8:21, 22 we are told of
physicians, who treat wounds and bandage them. In Ezekiel 30: 21 the treatment of a broken arm is described. King
Asa refused to pray for healing, but
relied solely on physicians to cure the
severe trouble in his feet (2 Chronicles
16:12).

In later centuries physicians and
medicine came to be of greater importance also among the Jews (Matthew
9:12; Mark 5:26). In the New Testament one of the apostle Paul's co-
workers, Luke, was a physician (Colossians 4:14).

Some medicines that were generally
used were: cakes of figs (Isaiah 38:21);
balm (Jeremiah 8:22); oil and wine
(Isaiah 1:6; Luke 10:34, 1 Timothy
5:23).
See also Disease, Healing

MEDITERRANEAN

The Israelites called the Mediterranean
the Great Sea. This was the only sea
known to them (Numbers 34:6; Joshua
1:4).

MEMPHIS

At various times in Egypt's history,
Memphis was one of its largest cities. It
was the capital city during the reign of
certain of its pharaohs. The city was
situated on the river Nile in northern
Egypt.

In older versions the city is called
Noph, but RSV changes this to Memphis. Not much remains of Memphis
nowadays.
See Isaiah 19:13; Jeremiah 2:16; Hosea 9:6.

MENE, MENE, TEKEL, PARSIN

In the fifth chapter of the Book of Daniel we are told that the Babylonian king Belshazzar at a feast brought out the vessels taken from the Temple in Jerusalem. During the banquet a hand appeared which wrote these four words on the wall in the palace. They are the names of weights, i.e. a mina, shekel, and half-shekels. Daniel interpreted the writing by taking the root meanings of the words, Numbered, Weighed, Divided as follows: 'God has numbered the days of your kingdom and brought it to an end; you have been weighed in the balances and found wanting; your kingdom is divided and given to the Medes and Persians'. Thus, the Babylonian kingdom was soon to fall, and in fact the Persians took Babylon that night.

MERCY SEAT

The golden covering of the Ark bearing two cherubim within the Holy of Holies. See Ark of the Covenant

MESOPOTAMIA

Nowadays the name Mesopotamia is taken to mean the whole area between the rivers Euphrates and Tigris. In biblical times Mesopotamia was the name of the area between the upper reaches of these two rivers.
See Genesis 24:10; Deuteronomy 23:4; Judges 3:8; Acts 2:9.

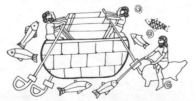

Syrian relief showing a boat on the river Tigris

MESSIAH

The word Messiah was properly a title used by the king. It is a Hebrew word, which means 'the anointed one'. When the king was consecrated for his royal office, he was anointed with oil. It was thought that the king, by having been anointed, received divine spirit, wisdom to rule and lead his people and power to defeat his enemies. Priests and, perhaps, prophets were also anointed.

The Greek word for Messiah is Christ. The idea of a Messiah is found quite early in Israel. King David was regarded as the greatest of the kings of Israel. The Messiah was to come from his family, and so in the first place he would be the Messiah of Israel.

It was primarily the prophets in the Old Testament who repeatedly reminded the people about the Messiah. They wanted to teach Israel that the Messiah one day would come and establish his perfect kingdom. The prophets wanted the people to look forward to the future, 'that day' or the 'day of the Lord'. The expectation was for a spiritual and national deliverer – both ideas were strong when Jesus was born. One of the most important ideas in the New Testament is that Jesus is the Messiah, fulfilling the Old Testament expectations. He is also the Prophet, Priest and King as the book of Hebrews explains. Jesus was of the family of David and was born in David's city, Bethlehem. Jesus did not speak openly about himself as the Messiah. But when the high priest asked: 'Are you the Christ?', Jesus answered: 'I am' (Mark 14:61–62).

At Caesarea Philippi Peter declared that he believed Jesus to be the Christ (Matthew 16:13–17).

Through his passion and death on the cross Jesus showed that the Messiah must die at the hands of men as he warned his followers. This went right against the political and national hopes of many Jewish people. Jesus as Messiah/Christ is ruler of the kingdom of God. This kingdom of God, or messianic kingdom, will extend across the borders of Israel and not be tied to any particular people or country.

See also Jesus Christ, Son of Man, Ointment

The prophets and the Messiah

Amos	says that the Lord in that day will raise up the booth of David that is fallen (Amos 9:11–15).
Hosea	explains that in the future the house of David will be of great importance (Hosea 3:5).
Isaiah	describes the Messiah as a person with divine qualities. The Book of Isaiah also speaks of him as the suffering servant of the Lord (Isaiah 9:2–7; 11:1–10; 32:1–5; 53).
Micah	mentions that the Ruler, the Messiah, will come from Bethlehem, the city of David (Micah 5:2).
Joel and Habakkuk	have several descriptions of the time when the Messiah will come (Joel 2:1, 2; 3:18; Habakkuk 3:13).
Jeremiah	speaks of the Messiah, the King of the house of David, who will 'execute justice and righteousness in the land' (Jeremiah 23:5–8).
Ezekiel	describes the future Messiah as a true shepherd, who will take his flock to good pastures. This shepherd will come from the family of David (Ezekiel 34:11–16, 23).
Daniel	depicts the Messiah as the Son of Man. When he comes, an eternal kingdom will begin, which will never be destroyed (Daniel 7:13, 14).

MICAH, BOOK OF

Micah was a prophet from Judah, who lived at the time of Isaiah, about 700 BC. He appeared in Jerusalem with very harsh prophecies of judgement.

Micah warned the people against God's judgement and punishment with sharp and merciless words. But the prophet also awaited the coming of the

Messiah and prophesied that he would be born in Bethlehem.

The Book of Micah may be divided into different sections as follows.

Words of judgement against Israel and Judah	Micah 1–3
Israel's salvation through the Ruler from Bethlehem	Micah 4–5
Judgement prophecies against the whole of Israel	Micah 6–7:6
Promise of a new and better era	Micah 7:8–20

MIDIAN, MIDIANITES

In the Book of Genesis it is said that the Midianites originally came from the family of Abraham (Genesis 25:1–6). They lived in the desert areas of north-western Arabia, and were nomads, desert dwellers who on their camels went on expeditions of plunder and trade to neighbouring countries (Genesis 37:28; Judges 6–8).

After his escape from Egypt Moses stayed with the Midianites. His wife, Zipporah, came from Midian (Exodus 2:15–22).

MILETUS

was a port in Asia Minor. Paul visited the city on his last journey to Jerusalem (Acts 20:15–17).

MILK SEE FOOD AND DRINK

MILL SEE HOME, BREAD

MINT SEE HERBS AND SPICES

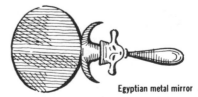

Egyptian metal mirror

MIRRORS

were used in both Old and New Testament times. They were cast from metal and had to be polished constantly. These metal mirrors gave a somewhat blurred reflection, so that Paul speaks of seeing 'in a mirror dimly'.

See Exodus 38:8; Isaiah 3:23; 1 Corinthians 13:12; James 1:23.

MISHNAH SEE TALMUD

An old Roman road built of large stone blocks

MISSION

In the time of the Old Testament the people of Israel considered the Lord to be primarily the God of Israel only. It sometimes happened that Gentiles were converted to Judaism, and became proselytes (See PROSELYTE). Judaism was not an active missionary religion, but the standards of Judaism, especially in Alexandria, influenced many pagans to adopt the Jewish faith. In the New Testament Jesus commands his disciples, in the Great Commission, to 'go and make disciples of all nations' (Matthew 28:18-20).

Immediately after Christ's resurrection, the disciples began to spread the gospel in different directions in the world, i.e. those parts of it which were known at that time.

When the apostles Peter and Paul suffered martyrdom in about AD 60, there were already Christian churches in many parts of the Roman empire.

Thanks to the roads which the Romans built for their armies, it was easier for the Christian missionaries to travel. Moreover, the Greek language was spoken by all educated people living in the countries around the Mediterranean. Mission is not only preaching but communicating God's caring love to people.

See also Apostle.

MOAB, MOABITES

Moab was the name of a country east of the Dead Sea. It is a high plateau, with the river Arnon running through it into the Dead Sea. According to Genesis the Moabites were descendants of Lot (Genesis 19:37). During certain periods in the Old Testament relations were peaceful between Moab and Israel (Ruth 1:2; 1 Samuel 22:3, 4). At other times there were wars between the two countries (2 Kings 3:4-27). During the reign of king David, Moab was a vassal kingdom under Israel (1 Samuel 14:47; 1 Chronicles 18:2). At the time of Christ another people, the Nabataeans, lived in the country of Moab. Ruth, the Moabitess, was the great-grandmother of David, and so in the line of the Messiah (Ruth 4:21, 22; Matthew 1:5).

MOLECH (OR MOLOCH)

His name appears to be a variant form of the Hebrew word for King.

In the Old Testament Molech is described as a god, to whom the Israelites at various times offered human sacrifices. It seems that a fierce fire was lit in front of his image or his image was heated, and children were then burned alive in the fire or in his arms (Leviticus 18:21; 1 Kings 11:7).

The Valley of Hinnom became the chief place of this practice (2 Chronicles 33:6: Jeremiah 19; 32:35; Ezekiel 23:37–39).

See Gehenna, Hinnom

MONEY

At the time of the Old Testament people did not use coined, ready-made money as we do now. Bartering (trade by exchange) was a common way of buying. People might also pay with pieces of metal of a certain weight. The basic unit of weight was called a shekel, which weighed about 14 g ($\frac{1}{2}$ oz). With modern fluctuations in exchange rates it is impossible to give the values of each denomination.

Denomination	Worth in shekel	Approx. weight
shekel		14 g ($\frac{1}{2}$ oz)
beka	$\frac{1}{2}$	7 g ($\frac{1}{4}$ oz)
gerah	1/20	0.7 g
mina	60 or 50	0.85 kg or 0.7 kg ($1\frac{3}{4}$ or $1\frac{1}{2}$ lbs.)
talent	3,600 or 3,000	$50\frac{1}{2}$ or 42 kg (110 or $92\frac{1}{2}$ lbs.)

Coin denomination	Metal	=	Approx. weight
denarius	silver		8g ($\frac{1}{4}$ oz)
drachma	silver		8g ($\frac{1}{4}$ oz)
double drachma	silver	2 drachma	
stater	silver	4 denarii	
mina	silver	100 denarii	$\frac{1}{2}$ kg (1 lb)
talent	silver	6,000 denarii	30 kg (66 lbs)
assarion	copper	1/16 denarius	
quadrans	copper	$\frac{1}{4}$ assarion	
lepton	copper	$\frac{1}{2}$ quadrans or libra	
litra = Roman pound was only used as a weight			325 g (12 oz)

After the Babylonian exile money came into use, consisting of ready coins of particular weights and fixed values. The Persian daric was a gold coin, 8 g (just over ¼ oz) in weight.

The Assyrian drachma was of approximately the same weight and value.

In the time of the New Testament a number of foreign coins were in use in Palestine.

Jewish shekels as used for offerings in the Temple

MONEY-CHANGER

All the gifts of money which were given to the Temple had to be offered in Jewish or Tyrian coins. In the Court of the Gentiles people could go to the money-changers and get the coins which were needed.

The reason for allowing Tyrian coins, and not Roman or Greek, may be that the Jews would not use for sacred purposes the coinage of any nation that had ever subdued them. The Jews themselves did not mint any silver coins.

In Jesus' opinion the money-changers were blaspheming against God by working within the walls of the Temple. They may also have been making unfair profits in their rate of exchange to the poor. Jesus became justly angry and threw them out (Matthew 21:12; John 2:15).

MONTH SEE FESTIVALS

MOTH SEE ANIMALS, INSECTS

MOUNT OF OLIVES

(also called Mount Olivet) is the name of the hill which is due east of Jerusalem.The hill has several peaks, and the Mount of Olives is, properly speaking, the name of that peak which is situated east of the Temple area.

Between the city and the hill was the Kidron Valley. The highest point of the hill is about 2,660ft (810 m) above sea level. The hill has probably been given its name because of the olive orchards which were there in the past.

The most significant mention in the Old Testament is Zechariah 14:4 as the place where the Lord's feet stand at his coming.

Jesus often went to the Mount of Olives (Luke 22:39). It was from there that he made his entry into Jerusalem, (Matthew 21:1). The garden of Gethsemane was close by the Mount of Olives.

The Ascension took place on the Mount of Olives (Luke 24:50; Acts 1:12).

MOUNT OF TRANSFIGURATION

is the name given to the mountain where Jesus was transfigured before three of his disciples and appeared in white and shining garments. Moses and Elijah appeared with him and spoke with Jesus about his coming death. The disciples heard a voice which said: 'This is my beloved Son ... Listen to him'. The Mount of Transfiguration is usually identified with Mount Tabor west of Lake Gennesaret.

See Matthew 17:1–8; Mark 9:1–8; Luke 9:28–36.

MOUNTAINS OF ISRAEL

Israel is a hilly country. Two mountain ridges cross it from north to south on either side of the river Jordan. Along the Mediterranean there is a coastal plain, which is up to 12½ miles (20 km) wide.

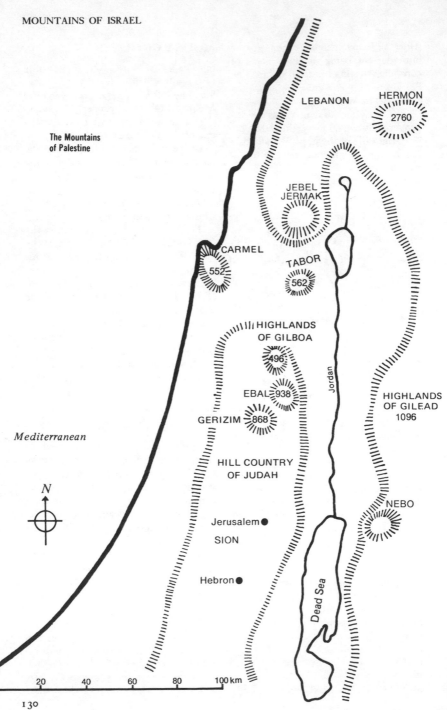

The Mountains
of Palestine

LEBANON

HERMON
2760

JEBEL
JERMAK

CARMEL
552

TABOR
562

HIGHLANDS
OF GILBOA
496

EBAL 938
GERIZIM 868

HILL COUNTRY
OF JUDAH

HIGHLANDS
OF GILEAD
1096

Mediterranean

N

NEBO

Jerusalem ●
SION

Hebron ●

Jordan

Dead Sea

0   20   40   60   80   100 km

The mountains often were holy places to the Israelites, where they built altars and sanctuaries, and where sacrifices and worship took place (see High Place).

Some of the more important mountains in the Bible

On **Mount Sinai** (outside the borders of Palestine) the Lord made a covenant with Israel. There Moses received the tables of the Law (Deuteronomy 5:1–5).

Mount Gerizim was Israel's holy place in Canaan in the beginning (Deuteronomy 11:29).

Mount Tabor was the centre of worship for the northern tribes.

Mount Zion in Jerusalem became the site of the Temple, the Temple Mount, for the whole of Israel (Psalm 74:2; 76:1–3).

On **Mount Carmel** the prophet Elijah built his altar to the Lord and demonstrated to Israel that the Lord, and not Baal, was God (1 Kings 18:19–39).

The Ascension of Christ took place on the **Mount of Olives** east of Jerusalem (Acts 1:9–12).

See also High Places

MOURNING SEE FUNERAL

MULE

A mule is a cross-breed between a mare and a donkey. It has the strength of a horse and is persistent and patient like the donkey. The Law banned breeding to produce mules (Leviticus 19:19), so mules had to be imported (1 Kings 10:25). They were ridden by important people.

See 2 Samuel 13:29; 18:9; 1 Kings 18:5; 2 Kings 5:17; Psalm 32:9.

MURDER

The fifth commandment (Exodus 20:13) says: You shall not kill and this refers primarily to murder. The murderer himself was put to death (Genesis 9:6). This was brought about through the rule of blood vengeance, which meant that the relatives of the murder victim had legal right to kill the murderer.

Gradually certain cities were designated sanctuaries. A person who had killed another by accident or unintentionally could flee to the sanctuary. There he would be tried, would be protected from blood vengeance according to the law (Numbers 35:9–34; Deuteronomy 19:1–13).

Although the Law did not allow compensation as a substitute for capital punishment (Numbers 35:31), some think that later on the relatives might receive a sum of money in recompense; this is allowed by Islamic law. But murder remained a capital crime to be tried by the courts (2 Chronicles 19:10; Luke 23:19, 25). Jesus gives the fifth commandment an even more pointed meaning. One who is angry with or hates his fellow man is under the same judgement as the murderer (Matthew 5:21, 22). It is not the act itself that is decisive, but the evil thought too.

See Genesis 4:10; Exodus 20:13; Numbers 35:9–34; Matthew 5:21,22.

See also Blood Vengeance

MUSIC

The Israelites were known to be skilled singers and musicians. The first mention of different musical instruments is in the very beginning of the Old Testament (Genesis 4:21); and throughout the history of the Jewish people there was singing, playing and dancing. David was a skilled musician (1 Samuel 16:18).

The people sang while working – for instance when they trod the grapes in the wine-press, at weddings, funerals and other ceremonies and festivals. Many of the Psalms were composed for worship in the Temple. Songs were also sung when a victory had been won over some enemy (Exodus 15; Judges 5).

Jewish music was strongly rhythmical and melodic, but had little harmony. Musical instruments were the lyre (1 Samuel 16:23; Psalm 137:2), pipe or oboe (1 Kings 1:40), small pipe or flute

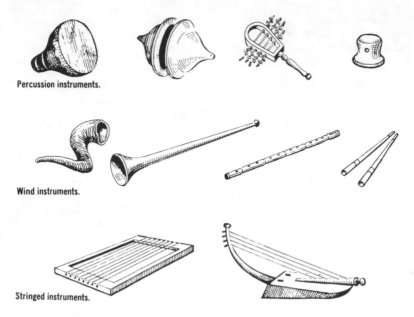

Percussion instruments.

Wind instruments.

Stringed instruments.

(Job 21:12; Psalm 150:4), timbrel or tambourine (Exodus 15:20), harp with resonant body, or of zither type, formerly translated as psaltery (1 Samuel 10:5; Isaiah 5:12; Amos 6:5), cymbals (Psalm 150:5), trumpets of silver or copper (Numbers 10:2; 2 Kings 11:14). The *shofar*, or ram's horn, which is still blown at festivals, is hardly a musical instrument in the usual sense (Joshua 6:4; Psalm 81:3; Zechariah 9:14). Babylonian instruments are listed in Nebuchadnezzar's orchestra (Daniel 3:7), where RSV rightly changes AV *sackbut* to *trigon*, which was probably a triangular harp, although we do not know its size or number of strings.

MUSTARD SEE HERBS

MYRRH

A sweet-smelling resin which is found on small shrublike trees in the desert areas of Arabia. The resin drips from the tree on to the ground, where it solidifies into small round balls. Its scent is reminiscent of lemon and turpentine. It was used to mix with other ingredients for an anointing oil (Exodus 30:23). It was one of the gifts which the wise men brought to Jesus (Matthew 2:11). As a pain killer it was mixed into the wine which was handed up to Jesus on the cross (Mark 15:23). When Jesus was put into the tomb, Nicodemus brought a mixture of myrrh and aloes to bind up with the grave-clothes (John 19:39, 40).

N

NAHUM, BOOK OF

Nahum lived about 650 BC. He came from Elkosh which was probably in Judah. His book is a prophecy concerning the destruction of the Assyrian capital, Nineveh.

Outline of Contents	Chapter
The Lord's wrath and the Lord's goodness	Nahum 1:1–8
Words of judgement against Nineveh	Nahum 1:9–14
Judah will be saved	Nahum 1:15
The fall of Nineveh	Nahum 2:3

NAIN

was the name of the city in which Jesus raised a widow's only son from the dead (Luke 7:11–17). It is thought that Nain was the present village of Nein, which is

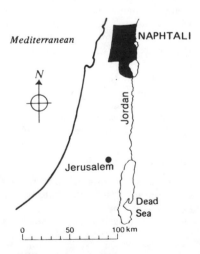

situated about 6 miles (10 km) south-east of Nazareth.

NAPHTALI

was one of the sons of the patriarch Jacob (Genesis 30:7, 8). Naphtali became the father of the tribe of Naphtali, one of the twelve tribes of Israel.

The area of Naphtali was a fertile district, situated west and northwest of Lake Gennesaret (Joshua 19:32–39). The Judge Barak came from the tribe of Naphtali. The prophecy of Isaiah 9:1 connects the Galilee area of Naphtali with the coming Messiah, and this was the main sphere of Christ's ministry.

NARD

(in the AV translated 'spikenard', in the RSV 'pure nard') is a fragrant oil derived from an aromatic plant which grows in India.

In the time of the Bible, nard was imported into Palestine (Song of Solomon 1:12; 4:13, 14). It was sold in alabaster bottles, and was used on special occasions as a perfume or ointment. In the New Testament we are told that Mary in Bethany anointed Christ's head and feet with nard.

NAZARETH

is mentioned in the New Testment as being the city where Jesus grew up (Matthew 2:23; Luke 2:51). Where the Nazareth of the Bible was, there is now a modern city called en-Nazira.

Nazareth was situated in the southernmost hills of the mountains of Galilee. From the hilltops near the city there was a wide view southwards across the plain of Jezreel.

The main caravan routes which were used by merchants and soldiers were close to Nazareth in Jesus' day. The Jews themselves regarded Nazareth as an insignificant small town (John 1:46).

The well at Nazareth

In the present day, tourists are shown several sites in Nazareth where biblical events are supposed to have taken place. From the city's well, the old Well of Mary, the mother of Jesus probably carried water to her house. It is impossible to know the sites of any other holy places in the city with absolute certainty.

NAZIRITE

The name comes from a Hebrew word which means 'set apart', 'consecrate'. The Nazirite was a person who was especially consecrated to serve God in various ways. He could be a Nazirite for a shorter period, but he could also take the Nazirite vow for the whole of his lifetime. The Nazirite was not allowed to drink wine or to have contact with a dead body. Nor was he allowed to cut his hair.

When the period of his vow had expired, his hair was cut and burnt on the altar (Numbers 6).

The first Nazirite of the Old Testament was Samson (Judges 13:4, 5).

Nazirites were well known in the time of Amos (Amos 2:11, 12). John the Baptist in the New Testament had taken Nazirite vows for life (Luke 1:15).

NEBO

Moses led the people of Israel out of Egypt. He was the leader of the people during the wandering in the desert but was not himself allowed to take the people into Canaan. From Mount Nebo he could look into the country before he died (Deuteronomy 34:1–8).

It is believed that Mount Nebo is the hill now called Jebel-en-Neba east of the river Jordan, opposite the city of Jericho. Nebo is also the name of the Babylonian god of science and learning (Isaiah 46:1).

NEHEMIAH, BOOK OF

Nehemiah was a Jew who had been given an important post at the court of the Persian king. He was the king's cup-bearer and looked after his supply of wines.

Earlier, a large group of Jews had been freed from captivity and been allowed to return to their own country. Their leader had been the priest Ezra.

Nehemiah's brother sent a message that those who had returned to Jerusalem were in grave difficulties. They suffered want. Their position was precarious because the walls around Jerusalem were torn down and their gates burnt.

The Persian king promised Nehemiah that he could go to Jerusalem. With help from the people he would rebuild the walls and set up new gates.

Nehemiah was appointed by the Persian king to be governor or ruler of Judah. Subsequent events in Jerusalem are told in the book of Nehemiah.

NEW MOON SEE FESTIVALS

NINEVEH

The last capital of Assyria. All that remains today are ruins. It was the capital of Assyria after Asshur. The city was rebuilt extensively by Sennacherib. To give water, he built a thirty mile canal from a dam on a river to the North. The walls of his palace were decorated with pictures of the siege of Lachish, and have survived to this day and now rest in the British Museum. King Hezekiah of Judah sent tribute money to Sennacherib at Nineveh (2 Kings 18:15). Nahum and Zephaniah, two of the Minor Prophets, predicted the Fall of Nineveh. It happened in 612 BC when an alliance of enemy powers successfully besieged the city. Flooding rivers helped to weaken the city's defences (Nahum 2:6) leaving the Medes to plunder it. The remains of the city were left to fall into complete ruin.

The city was already a desolate heap as early as the 4th century BC. Today the site where the Assyrians built their proudest city is grazing land for sheep, just as Zephaniah foretold in 2:13-15. The modern name of the place is Tell Kuyunjik which means 'mound of many sheep'.

It was to Nineveh that God sent the very reluctant Jonah to preach the warning of disaster if the city did not turn to God. Many expeditions have excavated the city and the large library of tablets and literature has provided scholars with important information about Assyrian life.

See also Assyria

NOAH

In the Book of Genesis we are told about Lamech's son, Noah, who was a good and righteous man. Noah himself had three sons, Shem, Ham and Japheth.

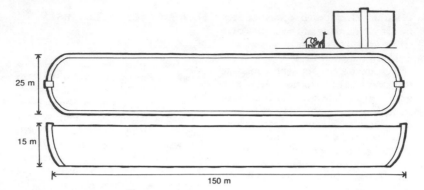

The Lord told Noah that he intended to wipe out all living things, because they had become filled with evil and violence. Only Noah was good and blameless before God. Therefore God wanted to preserve him as a 'remnant', and made a covenant with him.

Noah built an ark, a boat which would save him when the rains and the flood came.

The design and measurements of the ark are described in Genesis 6:15.

Length = 300 cubits = 490 ft (150 m)
Width = 50 cubits = 82 ft (25 m)
Height = 30 cubits = 49 ft (15 m)

Noah and his family were rescued in the ark, together with his cattle, birds and wild animals which had been brought on board the ark. At the end of the Flood, when the ark had gone aground on the mountains of Ararat, Noah built an altar and made a sacrifice to the Lord.

God used the rainbow in the sky as a sign of the covenant that he had made with Noah and with following generations (Genesis 6–9).

It is debated whether the Flood was universal or whether it was localized over a large area. Geological and other evidence has been produced on both sides.

NORTHERN KINGDOM SEE ISRAEL

NUMBERS

is the name of the Fourth Book of Moses. It is so called because of the census of the people of Israel, which is here recorded at the beginning and end of the wanderings in the wilderness (chapters 1 and 26). There is, however, much historical material in between the two numberings.

O

OATH

An oath might be a fairly simple declaration (Genesis 14:22) or taken in a court of law (Exodus 22:11). It might be accompanied by a solemn action, such as putting the hand under the thigh (Genesis 24:2, 3) or lifting up the hand to heaven (Deuteronomy 32:40). An oath might be taken by the name of the Lord (1 Samuel 24:21), by one's head (Matthew 5:36), or by the Temple (Matthew 23:16).

It is remarkable that the majority of references in the Old Testament are to God's oaths of promise to his people, e.g. the Patriarchs (Genesis 26:3; Exodus 13:5), and to David (Psalm 89:3), and culminating in the promise and oath concerning the Messiah (Luke 1:72–74). Jesus Christ urged his followers to be so transparently honest that their word would be accepted without an oath (Matthew 5:37).

OBADIAH, BOOK OF

The prophet Obadiah is the author of the shortest book of the Old Testament. We know little about him except that he was presumably a prophet of Judah probably living in the 5th Century BC. If this is true, then the disaster foretold of Jerusalem (11–14) would refer to the capture of the city by the Chaldeans in 587 BC (See Psalm 137:7).

Theme
1 – 14 Judgement of Edom
15 – 16 Universal judgement
17 – 21 Restoration of Israel

The similarity between Obadiah 1–9 and Jeremiah 49:7–22 suggests some literary relationship between the passages. Perhaps both prophets are quoting an earlier divine judgement against Edom. The language of Obadiah is strongly poetic, notably the pentameter metre (3 + 2). The perfect tense is used to describe events yet to happen, a device to show the certainty of God's promises.

OFFERING SEE SACRIFICE

OIL PRESS

In the oil press the oil was extracted

An oil press

from the olives (see Trees, Olive). The ripe olives were beaten down from the trees with long sticks or tubes (Isaiah 24:13). The fruits which were further down could be picked by hand.

The fruits were gathered in baskets and carried to the place where the oil press was set up. The simplest ways of getting the oil out were to tread the olives with bare feet (Micah 6:15) or to crush them with a stone in a mortar (= a stone vessel). The latter produced the 'beaten oil' of Exodus 27:20. Grad-

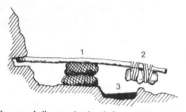

The second oil press showing, 1. Bags of olive pulp 2. Large stones 3. Extracted oil.

ually people learnt to make more elaborate mills, where the olives were crushed. The oil poured out of the mill into jars or vats. There was, however, a large amount of oil left in the olive-pulp that remained in the mill. This was packed in baskets which were then carried to a separate oil press of a different design. The second pressing produced oil of inferior quality.

OINTMENT

People needed to protect their skins in the hot and dry climate of Palestine. They rubbed their faces and hands with oil from the olive tree (2 Samuel 12:20; 14:2; Ecclesiastes 9:8).

Oil was used medicinally for healing wounds or soothing injured parts of the body (Luke 10:34). A sacred oil was used when a king was to be crowned (1 Samuel 10:1; 16:1; 2 Kings 9:3).

The anointing with oil was the most important part in the coronation ceremony (1 Kings 1:39). It was thought

that through the anointing the king was given spiritual wisdom to govern and lead his people and power to vanquish his enemies. After being anointed the king was given the title 'the Anointed One'; In Hebrew 'Messiah'. Priests also were anointed (Leviticus 8:30) and occasionally prophets (Isaiah 61:1).

OLIVES SEE TREES, OIL PRESS.

OMER SEE MEASURES

Golden headband from Ur

ORNAMENT

In Biblical times, women used a wide variety of ornaments from anklets, frontlets, bracelets, necklaces, earrings, hair ornaments, amulets, finger rings, nose rings to head-bands and veils (Isaiah 3:18–24). This jewellery could be made of gold, silver, precious stones, ivory, copper or bronze. Men wore signet rings, sometimes hanging from chains as pendants as well as on their fingers (Genesis 41:42; Numbers 31:50; James 2:2). Isaiah condemned over-indulgence in personal decoration (Isaiah 3:18–23) and Paul encouraged women to be sparing in their use of ornaments (1 Timothy 2:9; see also 1 Peter 3:4).

OVEN SEE BREAD

OX SEE DOMESTIC ANIMALS

PALESTINE
In Old Testament times

Sidon
Sarepta
LEBANON HERMON

Tyre

Dan

PHOENICIA

Mediterranean

Sea of
Galilee

CARMEL

Megiddo ● ● Jezreel
GILBOA

Jordan

N

Samaria ● Tishbe

● Shechem Jabbok
GERIZIM

● Shiloh

Joppa ● Bethel
Jericho ●
Anathoth ● Gilgal
Jerusalem ●
Ashdod Bethlehem ●
Ashkalon ● Tekoa ●

PHILISTIA

Lachish
Gaza Hebron ● En-Gedi ●

WILDERNESS OF JUDAH

Dead Sea

MOAB

● Beer-sheba

0 15 30 45 60 75 90 km

EDOM

PALESTINE

As divided among the
twelve tribes.

Mediterranean

PHOENICIA

DAN

NAPHTALI

ASHER

ZEBULUN

Sea of Galilee

ISSACHAR

MANASSEH

N

Samaria ●

Shiloh ●

EPHRAIM

GAD

DAN

● Bethel

BENJAMIN ● Jericho

AMMON

● Jerusalem

PHILISTIA

REUBEN

JUDAH

Dead Sea

MOAB

● Beer-Sheba

SIMEON

0   15   30   45   60   75   90 km

PALESTINE
In New Testament times

Mediterranean

PALESTINE

LEBANON

HERMON

Damascus

Sidon

Tyre

Caesarea Philippi

Lake Huleh

Chorazin

Capernaum

Bethsaida

Magdala

Cana

Sea of Galilee

GALILEE

Tiberias

N

Nazareth

TABOR

Nain

Caesarea

Pella

SAMARIA

Jordan

Samaria

Shechem

GERIZIM

Sychar

Joppa

Arimathea

Lydda

Jericho

Emmaus

Jerusalem

Qumran

Bethany

Bethlehem

Machaerus

Dead Sea

Gaza

Hebron

JUDEA

Beer-sheba

0   15   30   45   60   75   90

PALESTINE

As divided among Herod's
sons.

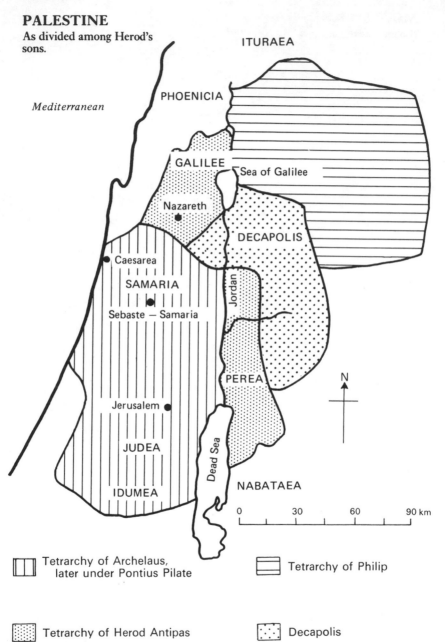

Mediterranean

ITURAEA

PHOENICIA

GALILEE

Sea of Galilee

Nazareth

DECAPOLIS

Caesarea

SAMARIA

Sebaste — Samaria

Jordan

PEREA

N

Jerusalem

Dead Sea

JUDEA

NABATAEA

IDUMEA

0   30   60   90 km

▯▯▯ Tetrarchy of Archelaus,
      later under Pontius Pilate

▭ Tetrarchy of Philip

▒ Tetrarchy of Herod Antipas

⋮ Decapolis

MODERN PALESTINE
(Boundaries as at 1948)

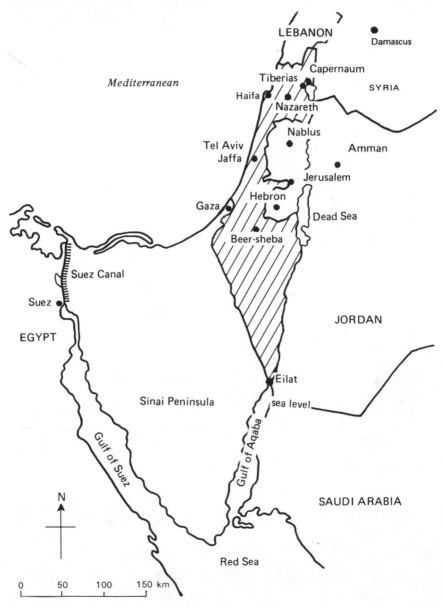

LEBANON

Damascus

Capernaum

Mediterranean

Tiberias

Haifa

Nazareth

SYRIA

Nablus

Tel Aviv
Jaffa

Amman

Jerusalem

Hebron

Gaza

Dead Sea

Beer-sheba

Suez Canal

Suez

EGYPT

JORDAN

Eilat

Sinai Peninsula

sea level

Gulf of Suez

Gulf of Aqaba

SAUDI ARABIA

N

Red Sea

0   50   100   150 km

P

PALESTINE

The name which is used for the Holy Land in the Old Testament is Canaan. It was only later that the country was called Palestine. The name Palestine originally referred to the area of the Philistines, a narrow strip of country along the coast of the Mediterranean. The modern Jewish State, which was founded in 1948, was called Israel, from the name of the old kingdom of Israel.

The length of Palestine, north to south, is about 155 miles (250 km), and its greatest width 87 miles (140 km).

Palestine may be divided into the following areas: The Jordan Valley with Lake Gennesaret and the Dead Sea are located along the line of a massive geological fault. The surface of Lake Gennesaret is 683 ft (208 m) below that of the Mediterranean, and the level of the Dead Sea is 1,275 ft (390 m) below the Mediterranean. This large and deep fault begins in the Taurus mountains north of Palestine and continues southward to the other side of the Dead Sea deep into Africa.

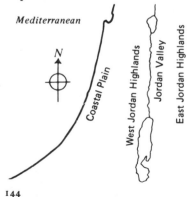

There are traces of volcanoes in many places along this massive crack in the earth's crust. More than 50 major earthquakes have been recorded as having taken place in Palestine since the beginning of the Christian era.

Nowadays there are no forests to speak of in Palestine. The forest was cleared away at an early date, with the unfortunate result that the country became largely arid and infertile.

The climate in Palestine is characterized by warm summers without rain and cold winters with frequent heavy rain (sub-tropical climate). There are fairly large differences in temperature and rainfall between the various parts of the country.

Many of the ancient army roads and trade routes went across Palestine. Because of its strategic importance, Israel was often occupied by the armies of foreign powers. The great powers of the time often went to war against each other and many of their great battles were fought on Palestinian soil.

The history of Israel and its people is told under the heading Israel, History of.

PALM SEE TREES

PAMPHYLIA

was a province in Asia Minor. The apostle Paul visited several cities in Pamphylia during his journeys (Acts 2:10; 13:13; 14:24).

PAPYRUS

An Egyptian reed which was cut into strips, stuck together crosswise, and used as writing material.
See Reed and picture under Birds

PARABLE

The Greek word *parabolē* has to do with a verb which means 'putting something beside something else in order to compare'. A parable in the New Testament sense was a story or event which had been invented for a particular purpose: that of showing something important about the Kingdom of God.

Jesus used parables in his teaching. Through his parables Jesus wanted to explain those things that were difficult to understand, that which was hidden or secret (Matthew 13:34–35). At the same time Jesus spoke to the people in parables 'so that they may indeed see but not perceive, and may indeed hear but not understand' (Mark 4:11–12). This word by Jesus may be understood to mean that only those who knew who Jesus was could understand his parables. Parables often have different layers of meaning, but have sometimes been over-elaborately interpreted.

Parables in the New Testament

The workers in the vineyard Matthew 20:1–16
The talents Matthew 25:14–30
The parable of the vineyard Matthew 21:33–43
The wise and the foolish maidens Matthew 25:1–13
The good Samaritan Luke 10:30–37
The coin that was lost Luke 15:8–10
The pearl of great value Matthew 13:45–46
The prodigal son Luke 15:11–32
The good shepherd John 10:1–16
The hidden treasure Matthew 13:44
The heartless servant Matthew 18:23–35
The rich fool Luke 12:16–21
The rich man (Dives) and Lazarus Luke 16:19–31
The lost sheep Matthew 18:12–14
The Pharisee and the tax collector Luke 18:9–14
The sheep and the goats Matthew 25:31–46
The marriage feast for the king's son Matthew 22:1–14
The lamp Matthew 5:14–16
The net cast into the sea Matthew 13:47–50
The weeds among the wheat Matthew 13:24–30
The salt Matthew 5:13
The mustard seed Matthew 13:31–32
The leaven Matthew 13:33

PARADISE

The original Persian word meant a garden with a wall. The Septuagint translation of Genesis 2:8 uses the Greek equivalent of the garden of Eden. It only took on an 'end-of-time' meaning when Jewish religion looked to the ultimate future as a kind of return to the days of Eden (Isaiah 51:3; Ezekiel 36:35). They also believed that paradise was a hidden place of the present, where the souls of the dead Patriarchs and chosen people were taken. In a sense it was the salvation part of Hades.

Paradise is mentioned three times only in the New Testament. Jesus told the repentant thief on the cross that he would be with him in Paradise today (Luke 23:43). Paul speaks of a man being caught up into Paradise (2 Corinthians 12:3) and Revelation 2:7 places the Tree of Life in the paradise of God. It is the place where believers go after death, a place of glory, a place of blessedness above the earth. It is something which exists now but is still to be revealed in its full glory at the end of time.

See also Eden, Kingdom of the Dead

PARCHMENT

Writing material made from the finely scraped and smoothed skin of a young calf, sheep or goat. Regularly used before the discovery of paper. Moses had plenty of suitable skins from the sacrifices on which to record the laws and records.

See also Pergamum

PARTHIANS

The Parthians were a people who are mentioned in connection with the day of the first Pentecost in Jerusalem when the Holy Spirit was given to the disciples of Jesus (Acts 2:9).

The Parthian kingdom was originally a small kingdom south-east of the

Caspian Sea. The power of the Parthians gradually became so great as to threaten the Roman empire itself. In the third century AD the Parthian kingdom lost its power.

PARTIES, RELIGIOUS AND POLITICAL

In New Testament times there were a number of different religious and political parties among the Jews.

Pharisees. The Pharisees, meaning 'the separated ones', were the most important of the Jewish parties, and were to be found in different parts of Jewish society. A Pharisee was expected to live according to the letter of the Law, and Pharisees were well-educated and highly intelligent. It has been calculated that there were from 4,000 to 5,000 Pharisees in and around Jerusalem in Jesus' day. Some (but not all) of them were among Jesus' most energetic opponents; others became Christians at an early date. They wanted to keep Judaism pure, but their method of strict regulation denied the real basis of the law.

Sadducees. The Sadducees were much more conservative than the Pharisees, accepting only the written Law (Torah), that is, the Pentateuch or first five books of the Old Testament; the Pharisees accepted the authority of the 'oral Law' – including many commentaries on Scripture – as well. Sadducees did not believe in the doctrine of the resurrection of the dead, nor did they believe in the existence of angels and spirits. Politically, they attempted to remain on good terms with the Romans, and did their best to prevent the Jewish people from revolting against Roman rule. Since the High Priest and other priests were members of this party, their influence was great; they virtually controlled the Sanhedrin (the Great Council), the highest Jewish court, of which the High Priest was chairman.

Scribes. Not really a party, the Scribes were more of a professional group, who were concerned with the study and teaching of the Law. Many Scribes were in fact attached to the party of the Pharisees.

Zealots. The Zealots were a group who were committed to making Israel into an independent state. However, their methods were violent, and they may be compared with the 'urban guerrillas' of today.

Assassins. The Assassins (in Latin *sicarii*, 'dagger-men') are mentioned only once in the New Testament, in Acts 21:38. They were the most extreme Zealots, who would even commit murder for the sake of their country.

Essenes. The Essenes were a disciplined order of men who lived in communities, one of which was situated at Qumran, on the Dead Sea. It is believed that there were some 4,000 Essenes in Jesus' day.

Herodians. The Herodians were a group of Jews who supported both King Herod and the Roman rule. Some of them were among Jesus' opponents.

See also Assassins, Essenes, Herodians, Sadducees, Scribes, Dead Sea Scrolls

PASSION OF CHRIST

When Jesus went up to Jerusalem for the last time to celebrate the Passover, he knew that he was going to suffer and die. This is known as his 'Passion'. At his entry into Jerusalem the people praised Jesus. It is thought that he entered the city through the 'Golden Gate' (see under this name), riding on an ass. (Mark 11:1–10.) The leaders of the Jews agreed to have Jesus killed. One of Jesus' disciples, Judas Iscariot, promised to deliver Jesus to them. The course of events was as follows. The numerals 1– 8 relate to the map.

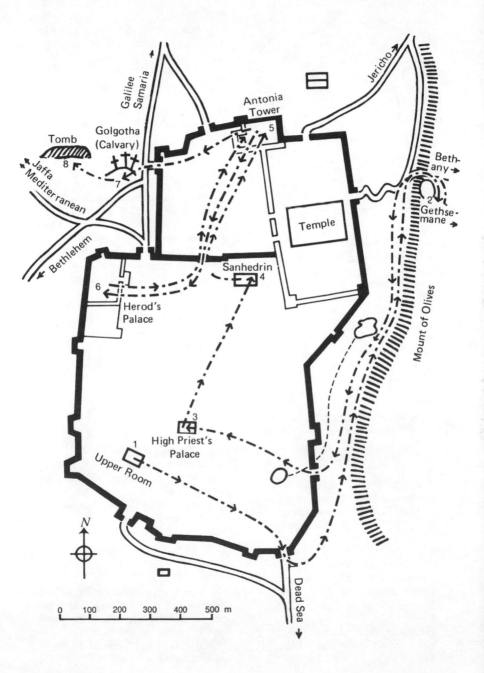

At the sixth hour (12 noon)

Darkness over the land

Friday

At the ninth hour (3 p.m.)

Jesus dies

At the third hour (9 a.m.)

Jesus crucified

Jesus arrested by Caiaphas' guards

Jesus taken to Pilate

Good Friday

Dawn (6 a.m.)

Fourth watch of the night

1
Jesus ate the Last Supper, the Passover lamb, together with his 12 disciples. Jesus instituted the Holy Communion (Mark 14:12–25; John 13).

2
Jesus and the disciples went to the garden of Gethsemane on the slope of the Mount of Olives. Jesus prayed. Judas Iscariot came with a group of armed men, and these arrested Jesus (Luke 22:39–54).

3
Jesus was taken to the house of the High Priest, Caiaphas. Jesus was interrogated during the night. Peter denied that he knew Christ (Luke 22:54–65).

4
The highest court of the Jews, the Sanhedrin, used to meet just below the Temple. Perhaps Jesus was interrogated here, too, by the Jewish leaders (Luke 22:66–71).

5
The Jews took Jesus to the Fortress Antonia, where the Roman governor, Pontius Pilate, lived. Pilate thought that Jesus was innocent (Luke 23:1–6).

6
Pilate sent Jesus to Herod Antipas, who was on a visit to Jerusalem (Luke 23:7–12).

7
Jesus was declared guilty and taken by the Roman soldiers out to the place called the Skull, Golgotha. Jesus was crucified and died (Luke 23:18–46).

8
Joseph of Arimathea and Nicodemus laid Jesus' body in Joseph's rock tomb near Golgotha (Matthew 27:57–61; John 19:38–42; Luke 23:50–53).

Jesus' seven words on the cross

1 Eli, Eli, lama sabachthani? = My God, my God, why hast thou forsaken me? (Matthew 27:46, c.f. Psalm 22).
2 Father, forgive them; for they know not what they do (Luke 23:34).
3 Truly, I say to you, today you will be with me in Paradise (Luke 23:43).
4 Father, into thy hands I commit my spirit! (Luke 23:46).
5 Woman, behold your son! Behold, your mother! (John 19:26, 27).
6 I thirst (John 19:28).
7 It is finished (John 19:30).

See also Atonement, Barabbas, Blood, Cross, Funeral, Gethsemane, Golgotha, Holy Communion, Praetorium, Punishment: Scourge, Resurrection, Salvation, Veil.

PASSOVER SEE FESTIVALS

PATMOS

A small island off the coast of Asia Minor, eight miles long and four miles wide. From this island the book of Revelation was written by the author in exile, traditionally John the apostle in his old age. The island is now called Patino, and today it is a part of Greece (Revelation 1:9).

PATRIARCH

The word patriarch means 'forefather', and although it is applied to the great men before the Flood, and to the twelve sons of Jacob, it primarily refers to Abraham, Isaac and Jacob, whose stories are found in Genesis 12–50.

In these stories we are told how God began to choose Israel for his own people. God established a covenant with Abraham, which he renewed with Isaac and Jacob. In this covenant the patriarchs were promised the land of Canaan and a future as a great people (see also Abraham, Isaac and Jacob).

The Patriarchal Age is likely to have been approximately 1900 to 1600 BC covering the life-spans of Abraham, Isaac and Jacob. It was a time when urban life was set beside the nomadic life of travel. Towns such as Ur, Shechem, Dothan, Hebron, Sodom and Gomorrah to name a few, were occupied as nomads settled down. The Patriarchs appear to be semi-nomadic, travelling with large flocks of sheep, herds of oxen, asses and even camels (Genesis 13). Nomads sometimes clashed with towns over water supplies and pasture (Genesis 21:22-34). The father was the family head over his sons and their families. The eldest son succeeded him and inherited his possessions and property by right of birth or birthright. Marriage was complex and polygamy was widespread (Genesis 16:4; 29:23-29).

The blessing of the father was considered very important and was the equivalent of making a will, but, once given it could not be withdrawn, e.g. Esau and Jacob (Genesis 27). The Patriarchs had a strong personal faith in God and were very faithful in their worship and sacrifices. Circumcision of babies was instituted by God as a sign that they were included in God's covenant relationship – in other words part of the family of God's promise (Genesis 17:9-14). Such was their trust in God, that the Patriarchs often named places after God's activity (Genesis 22:14), and children, too (Genesis 21:3-7). Some German scholars have attempted to discredit the Patriarchal records as non-historical and written up later by the Israelites. However, recent archaeological excavations at Mari, Nuzi and Alalakh have given much information to confirm the background of the records as they stand.

PEACEMAKER

This word is used in Matthew 5:9, 'Blessed are the peacemakers'. Jesus is here referring to those who make peace between two opponents, who put an end to enmity and effect a reconciliation between people.

THE PENTATEUCH

The first five books of the Bible – Genesis, Exodus, Leviticus, Numbers, Deuteronomy – form a third of the Jewish canon and are known as the book of the Law. The Greek *pentateuchos* means simply five-volumed book. In Hebrew it is called the Torah, meaning the Law (Galatians 3:10; Matthew 12:5; Luke 2:22, etc.). It covers the life of the family of Abraham and his descendants through to Moses' death. Contents: Given in more detail at the end of this article, there are six main divisions.

1 The origin of the world and the nations (Genesis 1-11).
2 The Patriarchs: Abraham to Joseph (Genesis 12-50).
3 Moses and the Exodus from Egypt (Exodus 1-18).
4 The Sinai history and the giving of the Law (Exodus 19-Numbers 10).
5 The wilderness wanderings (Numbers 10-36).
6 The final speeches of Moses (Deuteronomy 1-34).

Until the nineteenth century, it was universally accepted that Moses was the author. Since the 1870's the German Graf-Wellhausen theory that the Pentateuch is a collection of different writings by different authors at widely spaced historical periods, has dominated much theological and historical interpretation. This documentary hypothesis, as it is known, holds that the various different strands were written at a later date than Moses. The four main strands they refer to as J, E, D and P. There is no space here to begin to discuss arguments that have occupied volumes of books since the 1870's, but conservative and evangelical scholars have consistently defended the traditional view that Moses was the author of the Pentateuch. Such elements as the use of divine names, style, language and the evidence of archaeology have been taken into account in reaffirming the inner harmony of the five books. The arguments are very complex, but studies of the Egyptian world in ancient times have confirmed the genuineness of the biblical setting to the Exodus, and Moses remains the great lawgiver and the dominant figure of Israel's history.

Contents in Detail

Genesis

Exodus

Leviticus

Numbers

(Note: In between the historical records there are ritual laws.)

Deuteronomy

Deuteronomy 1–31	Moses' speech to the people
Deuteronomy 32–33	The song and blessing of Moses
Deuteronomy 34	Moses dies

PENTECOST SEE FESTIVALS

PEREA

was, in the time of the New Testament, the name of the area immediately to the east of the river Jordan. After the death of king Herod the Great, his son Herod Antipas reigned over Perea. Perea is not mentioned by name in the Bible, but, since the word means, *the other side*, it is represented by the translation 'beyond the Jordan' in Mark 10:1; John 10:40.

PERGA

was a city in Asia Minor which Paul visited on his first missionary journey. Paul's co-workers were Barnabas and John Mark. In Perga John Mark left the two others and returned to Jerusalem (Acts 13:13; 14:25).

PERGAMUM

(or Pergamon) was a city in western Asia Minor. One of the letters in the Book of Revelation is addressed to the Christian church there (2:12–17). The city of Pergamum has given the name to a type of fine writing material from prepared animal skins (in Greek *pergamēnē* 'of Pergamum'), which in English is called 'parchment'. Large amounts of this material were manufactured in the city. The actual use of skins for this purpose is much older, and the general Greek word is that from which our English *membrane* comes (2 Timothy 4:13).
See Parchment

PERSIA

East of the Persian Gulf, Persia was once an insignificant kingdom. It was Cyrus who made Persia an empire from about 550 BC onwards. Those peoples whom Cyrus defeated were treated in a completely different manner from that which was used by Assyrians and Babylonians. Cyrus allowed the defeated nations to keep a great deal of freedom and

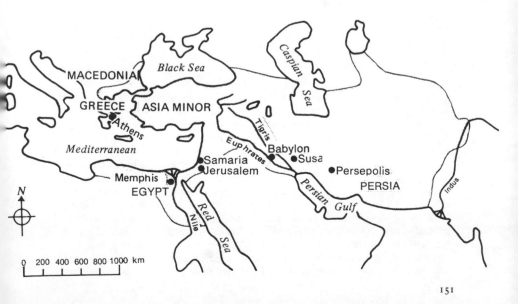

Approx. date	King	Particular events
550 BC	Cyrus	Under Cyrus Persia was liberated, after having been a vassal kingdom under Media. Cyrus now conquered Media
540 BC	Cyrus	Cyrus conquered Asia Minor
538 BC	Cyrus	The fall of the neo-Babylonian kingdom. The Jews who were captive in Babylonia were allowed by Cyrus to return to Palestine and start to rebuild their temple, which had been destroyed
529–522 BC	Cambyses, son of Cyrus	Widened the borders of the Persian Kingdom. Conquered Egypt
522–486 BC	Darius I, called the Great	Divided the country into 20 provinces (satrapies) each of which was governed by a satrap or governor. Persepolis became the capital of the country. A new temple was finished in Jerusalem in 516 BC, which is usually referred to as the second temple
486–465 BC	Xerxes = Ahasuerus	One of King Xerxes' wives was the Jewess Esther, whose story is told in the Book of Esther. Xerxes led his army into Greece. Athens was captured, but Xerxes was gradually driven out of Greece and Europe
465–424 BC	Artaxerxes I	The Jewish priest Ezra was commissioned by the Persian king to travel to Jerusalem in order to examine conditions there. The cupbearer Nehemiah was given permission to rebuild the walls of Jerusalem
423–405 BC 404–359 BC 358–338 BC	Darius II Artaxerxes II Artaxerxes III	The power of the Persian empire was declining
338–333 BC	Darius III	Alexander the Great defeated Darius III at Issus and Arbela in 333 and 331, and ended the Persian empire

independence. Peoples were not taken away in captivity and those who were prisoners of war were allowed to return to their homelands. Each nation was allowed to worship its own gods.

PETER, LETTERS OF

First Peter is written against a background of persecution. Almost certainly the full-scale persecution of Christians was reaching high proportions, and there are references to the fiery trial and ordeal throughout the letter. Peter shows how Christ had to suffer for man to be redeemed, and Christians must expect the same ordeals. A suitable date for First Peter would be AD 63 or 64 – just as Nero's persecution of Christians was breaking out. Written by Peter from Rome ('Babylon' in 1 Peter 5:13 is almost certainly a code-name for Rome), the letter contains many personal references to words of Christ, and it shares Mark's theme of suffering and glory. According to the account of the early historian Papias, Peter supplied Mark with the basis for his Gospel account while in prison at Rome (see Mark, Gospel of).

First Peter prepares Christians for persecution and suffering which was already very strong; Second Peter deals with the quite different problem of false teaching. As early Christians were dying, many believers could not understand why Christ had not returned to put an end to their suffering. Peter tackles this problem by reminding believers that God's dimension of time is totally different from our own (chapter 3). Nevertheless, Christ will return, Peter affirms. Christians must live a life prepared for that day, faithful to God's revealed truth and not led away by false teaching.

Outline of contents	Chapter
The letter is written to the Christians of different areas in Asia Minor	1 Peter 1:1
Thanks to God for His good gifts through Jesus Christ	1 Peter 1:3–12
Exhortation to lead a holy life	1 Peter 1:13–25
Jesus as the living stone	1 Peter 2:1–10
Obedience to authority, i.e. kings and governors	1 Peter 2:13–17
The obedience of servants to their masters, and the endurance of Christ	1 Peter 2:18–25
Exhortation to man and wife to lead a holy life	1 Peter 3:1–7
Admonition to a holy life	1 Peter 3:8–22
Spiritual liberation through suffering	1 Peter 4:1–6
Practise hospitality and serve each other with those gifts which every one of you has received	1 Peter 4:7–11
On being able to rejoice in suffering	1 Peter 4:12–19
Exhortation to the elders and leaders of the churches to be good examples	1 Peter 5:1–4
Humility and perseverance	1 Peter 5:5–9
Conclusion of the Letter	1 Peter 5:10–14

The Second Letter of Peter may be divided as follows:

Greetings	2 Peter 1:1–2
Exhortation to a fruitful faith and a firm belief in the prophecies and truths concerning Jesus Christ	2 Peter 1:3–21
Warning against false teachers	2 Peter 2
Jesus will return. Christians are admonished to lead a life of holiness and godliness	2 Peter 3

PHARAOH SEE EGYPT

PHARISEE SEE PARTIES

PHILADELPHIA

A city in Asia Minor, to which one of the seven letters in the Book of Revelation was addressed (Revelation 3:7–13). The letter contains words of encouragement and praise.

PHILEMON, LETTER TO

Philemon was a rich man who lived at Colossae in Asia Minor. Paul had converted him to Christianity. The Christians at Colossae used to meet in Philemon's house.

Paul wrote the Letter to Philemon when he was a prisoner in Rome. In this letter Paul asks Philemon to receive back a slave by the name of Onesimus who had run away from Philemon. The slave had met Paul in Rome and had become a Christian. The apostle Paul urges Philemon to forgive his escaped slave, and receive him back as his beloved brother in Christ.

See also Colossians 4:9.

PHILIPPI

Described in Acts 16:12 as 'the leading city of the district of Macedonia and a Roman colony'. Paul and Silas stayed at the house of Lydia, delivered a slave girl who was demon possessed and, after

Coins from Philippi with a portrait of the Roman Emperor

being arrested, were miraculously released from prison. An earthquake shook the prison and broke their chains, and the jailor was converted with his household. The magistrates were embarrassed to discover Paul had Roman citizenship and asked him to leave the town (Acts 16). The name Philippi comes from Philip of Macedon who took it from the Thasians about 300 BC. In 42 BC the famous battle of Philippi was fought; Antony and Octavian fighting against Cassius and Brutus. Nine years later, in 31 BC, Octavian defeated Antony and Cleopatra in the ancient world's most important sea battle, and Philippi received a colony of Antony's defeated Italian supporters. Octavian gave the town great civic rights as if it were on Italian soil. Today it lies in ruins.

PHILIPPIANS, LETTER TO

The Letter to the Philippians was written by the apostle Paul, probably during his imprisonment in the city of Rome. The letter is addressed to the Christian congregation at Philippi. A persecution of the Christians has evidently just started in the city.

In the letter Paul wants the congregation to understand that it is a privilege to be allowed to suffer for Christ (Philippians 1:29). Paul repeatedly exhorts the Christians to rejoice, even during suffering and persecution (Philippians 4:4). It is believed that the passage Philippians 2:5–11 is a hymn, which was sung in the early Christian churches to celebrate the Incarnation.

See Acts 16:12–40; 20:6.

Philistine vase with a swan pattern

PHILISTIA, PHILISTINES

In the time of the Old Testament Philistia was the name of a narrow coastal strip on the Mediterranean west of Jerusalem. The country of Philistia was, properly speaking, a league between five cities, namely Gaza, Ashdod, Ashkelon, Ekron and Gath. The Philistines were originally among the 'Peoples of the Sea' who invaded Syria and Egypt in the 12th Century. They came from Caphtor (Jeremiah 47:4; Amos 9:7) which is probably Crete and other Aegean islands. During the time of the Judges the Philistines were Israel's worst enemy. They had the upper hand until they were totally and thoroughly vanquished by king David (2 Samuel 8:1). Later on the Philistines were subjected to the empires which ruled Palestine, but they gave their name to Palestine itself.

Finds in excavations show that the Philistines were highly skilled potters and iron-smiths.

See Genesis 21:32; Joshua 13:3; Judges 13–16; 1 Samuel 4:1–11; 5; 7:7–13; 13:19; 28; 2 Samuel 5:17–25; Acts 8:26, 40.
See also Ashdod, Ashkelon, Ekron, Gath, Gaza

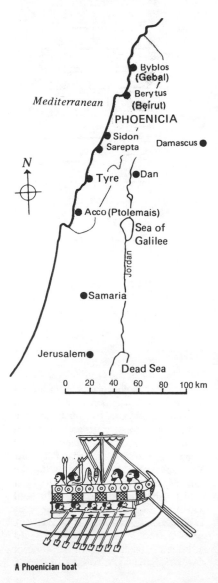

A Phoenician boat

PHOENICIA

In biblical times, Phoenicia was the name of a narrow stretch of country along the Mediterranean coast north of Palestine. In the Old Testament the people of this country were called Sidonians. There were several important cities in Phoenicia: Acco (or Ptolemais), Tyre, Sarepta, Sidon, Berytus (now Beirut) and Byblos (or Gebal). From the Amarna letters, dating from the 15th century BC, we learn that the coastal cities of Phoenicia went through a period of strife and disunity. Their citizens were more interested in increasing their riches by sea-faring and commerce, than in trying to unite their cities into a powerful nation of Phoenicia.

See Judges 3:3; 10:12; 18:7; 1 Kings 16:31; Mark 7:26; Luke 6:17; Acts 11:19; 15:3; 21:2.
See also Letters. For later history see Tyre

PHRYGIA

was the name of a province in Asia Minor visited by the apostle Paul. The cities Laodicea and Colossae were situated in this province (Acts 2:10; 16:6; 18:23; Colossians 2:1; 4:15; Revelation 3:14).

PHYSICIANS

There were physicians in Israel as early as in the time of the Old Testament. They treated external injuries, and could bandage wounds and cure fractures of arms and legs.

It was believed that internal and infectious diseases were often caused by evil powers and demons. They might also be a punishment for sins which the patient was guilty of. Therefore the doctor could do nothing about such illnesses. The sick person would have to reconcile himself with God. He often went to the priest or to the prophet to ask for help. In the New Testament we are told that Luke, the apostle Paul's co-worker, was a physician.

See Genesis 50:2; Isaiah 1:6; Jeremiah 8:22; Ezekiel 30:21; 2 Kings 1:16; 2 Kings 4:18–35; Colossians 4:14.
See also Disease, Healing, Medical Care

PIGEON SEE BIRDS

PILLAR

The word 'pillar' in the English Bible translations sometimes stands for the stone, or altar-like monument, which was erected to the male deity in Canaan. The asherah, or wooden pole, was put up as an image of the female deity (Exodus 23:24).

Pillar-like stones could also be used to mark boundaries (Genesis 31:51, 52) or to be memorials (Genesis 28:18–22; 2 Samuel 18:18). They were sometimes set up above graves (Genesis 35:20).
See also Asherah, High Place

PISIDIA

was an area in the south-west part of Asia Minor. Paul and Barnabas visited Antioch in Pisidia twice during the first missionary journey (Acts 13:13–52; 14:24).

PLOUGH SEE AGRICULTURE

PLUMB-LINE

A plumb-line (the word 'plumb' means 'lead') was a tool which was used in building. It consisted of a line with a weight at one end. With a plummet the builder could check that the walls and pillars were straight (perpendicular) (Zechariah 4:9, 10). By a reverse use the plummet could depict utter destruction without any walls left to check (Isaiah 34:11; Amos 7:7–9).
See also: Crafts and Craftsmen, Line.

A builder checking a wall with a plumb line

PODS

In the parable of the prodigal son we are told that 'he would gladly have fed on the pods that the swine ate.' (Luke 15:16.) These pods (or 'husks', as the Authorized Version translates the Greek word) were probably seed pods of the carob tree, which is common in Palestine. The pods were given mainly to the animals, but they could be dried and used for human food as well. The seed pods have a sweetish taste, and are sold in health stores as a form of cocoa.
See also Trees

POMEGRANATE SEE TREES

POOR, POVERTY

There were large numbers of poor people in the Orient (Matthew 26:11; Mark 14:7; John 12:8). They kept themselves alive by begging (Mark 10:46) often sitting around the Temple (Acts 3:2) or near the houses of the rich (Luke 16:20). Others had jobs which brought in very little money.

In Deuteronomy we find the wealthy under an obligation to help the poor. Widows and orphans were to be given special attention together with the Levites. This is reflected in the legislation. At the harvest some grain (Leviticus 19:9), grapes (Leviticus 19:10) and olives (Deuteronomy 24:20) were to be left for the poor. The tithe in the third year was specifically for the Levites and the poor (Deuteronomy 14:28, 29). In the seventh year the land was to lie fallow and the poor allowed to eat the food which grew (Exodus 23:10, 11).

In New Testament times heavy taxes made life harder for people than ever. Jesus' own parents were poor, and with the disciples he shared a common purse from which Judas took money (John 12:6). They were prepared to go without home comforts (Luke 9:58), but still gave to the poor and needy (John 13:29). It was to the poor that Jesus came to preach the good news (Luke 4:18) and much of his teaching focuses on this theme.

In the early Christian congregations there were many who were poor (1 Corinthians 1:26; James 2:5). Much of Paul's ministry was spent raising money to help the poor church at Jerusalem (Romans 15:25-29).

2 Corinthians 8 and 9 discuss poverty in relation to wealth with a spiritual context, looking at Jesus who though rich for our sakes became poor that we might be rich.

POOR IN SPIRIT

The Pharisees considered a person who carefully followed the Law to be rich before God. Standing before him, such a man or woman could point to a surplus of good deeds. Poor in spirit was the man who could not show any such good deeds, who felt himself to be totally unworthy and lacking everything that was worth praise. Jesus, however, explains that those who believe themselves to be spiritually rich only deceive themselves. He says: 'Blessed are the poor in spirit, for theirs is the kingdom of heaven' (Matthew 5:3; Luke 6:20; 18:9-14).

POSSESSION

Among the people who sought help from Jesus there were those who were possessed. The word means that a person is ruled by one or more evil spirits. The possessed individual could be mad, insane, mute, lame, blind, or show other signs of disease. The New Testament says that Jesus had special power over the evil spirits and could deliver those who were possessed by them.

Demon possession has been seen as particularly strong in Jesus' day as a real Satanic opposition to Christ. But it occurs to this day, and especially in countries and cultures where Christianity has never been strong; missionaries returning have reported severe demon disturbance. In places like Haiti, there is primitive Voodoo religion that actually seeks possession by evil spirits. The Christian testimony is of Jesus Christ, who came to destroy the works of the devil (1 John 3:8). Exorcism continues to be effective in cases of possession, but is always to be approached with the greatest caution and in consultation with Christian leaders. Exorcism is a demonstration of Christ's power and of his kingdom extending. Demon possession is not just illness, and the Gospel writers clearly see deliverance as a spiritual ministry of Jesus.

See Matthew 4:24; Mark 1:23; 5:9; Luke 4:33; 11:14; Acts 8:7.
See also Healing

POTTER SEE CRAFTS

POTTER'S FIELD SEE FIELD OF BLOOD

POUND SEE MEASURES

The area in which it is thought Pilate had his judgement seat

PRAETORIUM

The praetorium was the headquarters in a Roman army camp. The residence of the Roman governors also came to have the same name.

The 'game of kings' carved into the stone of the pavement

The governor Pontius Pilate, who conducted the trial of Jesus, had his praetorium in Jerusalem. It is thought that this was located in Fort Antonia

158

near the Temple. The place where Pilate's judgement seat was, was called *Gabbatha* or *Lithostroton*. The latter, which is a Greek word, means 'paved area' or 'pavement', and a large paved yard has been found in excavations in Fort Antonia.

Archaeologists found the 'board' for a game, 'the game of kings', carved into the stones of the pavement. The soldiers of the Roman guard would play this game to pass the time.

See Matthew 27:27; Mark 15:16; John 18:28–33; 19:9, 13.

PRAYER OF MANASSEH

The prayer of Manasseh is the name of an apocryphal book of the Old Testament. The book tells the story of king Manasseh as a prisoner in Babylon. He humbles himself before the Lord. The Prayer of Manasseh attempts to supply what is said in 2 Chronicles 33:12, 13, which records that his prayers were heard, and he then returned to Jerusalem.

PREPARATION SEE DAY OF PREPARATION

PRIESTS

In ancient Israel, during the life-time of the patriarchs Abraham, Isaac and Jacob, the head of the household, or the tribal chief, was also the priest (Genesis 12:8; 35:7; Job 1:5). It was he who offered the sacrifices at the various altars which had been set up in the country. Gradually particular priests were set apart to look after the order of worship and to conduct the necessary sacrifices.

Aaron and his sons of the tribe of Levi became the priests in Israel (Exodus 28) with the rest of the tribe as assistants (Numbers 3:5–13). The priest was to be the mediator ('go-between') between God and man (Leviticus 16). He had to tell the people the will of God (Malachi 2:7), and he had to carry the offerings, prayers and wishes of the people into God's presence (Leviticus 9:7).

The Pentateuch contains many rules concerning the priests and their tasks, especially in Leviticus and Deuteronomy. After the return of the Jews from their captivity in Babylon the importance of the priests gradually diminished, and the Scribes became the people's teachers.

In Jesus' day it was the Pharisees and the Scribes who taught the people the Law. The High Priest and the other high-ranking priests became involved in politics, although they continued to carry out their traditional functions in the Temple.

When the Temple of Jerusalem was destroyed in AD 70, the priests lost their importance completely. The worship continued in the synagogues, where no sacrifices were offered. The need for priests to carry out such functions was therefore no longer present.

For Christians the Epistle to the Hebrews shows that Jesus Christ has assumed the high priesthood through his one offering of himself on the cross (Hebrews 7–10).
See also High Priest

PRISON SEE PUNISHMENT

PROPHETS

The word 'prophet' means one who 'tells forth', or proclaims a message from God; it has also come to mean one who foretells the future. The task of a prophet was not mainly that of saying what was going to happen in the future, but to tell the people what was the will of God, for their particular time.

In the Old Testament, there were professional 'prophets' at the court of the king. Their task was to inform the king about the will of God (2 Samuel 7:1–17) and they might take part in advice about warfare (2 Kings 3). As a

professional class, they were not always reliable (1 Kings 22).

A prophet spoke freely a message which he believed that he had received from God. Believing that he was called by God, he felt himself compelled to speak, when the Word of God came to him: 'As the Lord lives, what the Lord says to me, that I will speak' (1 Kings 22:14).

A prophet employed at the court of a king might be both a professional prophet and a genuine prophet of God. But some were not genuine, and there are stories in the Old Testament about conflicts between the genuine and the false prophets (Jeremiah 28).

Some prophets were solitary figures, e.g. Jeremiah. Others gathered together in groups or schools, led by a senior prophet, in order to listen to him, to learn from him and pass his teachings on, memorizing his words and finally writing them down (Isaiah 8:16). There were groups of prophets connected with the Temple (1 Chronicles 25:1–3).

Some were followers of the religion of Canaan, not the religion of Israel, and conflicts arose between the two. The best known of these concerns the struggle between Elijah and the prophets of Baal (1 Kings 18).

Some of the prophets were critical of the official religion of Israel, or of some of the forms which it had taken. They criticized the complacent attitude towards worship which took place in the Temple, and particularly the sacrifices (Isaiah 1:10–17). Instead, they demanded that the worship of Israel should be centred on justice and truth, and on the sincere love of God. Their message, then, was one of purification – pure worship of God, without paying any attention to foreign gods, and a pure life: 'But let justice roll down like waters, and righteousness like an ever-flowing stream' (Amos 5:24).

Some of the prophets also foretold the

coming of the Messiah, the anointed King who would restore the true rule of God among the people.
See Messiah

PROSELYTE

is a Greek word which means 'new-comer', 'visitor'. In the Old Testament a proselyte was a Gentile who had become a Jew, and the Greek Septuagint uses the word in Exodus 12:48 to translate the Hebrew *stranger*. In order to be a proselyte he had to keep the Law of Moses, be circumcised, offer sacrifices and be baptized. There are only four references to proselytes in the New Testament (Matthew 23:15; Acts 2:10; 6:5; 13:43). There were other Gentiles who worshipped with the Jews without being circumcised (e.g. Acts 16:1-3; 18:7).

PROVERBS, BOOK OF

The Book of Proverbs in the Old Testament contains sayings and rules of life which are suitable not only for Jews in Old Testament times, but for non-Jews of all ages, too. It is a book of wisdom and great insight into human nature. Chapter 31, for instance, describes the perfect wife and mother. Many have believed that king Solomon collected or wrote the whole of the Book of Proverbs. Others would say this is partly true, and it is also possible that certain proverbs have come from courtiers at king Solomon's court. In any case, the book contains material from different periods. The Book of Proverbs may be divided into different sections:

Outline of Contents	Chapter
Introduction. Advice and warnings, especially to a young man	Proverbs 1-9
The first collection of the Proverbs of Solomon, numbering 375	Proverbs 10-22
The sayings of the wise	Proverbs 22-24

Proverbs of Solomon, 119 in number, collected by Hezekiah	Proverbs 25-29
The words of Agur	Proverbs 30
The words of Lemuel	
The praise of a good wife	Proverbs 31

PSALMS

The Psalms are poems, most of which are intended to be sung in public worship. The 150 psalms are divided into five 'books' or sections. This division (after the analogy of the Five Books of Moses, the Pentateuch) was probably made at a fairly late date. These five books are Book 1 Psalms 1-41, Book 2 Psalms 42-72, Book 3 Psalms 73-89, Book 4 Psalms 90-106, Book 5 Psalms 107-150.

Most of the psalms have headings, in which the author's names, according to ancient Jewish tradition, are given. Mention is made of Moses, David, Solomon, Asaph, Ethan and the Sons of Korah. Nearly half of the psalms are ascribed to king David. Only 50 psalms lack this kind of statement.

The psalms are not arranged in any particular order, although there are some groups, such as those celebrating God's reign (92-100) and the songs of Ascents (120-134).

There are different kinds of psalms: doctrinal psalms, psalms of comfort, prayer, and thanksgiving; penitential psalms and prophetic psalms. It is not known who collected the psalms and made the selection of those 150 which are contained in the Book of Psalms.

Besides these 150 psalms there were probably numerous other songs and psalms. For example, there are two quotations from the poetical Book of Jasher (Joshua 10:13; 2 Samuel 1:18). Note also Numbers 21:27-30. The psalms were used in the Jewish worship, a fact which shows that worship in the time of the Old Testament was not exclusively of a sacrificial type. Jesus referred to the psalms from time to time

(Matthew 21:16, 42; 22:43, 44), and perhaps on the cross recited Psalm 22, although only the first verse is mentioned (Matthew 27:46). The importance of the psalms cannot be exaggerated. They show us the nature of true worship in spirit and in truth. They glorify God in every situation, from shame and sin (Psalm 51), from love of creation (Psalm 8 and 104), from love of his word (Psalm 119). For every situation of human life, from the most ecstatic joy to the most painful grief and suffering, man can praise his maker. The psalms above all show this to be true and also give great importance to the place of public worship and Christian fellowship.

PSALTERY

A term used by the older translations. The Hebrew indicates a harp or zither of ten strings.
See Music.

PUBLICAN SEE TAX-COLLECTOR

PUNISHMENT

When a Jewish court of law had announced a verdict, the defendant, if found guilty, received his punishment immediately. The judge himself, the witnesses before the court, and others present joined together in carrying out the sentence.

Death sentences were common. There had to be two or three witnesses in order to sentence someone to death (Deuteronomy 17:6; 19:15), or in the New Testament for excommunication (Matthew 18:16).

Stoning to death was the commonest death penalty (Exodus 17:4; Joshua 7:25; 1 Kings 21:10; Acts 7:58). Crucifixion was a form of execution which the Romans used on non-Romans. A Roman citizen who was sentenced to death was executed by the sword, through beheading.

In Israel, capital punishment was used in cases of

Breaking the sabbath laws (Exodus 31:13–14).
Blasphemy against the name of God (Leviticus 24:11–16).
Image-worship (Deuteronomy 17:2–7).
Purifying Israel from the evil influence of rebellious sons in order to protect family unity (Deuteronomy 21:18–21).

In cases of murder or manslaughter, the family or relatives of the dead man used to settle the affair with the family of the murderer through blood vengeance (Deuteronomy 19; 2 Samuel 14:6, 7). The vengeance that could be exacted was strictly limited: the vengeance could not exceed the original injury (Exodus 21:12, 23–25; Leviticus 24:17–20).

Prisons were used chiefly for keeping the suspect or criminal under arrest until he was brought before the court and tried. The prisoner might be put in the stocks in or outside of the prison. The stocks were large blocks of wood with holes for his arms, legs or neck which were locked around him and restricted his movements (Jeremiah 20:2; 29:26; Acts 16:24).

Whipping or flogging was a common form of corporal punishment. In Jewish

The Jewish scourge consisted of three straps of leather fastened to a handle

Flogging as shown on an ancient Egyptian picture

law, flogging was limited to 40 strokes (Deuteronomy 25:3). In practice, in later years at least, the flogging was 39 strokes in case of a wrong count (2 Corinthians 11:24). Whips, canes or sticks were used for flogging.

The scourge, which was used by the Romans, was made of plaited leather straps, into which sharp pieces of iron and bone had been inserted. An unlimited number of lashes was allowed. It was not permitted to scourge a Roman citizen.

See Isaiah 9:4; Mark 15:15; Acts 5:40; 22:24, 25.

PURIM, FEAST OF, SEE FESTIVALS

PURPLE

The name of a dye which is derived from certain shell fishes found along the coasts of the Mediterranean. The Phoenicians were masters of this dye from early times, and indeed Canaan means Land of the Purple. In the ancient world it was used for dyeing fabrics and textiles (Acts 16:14). Each shellfish produces only one drop of the finest colour, although further pressing can give a dye of inferior quality. The finest dye was therefore very precious and very expensive, and only the rich could afford to buy and wear purple clothes. Kings and important officials wore purple as a sign of their high rank (Judges 8:26; Esther 8:15; Proverbs 31:22; Luke 16:19; Mark 15:17). Different shades of purple are mentioned in the Pentateuch: dark red, blue or violet, and purple cloth was used in the Tabernacle (Exodus 26:1) and in the Temple (2 Chronicles 2:14; 3:14).

Q

QUAIL SEE BIRDS

QUMRAN

is an archaeological site south of Jericho near the Dead Sea in the Judaean desert. It was here that, in 1947, a large number of 2,000-year-old scrolls, containing texts from the Old Testament, were found in hill caves. These scrolls were once the property of a Jewish organization similar to a monastic order. Its members were called Essenes. Their monastery, with a number of buildings, has been excavated at Qumran.

See also Dead Sea Scrolls, Dead Sea, Essenes

R

RABBI, RABBONI

In the New Testament the teachers of the Law or the Scribes were called 'Rabbi', transliterated from the Hebrew. This word means 'my lord', or 'my master', as a title of respect. The title 'rabbi' was also given to Jesus, (Matthew 26:25; Mark 9:5; John 3:2). Its use within the Church fellowship was forbidden by Jesus (Matthew 23:8). Rabboni (John 20:16) is an Aramaic variation of the word.

RAIN SEE CLIMATE

RAVEN SEE BIRDS

RECONCILIATION

In modern speech, reconciliation can mean a compromise. In the New Testament Greek it means something quite different; God breaking down the wall of separation caused by man's rebellion. This is God destroying for ever the power of evil and sin which caused the breakdown in relations. Four passages describe this work of reconciliation so essential to our understanding of why Christ died. They are Romans 5:10 ff; 2 Corinthians 5:18 ff; Ephesians 2:11 ff and Colossians 1:19 ff. God makes the offer, and our part to complete the reconciliation is to turn to him in faith and accept the gift which he offers in Christ.

RED SEA

That part of the ocean which separates Africa from Asia is called the Red Sea. It is about 1,425 miles (2,300 km) long. It is situated in one of the hottest areas in the world. The northern end of the Red Sea is divided by the Sinai peninsula into two gulfs: the Gulf of Suez and the Gulf of Aqaba.

In the Bible the Red Sea is known through the story of the Israelites' escape flight from Egypt. According to this account the sea was divided when Moses raised his staff. The place of crossing was 'the sea of reeds' just north of Suez. A dry road was formed through the waters, and the children of Israel arrived safely on the other shore. But Pharaoh and his soldiers, who pursued them into the sea, were drowned when the waters flowed back again.

See Exodus 14.

REED

When the word 'reed' is used in the English Bible translations, it sometimes refers to a species of rush, the papyrus reed. This plant can grow to a height of 10 to 15 ft (3 to 5 m). It has pithy, triangular stems and sword-shaped leaves, 3 ft long, which grow from the base of the stem. At the top of the stem there is a brush-like umbel of insignificant flowers. The papyrus reed is a tropical plant which flourishes in damp bogs and on the shores of lakes and river banks. It grew in abundance along the banks of the Nile in Egypt.

The stems of the papyrus were used for walking-sticks, fishing rods, measuring-rods, flutes, reed boats (light river boats), mats, shoes, clothes and fuel. The papyrus was however of greatest importance for the manufacture of writing materials and scrolls.

See 2 Kings 18:21; Job 8:11; 9:25–26; Isaiah 18:2; 35:7; 42:3; Ezekiel 2:9; Matthew 11:7.
See also Papyrus, Writing Materials

RESURRECTION

The Old Testament shows that God is able to bring an individual back from the kingdom of the dead into life (1 Samuel 2:6; Psalm 17:15). Isaiah and Daniel speak of a resurrection at the end of time (Isaiah 26:19; Daniel 12:2).

The important good news which the apostles and the first Christians at the time of the New Testament could proclaim was that Jesus had risen from the dead and was therefore alive (Luke 24:34; Acts 1:22; 17:31; 1 Corinthians 9:1. 1 Corinthians 15 especially). It is important to remember that the word resurrection always involves the body. It is not simply the survival of the spirit (Luke 24:40). Thus every reference to the resurrection of Jesus implies the empty tomb.

The New Testament says that just as Jesus rose from the dead, those who believe in him will rise again and afterwards always be with him (Acts 23:6; 1 Thessalonians 4:14–17), but the transformation will not be effected until the Second Coming (1 Corinthians 15:51, 52; Philippians 3:20, 21). In the last book of the Bible, the Revelation to John, we are told that death and the kingdom of the dead will give up all their dead. There will be a general resurrection. Everyone will then stand before the throne of God to be judged by him, 'the last Judgement' (Revelation 20:11–13). Although true believers are not then judged for their salvation (John 5:24), they must give account for their use of their opportunities and gifts (Matthew 25:14–30; 1 Corinthians 2:10–15; 2 Corinthians 5:10). On this basis they will apparently receive rewards of further opportunities of service (Matthew 25:21; Luke 19:17; 1 Corinthians 3:14).

REUBEN

was the eldest of the patriarch Jacob's sons (Genesis 29:32). He became the father of the tribe of Reuben. Their

tribal area was east of the Dead Sea, and consisted of a very fertile plain (Numbers 32:1–5).
See Genesis 29:32; 37:21; Deuteronomy 3:16; Joshua 12:6.

REVELATION BOOK OF

The Revelation of John (also called the Book of the Revelation, or the Apocalypse) is the last of the books of the New Testament. It has the form of a letter from John to seven churches in Asia Minor, and in it he writes what Christ has shown him through revelations (1:1–3).

According to some ancient sources the book was written during the reign of the Roman emperor Domitian, in about AD 95–96. Traditionally the author is the apostle John. The book itself does not identify the author. There is much symbolism and picture imagery that is hard to interpret. The writer was in exile on the island of Patmos, west of Asia Minor, when he saw the visions described in the book (1:9). During the difficult periods of persecution, the suffering

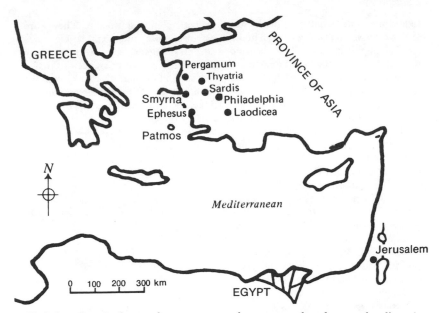

GREECE

PROVINCE OF ASIA

Pergamum
Thyatria
Sardis
Smyrna
Philadelphia
Ephesus
Laodicea
Patmos

N

Mediterranean

Jerusalem

0 100 200 300 km

EGYPT

Christians found solace and encouragement in the Book of Revelation.

Outline of the Contents	Chapter
Introduction with the greeting to the seven churches of Asia Minor.	Revelation 1:1–8
John is ordered to write down his visions.	Revelation 1:9–20
The letters to the seven churches in Asia Minor.	Revelation 2, 3
Visions and revelations which speak of coming events and demonstrate God's control of the whole of human history.	Revelation 4–22

RIGHTEOUS, RIGHTEOUSNESS

In the Old Testament the word 'righteousness' is similar in meaning to our word 'justice'. The Jewish Law speaks of accurate weights and measures as being 'just': 'You shall have just balance, just weights...' (Leviticus 19:36). These are pleasing to God, as is an act of sacrifice properly carried out: 'then wilt thou delight in right sacrifices' (Psalm 51:19). When a person is called 'righteous', this also means that he or she lives in accordance with the will of God, and is therefore pleasing to God. Because he wishes to do God's will, he does only that of which he knows God approves. Thus a righteous, or true, Israelite never turns to the worship of other gods, and plays a full part in the life of God's people.

Men and women are to behave in this way because God himself is righteous, and has shown his righteousness in the way he has behaved toward Israel. He has shown grace to Israel, and has given the people his help, blessing, victory and salvation. Because of this, the enemies of Israel experience the righteousness of God as judgement and even as punishment (Psalm 9:8).

This same judgement may, however, strike Israel, and does so when they abandon the worship of God for that of other deities. The Prophets often speak of the righteous judgement of God which will come upon the people of Israel unless they mend their ways (Isaiah 1:21–26). Later, the test of a person's righteousness was whether or not he was able to observe everything written in the Law (Philippians 3:6). This became more and more difficult as time went on, and extra laws were added to the list (Matthew 23:4).

The apostle Paul teaches that because of this, it is impossible for anyone fully to observe the Law. Therefore no one can be entirely righteous, except by faith in God: 'the righteousness of God is revealed through faith for faith' (Romans 1:17). The sufferings, death and resurrection of Christ are the means by which God makes men righteous, and righteousness is therefore a direct gift from God. Whoever has faith is made righteous by God. Another word for this is 'justified': whoever believes in Jesus Christ is justified by faith. There is an exchange, as it were, between Christ's righteousness and man's sin (Romans 5:18; 1 Corinthians 1:30; 2 Corinthians 5:21). The believer is pardoned, his sins are forgiven, just as though he were a criminal offender who has been declared 'not guilty'. He is acquitted, to use the words of Paul (Romans 5:18). The sinner then escapes the final consequences of his sin, and he is set free. 'This was to show God's righteousness ... it was to prove at the present time that he himself is righteous and that he justifies him who has faith in Jesus' (Romans 3:25, 26).

See also Romans 5:1.

Old ear-ring from Syria

RINGS

were worn in different ways as ornaments

by both men and women. They wore earrings, nose rings and ankle rings (anklets). Finger rings were not very common. The seal or signet ring was a special kind of ring, which was used for stamping seals. It was either worn on the finger, or on a chain or strap round the neck or the arm.

See Genesis 41:42; Esther 3:10; Luke 15:22; James 2:2.
See also Ornament, Seal

RIVER

In Israel there are only a few watercourses large enough to be called rivers. Many of them are filled with water only during the rainy season. People waded across the rivers in fords where the water was shallow. The Romans built bridges across the rivers, but later these were allowed to fall into disrepair. The most important rivers are the Jordan, the Jabbok, the Arnon and the Yarmuk. There are also frequent references to the Nile and Euphrates.

ROADS SEE TRAVEL

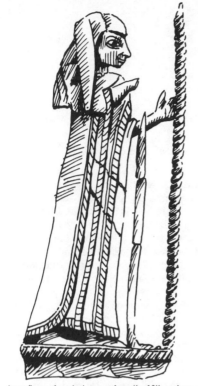

Ivory figure of a robed woman from the 13th century BC found at Megiddo

ROBE

A robe was a full-length garment, which was worn by high-ranking officials and other important people. The patriarch Jacob gave a robe to his favourite son, Joseph (Genesis 37:3). Jesus was given a purple robe – the imperial colour – as an act of mockery (Mark 12:38;16:5; Luke 20:46). Believers will be given white robes as a sign of approval and purity (Revelation 3:5; 6:11; 7:9).

ROMAN CITIZEN

In New Testament times all free-born people in the Italian peninsula had the right of citizenship in the Roman empire. Whole provinces in the Roman empire

might be given the right of Roman citizenship. A person who had been of great service to the Emperor could be rewarded with Roman citizenship. It was also possible to buy the right to be called a citizen of Rome (Acts 22:28).

The punishment of beating or scourging was not allowed in the case of a Roman citizen (Acts 16:37–39). He also had the right to contest a sentence and have it tried by Caesar (Acts 25:11, 12). The apostle Paul was a Roman citizen from birth (Acts 22:28).

ROMANS, LETTER TO

The letter to the Romans is one of the apostle Paul's letters. It is thought that the letter was written in about AD 58. It is highly likely that Paul was in Achaia (another name for Greece) at the time – most probably Corinth (Acts 20:2, 3). In the letter Paul speaks of his plans to leave the eastern part of the Mediterranean and to preach the gospel in Rome and Spain (Romans 1:9–15; 15:24, 28).

The city of Antioch in Syria had been the point of departure for the apostle's travels in the eastern parts of the Roman empire. Paul thought that Rome might, in the same way, become the starting-point for his missionary work in the western parts of the Roman empire (Romans 15:28). In the letter to the Romans Paul gives a detailed summary of his understanding of the gospel of Jesus Christ.

The letter to the Romans may be divided into different parts:

Outline of Contents	Chapter
Introduction	Romans 1:1–17
Jews are under God's judgement as well as Gentiles and God's judgement is just and righteous.	Romans 1:18–3:20
Righteousness is a gift received through faith	Romans 3:21–5:21
A new life with Christ is to be lived in holiness.	Romans 6–8

Israel has not wanted to
believe the gospel and has
therefore been rejected,
but God will finally save
all Israel.   Romans 9–11;
Exhortations to holiness,
humility and love. The
necessity of obedience to
authority.   Romans 12–16

S

Romans 5–8 show the basis of Paul's
theology and teaching. Chapter 8 ends
the section with a glorious exposition of
the Holy Spirit and the love of God.

RUE SEE HERBS AND SPICES

RUTH, BOOK OF

The chief character in this book is Ruth
herself. She lived in the country of Moab,
where she married one of the sons of
Naomi, who had come with her family
from Bethlehem during a famine. Ruth's
husband died and they had had no
children. Her mother-in-law, Naomi,
wanted to return to Jerusalem and Ruth
asked to be allowed to accompany her,
whereas her widowed sister-in-law, Or-
pah, chose to stay in Moab.

In Bethlehem Ruth was shown great
kindness by the farmer Boaz, who was a
relative of Naomi's. Finally Ruth became
Boaz' wife. King David's ancestry went
back to Ruth's family in Bethlehem
(Ruth 4:17–22). The story told in the
Book of Ruth shows that a person who
trusts in the Lord will be rescued even
from the – apparently – most hopeless
situation. It is also thought that the book
was planned to show how David's
grandfather was born through a particular act of God.

God is at work in every situation to
work out his purposes.

SABBATH SEE FESTIVALS

SABBATICAL YEAR

Every seventh year was a sabbatical year,
called a sabbath of rest for the land
(Leviticus 25:4, 5). In Exodus 23:10–
11 there is a clause of the Law which
says that in the seventh year the land
should rest and lie fallow. This rule also
governed the vineyard and the olive
orchard. The poor and the wild animals
were then allowed to eat freely of the
ripe harvest.

Every 50th year or every seventh
sabbatical year was called a year of
liberty or a year of jubilee (Leviticus
25:8–12). The soil was to rest unculti-
vated, and all Israelites were to be given
back any property which had been lost
or sold. Slaves were to be set free
(Deuteronomy 15). It is not known how
strictly these laws concerning sabbatical
years, years of liberation or of jubilee
were observed, if at all.

SACRIFICE (OFFERING)

The offering of various kinds of sacrifices
was an important element in Israelite
worship. Originally sacrifices were made
in a number of different places in the
country (Exodus 20:24, 25), but eventually the only proper place of sacrifice
became the Temple in Jerusalem (Deuteronomy 12:10–14; 1 Kings 8:27–30;
John 4:20).

Temple sacrifices were offered every
day. At seasonal festivals, special sacrifices took place.

The meaning and purpose of sacrifice

could vary. Some sacrifices were simply gifts to God, which maintained a good relationship with God or gave the sacrificer a sense of fellowship with God. Other sacrifices were intended to restore a broken relationship with God; they made atonement for a sin which had been committed, removed the guilt which followed sin, and re-established the fellowship of man and God. Sometimes the offering of sacrifice could be a straightforward act of thanksgiving.

See also Altar, Worship, Temple

Type of Sacrifice	Notes	Purpose	Material	Reference
Incense offering	'The daily incense offering', lit every day at the incense altar.		Incense, made of sweet-smelling substances. See Incense	Exodus 30:1-8; Psalm 141:2
Burnt offering or whole offering	The entire offering was burnt. Took place every day in the Temple. Also called morning and evening sacrifice.	atonement and purification	cattle, sheep, goats and doves	Leviticus 1:1-17
Sin offering	The sin was confessed and the animal slaughtered and its blood smeared on the altar. Part of the offering was burnt on the altar.	atonement	cattle, doves	Leviticus 4:1-35
Guilt offering	This was reparation for breaking the law. Damage done had to be repaired, stolen goods replaced, and fines paid.	atonement	ram	Leviticus 5:15-6:7
Peace offering	Made as praise, in fulfilment of a promise, etc. Part was burned, the rest eaten. The priests were given some of it.	thanksgiving or for special wish	cattle, bread or flour	Leviticus 3:1-17
Wave offering	Was 'waved' back and front of the altar.			Leviticus 7:30-34
Cereal offerings	Part was burned, the rest eaten by the priests.	Served as sin offering for atonement for the poor	flour, oil, salt or incense	Leviticus 2:1-16; 5:11-13; 6:14-18
Drink offering RSV sometimes translates as *libation*	Probably the pouring of wine over the altar.			Genesis 35:14; Exodus 29:40; Leviticus 23:13

SADDUCEES

The Sadducees were members of a religious party among the Jews in Jesus' day. They included the High Priests, other high-ranking priests and rich and prominent people in Jewish society. The party of the Sadducees originated after the Captivity, but may have acquired their name from the High Priest Zadok, who lived during the reigns of David and Solomon. The Sadducees exercised a great deal of influence among the 71 men who together formed the Sanhedrin, the Supreme Court of the Jews. The High Priest was the leader or chairman of the Sanhedrin. The Sadducees did not believe in the doctrine of the resurrection of the dead, nor did they believe in the existence of angels and spirits. They accepted only the written Law (Torah), that is the Pentateuch, and disregarded the 'oral law', i.e. all the additional rules which the Pharisees attempted to follow.

The Sadducees were more co-operative with the Romans than other Jewish people, although they united with the Pharisees in opposing Jesus.

See Matthew 16:1, 12; Mark 12:18; Acts 4:1; Acts 23:6-10.
See also Parties

SALAMIS

was a seaport on the east coast of the island of Cyprus in the Mediterranean. It was the first place which the apostle Paul visited on his first missionary journey (Acts 13:5). This was not the famous Salamis where the Persian king, Xerxes (Ahasuerus), the husband of Esther, was defeated by the Greeks in a naval battle in 480 BC.

SALT

was a necessity for cooking and storage of food. In addition salt was used for certain sacrifices (Leviticus 2:13). New-born babies were usually rubbed with salt, perhaps as an antiseptic (Ezekiel 16:4).

Salt was mined on the southern shore of the Dead Sea (Genesis 19:26; Zephaniah 2:9). The Phoenicians obtained and traded salt from evaporation of sea water.

It was thought that those who had eaten a meal together at which salt in some form had been consumed were afterwards bound to maintain their friendship (Numbers 18:19). When Jesus spoke about his disciples as being the salt of the earth, he was probably thinking of the property of salt to purify and keep meat from going bad (Matthew 5:13). Salt preserves, it brings out flavour and savours the food. So, too, Christians are to be salt, preserving the morality of society and giving to it a Christian flavour to enrich it.

SALVATION

The words 'salvation' or 'deliverance' are used in the Old Testament to describe rescue from all kinds of perils and deadly danger. But the Old Testament also mentions salvation from sin, especially in certain Psalms (e.g. Psalm 51:1-14; Isaiah 12:2).

In the New Testament the word 'salvation' is a very important one. It means rescue, deliverance, liberation. It is a liberation from sin, death, Satan and the accusations of the Law.

According to the New Testament, the only real salvation is the act of salvation which God carries out through Jesus Christ. All attempts by man to save himself are entirely worthless and without effect.

To believe and trust in salvation through Jesus Christ is the only thing man can do. He receives this salvation as a gift. No one can buy or earn salvation for himself through kindness, helpfulness, righteousness or goodness (Romans 3:28; 4:4-5; 1 Corinthians 1:31; Galatians 2:16; Ephesians 2:8-9). Salvation is a gift, given through God's grace.

God has made salvation possible through the life, suffering, death and resurrection of Jesus Christ (Acts 4:12; 2 Corinthians 6:2; Ephesians 2:5; 1 Peter 1:18-19; 1 John 4:9-10).

SAMARIA

Samaria became the capital of Northern Israel during the reign of king Omri. The city was built on a hill which rose about 90 m (295 ft) over the plain around it. Omri built a palace and surrounded the city with a wall (1 Kings 16:24). Later the city was expanded by king Ahab, who also built a temple to the god Baal (1 Kings 16:32).

In 722 BC Samaria was conquered by the Assyrians. The city was not destroyed, but foreign peoples were moved into the city (2 Kings 17). Soon after the time of Nehemiah a rival temple was built in Samaria (John 4:4, 20). During the wars of the Maccabees, Samaria was burned to the ground. King Herod the Great rebuilt the city and beautified it, and renamed it Sebaste. But Sebaste-Samaria gradually lost its particular position of importance.

SAMARIA, SAMARITANS

The whole of the Northern Kingdom might be called Samaria after the capital (2 Kings 17:24; Acts 8:5). When the Assyrians conquered the city of Samaria in 722 BC, a large part of the population were taken away and strangers settled in Samaria (2 Kings 17). There was inter-marriage between the Israelites who had been allowed to stay in the country and the foreign settlers (Ezra 6:21). Their descendants were called Samaritans.

The Samaritans' worship of Israel's God was initially mingled with the ways in which the foreign settlers worshipped their gods (2 Kings 17:33; Ezra 4:2), but after this the worship was purged from these non-Israelite rituals, and the Samaritans built a temple on Mount Gerizim. Here the ritual of the Pentateuch was followed. This temple was destroyed during the time of the Maccabees. The Samaritans, however, continued to worship on Mount Gerizim without a temple.

In Jesus' day the Samaritans regarded themselves as being part of Israel. Their holy scripture was the Pentateuch, of which the Samaritans today still have some very old copies. Samaria became a province in the Roman empire. The Jews, however, did not want to have anything to do with the Samaritans. They would try to avoid travelling through Samaria. A Jew would not sit down to a meal with a Samaritan. At times Samaritans were even regarded as worse and more ungodly than Gentiles (John 8:48). So Jesus' parable of the Good Samaritan (Luke 10:29-37) cut right through the racial tension of the day to show a better way than race hatred.

See 1 Kings 13:32; John 4:42; Acts 1:8.
See also Galilee

SAMUEL, BOOKS OF

The books of Samuel cover one of the most important periods of Israel's history, with the beginnings of the Monarchy and the Kingdom emerging from the time of the Judges. The first book records the reign of Saul, the contest of David and Goliath, the story of David and Saul, David in hiding and the death of Saul. Second Samuel covers the reign of David and the rebellion of his sons.

1 Chronicles 29:29 suggests that the prophet Samuel may have been joint author with Nathan and Gad. 1 Samuel 10:25 shows that Samuel himself kept written records. Chapter 1 begins with the call of Samuel himself, and the books can be divided into the lives of Samuel, Saul and David. Historically the period is roughly 1050-950 BC.

SANCTUARIES

Certain cities in Israel were sanctuaries, where a man could seek refuge and escape vengeance, if he had killed someone. Only if it was a case of unpremeditated manslaughter, for instance in self-defence, was the murderer given the right of remaining in refuge in the sanctuary. The six cities were Kedesh, Shechem, Kiriath-Arba, Bezer, Ramoth and Golan.

See Numbers 35:13; Deuteronomy 4:41–43; Joshua 20:5.

SANHEDRIN

The word is rendered *Council* in English translations. It is a transliteration of the Hebrew and Aramaic term, which is itself a transliteration of the Greek *synedrion,* meaning literally 'a sitting together' and hence a council. The Sanhedrin in Jerusalem was the highest authority of the Jews for about 200 years. It ceased to function in AD 70, at the destruction of Jerusalem. The Sanhedrin consisted of 70-71 members, among which were the High Priests, other high-ranking priests, Scribes and 'elders'. The High Priest in office presided over the council. The term was also used of local councils.

The Sanhedrin dealt with all important matters that concerned the Jews:

political matters:
the relation to neighbouring peoples and to the nation which ruled Palestine at the time.

religious matters:
the Temple, the worship, the festivals, the Torah and the way in which it was to be interpreted.

legal matters:
cross-examination of witnesses, pronouncing judgement and putting the sentence into effect. During the Roman period the Sanhedrin was not allowed to carry out capital punishment. The Roman authorities had to ratify and carry out the sentence.

See Matthew 27:1–2; Acts 5:21; 6:12; 22:30.
See also: Court of law, Elders

SARDIS

was a city in western Asia Minor. One of the letters in the Revelation to John is addressed to the Christian church at Sardis (Revelation 3:1–6), and the soiled garments (v.4) may be an allusion to involvement in the degrading worship of Cybele, which was popular in Sardis.

SARGON

ruled Assyria from 722 to 705 BC. His predecessor, Shalmaneser V, had penetrated into Northern Israel with an army and laid siege to the capital city, Samaria, for three years. Shalmaneser died without having captured the city. In 722 BC Sargon succeeded in breaking the city's defence and defeating its army. Sargon carried a large number of people into captivity, as he himself tells us in an inscription which has been found by

Sargon as shown on a limestone relief

archaeologists: '27,290 of its (Samaria's) inhabitants I carried away'. His name occurs only in Isaiah 20:1 in the Bible, but he is the king in 2 Kings 17:6.

See also: Assyria, Samaria

SATRAPS

were the royal governors of the different provinces in the Persian empire. The satrap might almost be compared to a tributary king. He had the legal right to pass judgement, commanded the armies in his province, collected taxes and was responsible for the maintenance of public order in his province (Ezra 8:36; Esther 3:12; Daniel 3:2).

SAVIOUR

The term in the Old Testament describes God in his activity (2 Samuel 22:3; Isaiah 43:3). So also Luke 1:47. In the New Testament the Greek word meaning Rescuer describes Jesus Christ. In John 4:42 and 1 John 4:14 Jesus is spoken of as the Saviour of the world.

See Salvation

SCALES

were used in biblical times chiefly for the weighing of money. The scales consisted of two pans which were suspended from a beam. A merchant was forbidden to carry false weights mixed with true in case he was tempted to use the false (Leviticus 19:36; Proverbs 11:1; 20:23; Amos 8:5).

To be weighed in the scales of God was an expression which meant to be judged by him (Job 31:6; Daniel 5:27).

See also Measures

SCARLET

was a brilliant crimson dye which was extracted from a certain species of insect, *Coccus ilicis* (English cochineal), which the Arabs call *kirmiz* (English crimson). There is an early reference to a scarlet thread in Genesis 38:28 and the hangings in the tabernacle were dyed scarlet (Exodus 25:4). It was a popular colour for good clothes (2 Samuel 1:24; Proverbs 31:21), but could be overdone by bad women (Jeremiah 4:30; Revelation 17:4). The impossibility of removing the dye is used as a symbol for the near impossibility of removing sins (Isaiah 1:18).

SCHOOL

In antiquity the parents would look after the children's teaching and upbringing at home. The father would see to the boys' education, and the mother would instruct the girls.

Jewish boys learned the old stories from the history of Israel, the command-

Weighing of money as shown in Egyptian picture

A synagogue school with boys sitting on the floor around the teacher

Roman relief showing school with teachers and pupils

ments and regulations of the Torah and the contents and meaning of the service of worship. Sons would learn their father's profession by joining him at work. Corporal punishment was regarded as an aid to instruction (Proverbs 13:24).

A mother would teach her girls all the tasks and skills needed to look after a home and family.

In Jesus' day there were probably separate schools for the boys between five and thirteen years of age, at the village or city synagogue. They would be seated on the floor in a circle around their teacher, who was seated on a chair. They learnt the Pentateuch by heart, through listening and repeating after the teacher (Matthew 23:2). The girls were not allowed to go to school in this way.

In AD 63, it was decreed that there should be schools for children in every city or village. In a work by Josephus, who lived in about AD 37–100, he stresses how important it is for Jewish boys to learn how to read and write, so that they will be able to study the Torah (Law). In Greek families it was common for an elderly slave to look after the children and be their constant guardian, instead of their father (Galatians 3:24). One of his duties was to see to it that the children got to their schoolmaster who took care of the actual teaching.

Those who wanted to and could afford to do so, could go on to study in one of the rabbinical schools in Jerusalem. Teachers of the Torah, or rabbis, taught in these schools. The apostle Paul was taught by the rabbi Gamaliel (Acts 22:3).

In addition there were wandering philosophers who often gathered their audiences at the city gate. They wanted to teach not only matters connected with God and the worship of him, but to impart knowledge of other things as well (Proverbs 1:20; Ecclesiastes 12:9, 10). In addition to having Christian teachers (Romans 12:7; Hebrew 5:12; James 3:1) the church continued to stress the importance of education in the home (Titus 2:3).

SCRIBES

The Scribes were a professional group in Israel. Their task was to study the Law, to teach it and to explain it (Ezra 7:6; Matthew 23:2). The Scribes were also called lawyers, teachers of the Law or rabbis. Jesus criticized them for their additions to the Law (Matthew 23; Mark 7:1–23).

The Scribes were not allowed to ask for payment when they carried out their work of interpreting the Law. Therefore a Scribe had to make his living from some other profession.

The Scribes were employed by different parties, above all the Pharisees, but also the Sadducees.

See also Parties

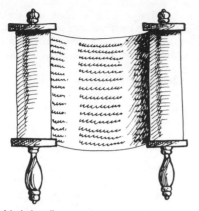

A typical scroll

Cylinder seal

sealing impressions were made with a signet ring, which was worn on the finger or on a band around the neck (Jeremiah 22:24; Haggai 2:23). The official whose duty it was to carry the

Signet-ring

SCROLL

The long rolls of papyrus or parchment on which people wrote could be up to one foot wide, and perhaps as much as 30 ft. long. If the roll was long enough, each end was fastened to a stick or wooden pin, around which it could be rolled and unrolled for reading.

Scrolls containing the Law and the Prophets were found in every synagogue. The book out of which Jesus read in the synagogue at Nazareth was a scroll of the Book of the Prophet Isaiah (Luke 4:16–20).

See also Dead Sea Scrolls, Writing, Writing materials

SEAL

The impression of a seal on wax or clay was valid instead of a signature in letters and on documents. It was used for closing something in such a way as to prevent unauthorized persons from seeing it (Daniel 12:4) or tampering with it (Jeremiah 32:14). The tomb of Jesus was sealed in this way (Matthew 27:66).

The seal was often made of soft stone and like an ordinary rubber stamp. It might also be made as a cylinder, which was rolled over the clay or wax. Smaller

royal signet ring was trusted completely and implicitly by the king. He could make decisions in the king's name (Esther 3:10–12).

The seal of Jeroboam as found in Megiddo

The seals most often had pictures but no text. The text which is sometimes found on seals was the name of the seal's owner. The oldest seals which have been found in Palestine date from about 2000 BC.

SECOND COMING SEE JESUS CHRIST

SEED

Apart from its agricultural context, the word 'seed' is used figuratively in the Bible to mean children, descendants, offspring and is commonly so translated in RSV, though it is retained in Genesis 3:15.

SELAH

is a word which is used 71 times in the Psalms and also in the psalm in Habakkuk 3. Scholars have attempted to explain this term in many different ways. It might be a musical term perhaps to indicate a place for the instruments to extemporize; have the same meaning as the word 'amen'; be a sign for a 'pause' or break for meditation; or a repeat sign which indicated that part of the psalm should be sung again. There is however no definite solution.

SELEUCIA

was a city in Syria on the coast of the Mediterranean. It was the seaport of the Syrian city of Antioch. Paul and Barnabas travelled this way, when they set out on their first missionary journey (Acts 13:4).

SENNACHERIB

ruled Assyria from 705 to 681 BC. He mounted many large military campaigns in order to strengthen his large empire. One of these campaigns was directed against Palestine and the surrounding countries. Sennacherib conquered several Israelite cities. He made his headquarters in the city of Lachish in Judah. Sennacherib was however unable to conquer Jerusalem, which was defended by forces under King Hezekiah's command. The prophet Isaiah spoke words of encouragement to King Hezekiah during this siege (2 Kings 18; Isaiah 36; 37). During Sennacherib's reign Nineveh replaced Asshur as the capital of the

Assyrian empire. The king was very interested in architecture and had several impressive buildings constructed and beautified with works of art of various kinds.
See also Assyria, Hezekiah, Lachish

SERAPHIM, SERAPHS, SEE ANGELS

SERMON ON THE MOUNT

In the Sermon on the Mount in Matthew 5–7 we find the central themes of Jesus' ethical teaching. The teaching describes the life of God's Kingdom, a life-style and basis that marks out the Christian as different. His life is characterized not by strict regulation like the Pharisees, but by love that goes a step further, that turns the other cheek, and forgives. The man who lives God's way will be a man of prayer, who knows God as Father in the intimate way in which a son and father know one another. A Christian prayer is to God as Abba, Father, an ancient Hebraic word showing how a man can have personal, close yet respectful access to God (Romans 8:15; Galatians 4:6). In the Sermon Jesus summarizes the whole of the Old Testament Law in the command to love God totally and your neighbour as yourself. This is the essence of true Christianity, not the petty regulations of the Pharisaic religion.

The parallel passage in Luke 6 is called the Sermon on the Plain or Level Place. If it refers to the same event, then the different descriptions might imply that Jesus stood on a plateau on the mountain.

Contents	Chapter

| giving, praying and fasting. Be not anxious, trust God and live in love | Matthew 6:1– 7:12 |
| A challenge: the way is narrow, bear good fruit, hear and do | Matthew 7:13–29 |

SERVANT SEE SLAVE

SHARON

was the name of a plain on the coast of the Mediterranean south of mount Carmel. The area was famous for the abundance of its harvests and the variety of its flowers, especially the roses.
See Song of Solomon 2:1; Isaiah 35:2.

SHEBA

In the Old Testament Sheba is the name of a kingdom in south Arabia. Sheba was a prosperous nation, and had trade connections with India. Its peoples, known as Sabaeans, are mentioned in Scripture as raiders (Job 1:15) and traders (Isaiah 60:6; Ezekiel 27:22). The Queen of Sheba came to visit King Solomon, to find out if he was as wise and as rich as was his reputation. She may also have wanted a trading pact (1 Kings 10:1–10).

SHECHEM

Shechem was an ancient holy place, situated between the mountains Ebal and Gerizim in the tribal area of Ephraim. Shechem was one of the places in which the patriarch Abraham made his camp, when he immigrated into Canaan, and here he built an altar to the Lord (Genesis 12:6).

Jacob settled at Shechem after having returned from his work for his uncle Laban at Haran (Genesis 33:18; 35:4). Joseph's final resting-place was at Shechem (Joshua 24:32). Joshua gathered Israel at Shechem to renew the covenant with the Lord (Joshua 24) and he made it one of the cities of refuge (20:7). Abimelech made himself king of Shechem in the time of the Judges (Judges 9).

It was at Shechem that ten of the northern tribes in Israel decided, after Solomon's death, to choose their own king, Jeroboam (1 Kings 12). During the first years of king Jeroboam's reign Shechem was his capital city. Jeroboam fortified it (1 Kings 12:25). Later Samaria became the most important city of the Northern Kingdom. Shechem was destroyed in 128 BC, during the time of the Maccabees. In Jesus' day it was of no great importance. Sychar, which is mentioned in John 4, was probably a village just north of Shechem. Excavations have revealed the site of the old city of Shechem.

SHEEP SEE DOMESTIC ANIMALS, SHEPHERD

SHEEP GATE

The Sheep Gate was one of the gates in the city wall surrounding Jerusalem. It was probably situated in the north-eastern part of the wall.
See Nehemiah 3:1, 32; 12:39; John 5:2.

SHEKEL SEE MONEY

SHEOL SEE KINGDOM OF THE DEAD

SHEPHERD

The domestic animals of the Israelites were looked after by the sons and daughters of the household. A slave or a shepherd might also be employed specially to look after the animals. The shepherd's job was regarded as a very good one. It involved many things: calling the flock together in the mornings; taking the animals to good pastures; finding springs or brooks where the animals could drink water; walking in front of or behind the flock when it

A Palestinian sheep fold

A typical Palestinian shepherd

Shepherd's sling

Water-bottle made from a hollowed out gourd

was to be moved. Usually a sheepdog helped the shepherd, who would take the animals out to pasture at all times of the year; protecting them against robbers and predatory animals (1 Samuel 17:34, 35; John 10:12) bringing his crook, staff and sling for the defence of the flock; making sure of having enough food supplies; taking the animals back to the stable or enclosure at the end of the day (John 10:3, 4, 9); counting the animals when they went into the stable or enclosure; going out to look for missing animals which had strayed from the herd (Ezekiel 34:12; Luke 15:4–6). His equipment included:

A Crook, (translated staff) about 6½ ft (2 m) long, smooth, sometimes with a hook at the top end, was used as a defensive weapon, as a help in climbing in the mountains, for beating green leaves off the trees, for chasing slow sheep and goats forward, for leaning against during long hours of watching.

The Club (translated rod) which was about 2½ ft (70 cm) long, and looked like a club with nails hammered into the thick end. It was hung from the belt and used as a weapon (Psalm 23:4).

A Satchel, like a large bag, made of kidskin, hung at the shepherd's side. That is where he kept his supply of bread, olives, cheese, raisins and dried figs (1 Samuel 17:40).

The shepherd was such an essential part of Jewish life that the Psalmist could refer to the function of the shepherd and know that everyone understood him (Psalm 23:80; similarly Isaiah 40:11). John 10 records a long passage where Jesus describes himself as the Good Shepherd who knows his flock by name, calls them and looks for them when they are lost until they are safe back in the fold. His loving care and protection for those who belong to him is very beautifully illustrated in this chapter. He is

called 'the great shepherd of the sheep' in Hebrews 13:20. Note also 1 Peter 2:25.

SHEWBREAD 'SHOWBREAD'. SEE BREAD OF THE PRESENCE

SHILOAH SEE SILOAM

SHILOH

After the entry into Canaan Shiloh became the most important place in Canaan to the Israelites. Here the ark and the tabernacle from the wandering in the wilderness were set up (Joshua 18:1). When the Philistines captured the ark in the time of Eli, they also destroyed the place (1 Samuel 4; Jeremiah 7:12), as archaeology has shown.

SHIP SEE TRAVEL

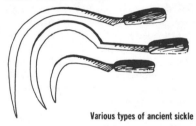

Various types of ancient sickle

SICKLE

A sickle was a curved implement which was used in farming for harvesting the ripe grain (Deuteronomy 16:9; Joel 3:13). It is applied to God's harvest of judgement in Mark 4:29; Revelation 14:14–19.

SIDON

was a city on the Mediterranean coast in the country of Phoenicia. Sidon was the largest of the Phoenician cities, and a very important port. Because of its strategic situation on the coast, Sidon was ruled by many foreign powers. Jesus visited the areas around Sidon, and people from the city came out to Jesus to ask his help (Matthew 15:21; Mark 3:8; Luke 6:17). When the apostle Paul was on his way to Rome as a prisoner, he was permitted to visit friends in Sidon (Acts 27:3).

See also Phoenicia

SILOAM

The Pool of Siloam was a pool or spring in the south-eastern corner of Jerusalem. King Hezekiah had a tunnel constructed, which carried water from the Gihon Spring outside the city wall to the Pool of Siloam (2 Kings 20:20; 2 Chronicles 32:30). Where the aqueduct from the Spring of Gihon opens out into the Pool of Siloam an inscription in Hebrew was found in 1880, describing the work on the tunnel.

The Pool of Siloam was additional to an earlier pool, known as the Pool of Shelah, or the King's Pool, in the King's Garden in Jerusalem (Nehemiah 2:14; 3:15). The aqueduct that carried the water was called Shiloah (Isaiah 8:6). It was replaced by King Hezekiah's tunnel, which followed a different course. Scholars think that the Pool of Siloam in the Gospel story is this old pool (John 9:7–12).

Ancient Persian drinking horn made from silver

SILVER

From an early date silver was regarded as a precious metal. There were no silver mines in Palestine, but silver was mined in northern Syria and parts of Asia Minor (Job 28:1). Silver was used for jewellery, ornaments, sacred vessels for use in the Temple (Numbers 10:2), and as currency, first in pieces of silver and later in coins (Genesis 23:16). Refining is referred to in Psalm 12:6; Jeremiah 6:29, 30.

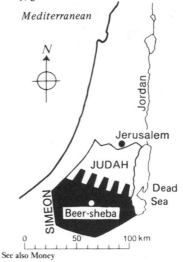

See also Money

SIMEON

was one of the sons of the patriarch Jacob (Genesis 29:33). Simeon became the father of the tribe of Simeon, one of the twelve tribes of Israel. The area where the tribe of Simeon lived was south of Canaan and properly speaking outside its boundaries (Joshua 19:1–9). The tribe of Simeon was counted among the least important of the twelve tribes. Gradually it came to be included in the tribe of Judah.

SIN

was the name of a desert in the Sinai

Skins used for carrying liquid

peninsula, which the Israelites walked across after the exodus from Egypt (Exodus 16:1).

See Wandering in the Wilderness

SIN OFFERING SEE SACRIFICE

SINAI

The name of the mountain in the Sinai peninsula where God revealed himself to Moses, where Moses received the Ten Commandments and where God made a covenant with Israel. This mountain is also called Mount Horeb in the Bible. The exact situation of the biblical Mount Sinai is not known. An old text identifies the mountain Jebel Musa, about 2200 m (7225 ft) high, in the southern part of the peninsula, as the Mount Sinai of the Bible. This is however far from certain.

See also Wandering in the Wilderness

SIRACH SEE ECCLESIASTICUS

SKINS

were used as containers for different kinds of liquid. They consisted of a whole skin from a goat or sheep. After the tanning process, the leg openings were sewn together. The hole at the neck was retained as the opening of the sack. In these skins people kept water (Genesis 21:14), wine (Joshua 9:4; Luke 5:37–38) and milk (Judges 4:19).

SKULL, PLACE OF THE, SEE GOLGOTHA

SLAVERY

Slavery was widespread throughout the ancient world. When the English Bible translations use the word 'servant', it usually refers to slaves or serfs. Prisoners of war were used as slaves (2 Chronicles 28:8). Poor people who had fallen into debt and who were unable to repay it, were forced to give themselves or sell

181

someone in the family into slavery (Exodus 21:1–7).

In Israel the slaves were in a better position than in many other countries, since there were regulations in the Law of Israel concerning the treatment of slaves (Exodus 21:26, 27; Deuteronomy 21:10–14). According to the Law an Israelite slave was supposed to be set free after six years' service in Israel (Exodus 21:2), but it is far from certain that this was always carried out. In the Christian household distinctions between slaves and masters became meaningless (Galatians 3:28; Colossians 3:11).
See also Philemon

SLING

Carried by shepherds (1 Samuel 17:40) and also used in battle (Judges 20:16; Zechariah 9:15).
See also Shepherd

SMITH SEE CRAFTS

SMYRNA

was a seaport on the west coast of Asia Minor. One of the letters in the Revelation to John is addressed to the Christian church there (Revelation 2:8–11). Today it is the largest city in Asiatic Turkey and is called Izmir. It was here that in AD 155 Bishop Polycarp was martyred for his Christian faith.

SNAKES

Snakes were common in the countries of the Bible. In the Bible specific mention is made of snakes which could be charmed (Psalm 58:4; Jeremiah 8:17). Although the word here is commonly translated as adder, adders are not used for charming, and the cobra is more likely. Many of the species of snakes were highly poisonous (Amos 5:19), and these are included under another common Hebrew word, which is used of the serpent in Eden (Genesis 3) and the serpent of brass (Numbers 21:6–9). Christians are to be wise as serpents (Matthew 10:16).

SODOM AND GOMORRAH

were two cities, which are mentioned in the story of Lot, Abraham's nephew. Lot lived in Sodom, but the Lord told him to flee from the city. Sodom had become so filled with evil and unrighteousness, that God's punishment was to fall on it.

After Lot's departure from Sodom sulphur and brimstone fell over the two cities Sodom and Gomorrah, which were totally destroyed.

It is possible that the cities Sodom and Gomorrah are now on the bottom of the Dead Sea, in its southern part. This part of the Dead Sea is considerably shallower than its northern end.
See Genesis 13:10–13; 14:8–12; 19:1–29.
See also Dead Sea

SOLOMON'S PORCH SEE TEMPLE

SON OF GOD

In the New Testament, Jesus is called 'the Son of God'. This means, first, that the relationship between Jesus and God was as close as that of a son to his father, and secondly, that Jesus was something more than an ordinary man. He was, and is, also divine, of the same nature and substance as God. John 1:12: Christians can share a sonship relationship with God the Father through Jesus the son.

Jesus as the Son of God

He will be great, and will be called the Son of the Most High. Luke 1:32.

This is my beloved Son. Matthew 3:17; 17:5.

If you are the Son of God, throw yourself down. Matthew 4:6.

Rabbi, you are the Son of God. John 1:49.

Truly you are the Son of God. Matthew 14:33

And whenever the unclean spirits beheld him, they fell down before him and cried out, 'You are the Son of God'. Mark 3:11.

You are the Christ, the Son of the living God. Matthew 16:16.

Are you the Son of God, then? Luke 22:70.

But when the time had fully come, God sent forth his Son. Galatians 4:4.

SON OF MAN

is an ancient name for a figure of the future – the king who will come in order to establish the rule of God on earth (the Messianic Kingdom). In Daniel 7:13–14, we read how the son of man will come on the clouds of heaven, and receive 'domination and glory and kingdom, that all peoples, nations and languages should serve him'.

The name 'son of man' is found about seventy times in the New Testament; Jesus uses it on a number of occasions to refer to himself, giving it quite new significance. Mark 10:45 is particularly important. The Evangelists say about the son of man:

that he is divine and that he came directly from God; he has the power to forgive sins (Matthew 9:6);

when he came, he was not recognized by the people, but lived in poverty and obscurity (Matthew 8:20);

that he suffered, died, rose again and then returned to God, from whom he had come (Mark 9:31);

that at the end of time he will return to rule and establish his eternal Messianic kingdom (Luke 21:27).
See also Messiah

SONG, SINGING, SEE MUSIC, PSALMS

SONG OF SOLOMON

This book is also called the Song of Songs, or Canticles. Traditionally King Solomon is said to be the author; some scholars regard it as a collection of pastoral popular poems or folk-songs celebrating love.

Certainly the book describes the love between man and woman in highly poetical and expressive language. It belongs to the finest and most beautiful poetry ever written.

The descriptions in the Song of Songs have also been interpreted as an allegory of the relationship between the Lord and the people of Israel, where the Lord God is the bridegroom and Israel is the bride.

In the Christian church the Song of Solomon has often been applied to the love between Christ and the church, or between Christ and the individual soul, Christ being the bridegroom.

SORCERY

Sorcery, magic and witchcraft were forbidden in Israel (Exodus 22:18; Leviticus 20:27; Malachi 3:5). Since there are such strict prohibitions to be found in the Law, there must have been many temptations to follow Canaanite magical practices. Simon Magus (Acts 8:9) and Elymas (Acts 13:6, 8) are two magicians named in the New Testament.

SOUL

The soul is the life principle (Hebrew *nephesh*). The Bible does not treat man as divided into body and soul. Body and soul are united and mutually dependent on each other. The soul is given expression in the body. The body is given life by the soul. This can be understood in the light of modern psychology. A person's soul is his nature and character, his self, his life. Hence RSV 'man became a living being' (Genesis 2:7). Inasmuch as life is in the blood, the soul is closely linked, in a special way, with the blood. The pouring out of the blood is the sacrifice of the life (Leviticus 17:11; Isaiah 53:12).

The New Testament views the relationship between body and soul in the same way. Body and soul belong together. The body needs salvation as well as the soul (Matthew 10:28). The apostle Paul contrasts those who are simply natural (lit. *'soulish'*) with those who believe in Christ, and so become 'spiritual' (1 Corinthians 2:14, 15). He speaks of man as being composed of spirit (*pneuma*), soul (*psyche*) and body (*sarx*) (1 Thessalonians 5:23). Man's spirit is the site of that new life which he receives through Jesus Christ.

SPEAR SEE WEAPONS

SPECIES SEE HERBS

SPIKENARD SEE NARD

SPIRIT

The Hebrew word for 'spirit' used in the Old Testament is *ruach* (Genesis 2:7) which means 'wind', 'breath', and is so translated in certain contexts. The spirit was that power in man which forced him to action. To be filled with the spirit was to be filled with power and energy.

The Spirit of God could descend on a human being, who then received divine power and wisdom (Judges 6:34; Isaiah 11:2).

In the New Testament there is a close link between the Holy Spirit and the regenerated human spirit (John 3:6; Romans 8:9; 1 John 3:24). Acts chapter 2 describes how the Holy Spirit came upon the disciples at Pentecost.

Through the Spirit the living Christ was with his disciples after his resurrection, leading them and helping them to spread the Christian message to others.

STEWARD

In the Bible, the steward is the person who on his master's behalf looked after a house, a business or workers on a farming estate. Isaiah 22:15–25 speaks of a royal steward. The steward was often one of the slaves. Stewards and stewardship are mentioned in some of Jesus' parables (Luke 16:1–8). Christian ministers are stewards of the Gospel (1 Corinthians 4:2; 1 Peter 4:10).

STOICS

The followers of the Greek philosopher Zeno were called Stoics, because they originally met in a porch (in Greek, *stoa*). The Stoics wanted to teach men that the one important thing in life was doing one's duty. Fortune, happiness and health were unimportant to man. The Stoics frequently spoke about the importance of a loving attitude towards all people, to whatever nation or social class they might belong.

The Stoic had to be on his guard against strong feelings. He had to keep calm in all situations. There were Stoics among the apostle Paul's audience in Athens (Acts 17:18).

SYCHAR

was a city in Samaria near Shechem. It is mentioned only once in the Bible. Jesus met the woman of Samaria at Jacob's well outside the town of Sychar, and spoke to her about her life and about the right way of worshipping God (John 4).

SYNAGOGUE

In Jesus' day there were one or more synagogues in most villages and cities. The synagogue was not a temple, but was to remind the Jew of the Temple in Jerusalem, and the worship there. There were synagogues in Jerusalem, too.

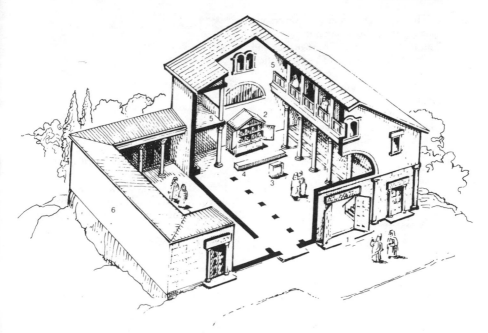

A typical synagogue showing,
1. Entrance facing towards Jerusalem, 2. The Torah
shrine, containing the scrolls, 3. Pulpit, 4. Elders'
bench, 5. Gallery for the women and children, 6.
Extension containing school rooms and guest rooms for
pilgrims

Services were held in the synagogue on the Sabbath and during the great Jewish festivals. In addition, the synagogue was open for prayer three times a day. It is believed that synagogues began to be built in Palestine after the return of the Jews from their captivity in Babylon.

In the large assembly room of the synagogue there was a Menorah (seven-armed lampstand) and a lamp of eternity. There was no altar in the synagogue. Sacrifices were not offered, so there was no need for priests to serve in their sacrificial function in the synagogue. Prayers, readings from Scripture and praise have always been the most important elements in the synagogue worship.

The sacred Torah-scrolls were kept in a cupboard, which was probably movable. The women and children were seated in a separate gallery.

In the larger synagogues there was an extension adjoining the assembly room itself, with smaller rooms grouped around an open courtyard. These small rooms might be used as classrooms or guest rooms for pilgrims.

A council consisting of ten elders chose the head of the synagogue (the Authorized Version calls him 'the ruler of the synagogue'). The Greek title is *archi-synagogos*.

In AD 70, when Jerusalem was conquered by the Romans after the Jewish revolt, all synagogues and most of the Jewish architecture in the country were destroyed. Synagogue remains have been excavated in Capernaum and Tiberias, among other sites.

The oldest known inscription from a synagogue has been found in Jerusalem. The text is cut into a stone plaque and reads: 'Theodotus, son of Vetenus, priest and archisynagogos, grandson of an archisynagogos, built the synagogue for the reading of the Law and for the teaching of the commandments and the guest house and the rooms and supplies of water as an inn for those who are in need when coming from abroad, which synagogue his fathers and the elders and Simonides founded.'

See also Prayer, worship, Sabbath, School

SYRACUSE

was a port in Sicily, where Paul's ship called during his voyage to Rome (Acts 28:12).

SYRIA

The name Syria usually refers to the country north of Palestine. In the time of the Old Testament Damascus was the capital of Syria.

During Jesus' lifetime Syria was a province in the Roman empire and was ruled by a Roman governor (Luke 2:2).
See also Antioch

TABERNACLE

The tabernacle was the movable sanctuary which the Israelites carried with them during their wandering in the wilderness. This sanctuary was also called the 'tent of meeting' (Numbers 11:16) or the 'tent of the testimony' (Exodus 38:21).

The tabernacle was put up in the

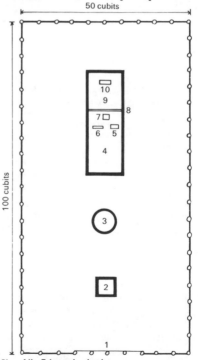

Plan of the Tabernacle, showing,
1. Entrance, 2. Altar of burnt offering, 3. The bronze sea, 4. The Holy Place, 5. The table of the presence, 6. The seven-armed lamp stand, 7. The incense altar, 8. The veil, 9. The Holy of Holies, 10. The Ark of the Covenant

TAX

centre of the Israelite camp (Numbers 2). It was made of fabric and leather, over a wooden framework. The tabernacle is described in Exodus 25-27 and Exodus 35-38.

Around the area of the tabernacle there was an enclosure of pillars. Large curtains of fabric were put up between them. The area inside this enclosure was called the court, and held the altar of burnt offering. The main section comprised the Holy Place and the Holy of Holies. The spiritual significance is expounded in Hebrews 9.

See also Ark of the Covenant, Temple

TABERNACLES, FEAST OF SEE FESTIVALS

TABOR

A mountain west of Lake Gennesaret. According to ancient tradition, Tabor is said to be the mountain where the transfiguration of Christ took place.

TALENT SEE MONEY

TALMUD

All Jews held that the Torah (the 'written law') must be observed. This was the whole of the Pentateuch. The Scribes and Pharisees interpreted the Torah, and required that their interpretation and additional laws and rules, the 'oral Law', should be kept, too.

In the third century of the Christian era this body of regulations and interpretations was written down. This work was called the Mishnah. The Pharisees then continued to interpret and explain the Law and the Mishnah. This rabbinical work of interpretation was also collected in a body of writings and this was called the Talmud. The word Talmud really means 'learning'.

TAMARISK

The tamarisk is a small cypress-like tree which grows in Palestine. The leaves look like those of heather. The tamarisk has red or white flowers.

See Genesis 21:33; 1 Samuel 22:6

TANNER See CRAFTS

TARES

or darnel. Resembles wheat in its early growth, and later cannot be weeded up without pulling up the wheat also (Matthew 13:24-30).

TARSHISH

Ships from Tarshish are mentioned in the Old Testament, so that it can be assumed that Tarshish was a place or a country by the sea. The prophet Jonah boarded a ship which was bound for Tarshish. It was also a country of mines and valuable ores. Tarshish may have been situated somewhere in Spain, possibly Tartessus. Since ships of Tarshish were built at Ezion-Geber (1 Kings 9:26; 10:22) from which Spain could not easily be reached, the term may have been used of any large ocean-going vessels, like the former English use of East Indiaman.

See 2 Chronicles 20:36; Jonah 1:3; Isaiah 66:19; Jeremiah 10:9; Ezekiel 27:12.

TARSUS

was an important centre of trade and seafaring, and one of the major cities of Asia Minor. The trade routes between east and west went through it. The most important industry in Tarsus was the weaving of tent-cloth (see under Crafts and Craftsmen). The apostle Paul grew up in Tarsus (Acts 9:11), and described it as 'no mean city' (Acts 21:39).

TAX

The Israelites paid tax to the Temple in Jerusalem. The temple tax was essentially a form of sacrifice. It had to be paid yearly, and was half a shekel (Exodus

187

30:13). Jesus told Peter to find a shekel in a fish's mouth, and use it to pay the tax for them both (Matthew 17:24–27).

The kings used to impose taxes and customs duties, because they needed money for wars, expenses at court and payments to more powerful rulers (2 Kings 15:20). At various times the Jews were obliged to pay taxes to rulers of different countries. In Jesus' day the Jews paid taxes to Rome (Matthew 22:15–22).

During the latter part of his reign Herod the Great levied very low taxes from the Jews. In order to change this and reintroduce a system of full taxation, Caesar Augustus arranged the enrollment (census) which is mentioned in Luke 2:1.

TAX-COLLECTORS

In New Testament times Jews were employed by the Romans to collect various taxes or the authorized toll-fees. In the AV (KJV) they are called 'publicans'. They collected tolls and taxes on the borders of countries and cities, at bridges, landing-stages and in several other such places.

The Jews hated the tax-collectors. They were thought to have become polluted through their contact with the Romans, the conquerors of Palestine. In addition, the tax-collectors often demanded larger amounts of tolls and taxes than were due.

In the New Testament the names of some tax-collectors are mentioned: Zacchaeus at Jericho (Luke 19:2–10), and Matthew at Capernaum. It surprised and shocked many people that Jesus associated with tax-collectors, and that he even ate with them. Eating a meal together meant a promise of friendship.

TEMPLE

During the Israelites' wandering in the wilderness they set up the tabernacle, i.e.

the tent sanctuary, in the different camps. There the Israelites celebrated services and worshipped their God. When they were settled in Canaan, the tabernacle soon lost its former importance. King David planned to build a proper temple to the Lord, the God of Israel. But the prophet Nathan prevented him (2 Samuel 7). Instead it was Solomon, David's son, who built Israel's first temple. Services of worship were celebrated every day in the Temple. Solomon's Temple was in existence between the years 940 BC and 587 BC. King Nebuchadnezzer destroyed the Temple when he occupied Jerusalem and took the people captive to Babylon.

When the Jews came back from the Babylonian captivity in 538 BC, they laid the foundations for a new Temple. Zerubbabel directed this work (Ezra 1–4). Zerubbabel's Temple was repaired and improved gradually, but remained without major alterations until the year 20 BC.

King Herod the Great had the Temple rebuilt over a number of years (John 2:20). His work gave the Jews a completely new Temple, which was a great deal larger than the Temples of both Solomon and Zerubbabel. Herod's Temple was destroyed in AD 70 by the Romans. There has never been a Jewish Temple in Jerusalem since.

Solomon's Temple was built with the help of skilled craftsmen from Phoenicia. The temple building itself was not large: 130 ft (40 m) long, including the porch, and about 49 ft (15 m) wide, including the storage areas. The Temple was built of stone and its interior was covered with

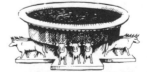

The bronze sea containing water used for the various cleansing rituals

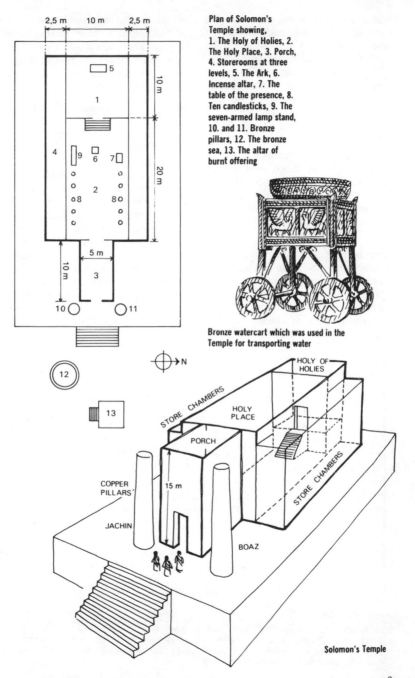

Plan of Solomon's Temple showing, 1. The Holy of Holies, 2. The Holy Place, 3. Porch, 4. Storerooms at three levels, 5. The Ark, 6. Incense altar, 7. The table of the presence, 8. Ten candlesticks, 9. The seven-armed lamp stand, 10. and 11. Bronze pillars, 12. The bronze sea, 13. The altar of burnt offering

Bronze watercart which was used in the Temple for transporting water

Solomon's Temple

cedar and cypress wood, large areas of which were covered in gold. Artists had carved patterns and decorations in the wood of the wall panels and the doors.

There is a description of Solomon's Temple and how it was built, in 1 Kings 5–8; 2 Chronicles 2, 3, 4; Ezekiel 40–42. Around the Temple building itself there was an inner forecourt surrounded by a stone wall.

The area which belonged to Solomon's Temple was much smaller than that which was needed later for Herod's Temple, at the time of Jesus. South of the Temple area, and close to it, was King Solomon's palace.

Zerubbabel's Temple was probably not smaller than Solomon's Temple, but lacked the precious ornamentation and expensive furnishings which characterized Solomon's Temple. The Ark was no longer in the room which was called the Holy of Holies. We are told in the Second Book of the Maccabees that the Ark had been saved from the Babylonian conquest and hidden in a cave. Later, people were unable to find it. And so there was a block of stone in the Holy of Holies, instead of the Ark.

Herod's Temple. King Herod began to rebuild the Temple of Zerubbabel in about 20 BC. This reconstruction changed the exterior of the Temple entirely. By extensive work on new foundations and filling in with soil, the temple area was doubled in size. The temple precinct was divided into different forecourts. Everyone was admitted to the outer courtyard, the Court of Gentiles. It was paved with stones and similar to a market. Buying and selling took place here, and here people could change their money into the special coins which were required for offerings and temple tax. Only Jews were allowed in the inner courts. There were warning inscriptions at their entrances, saying

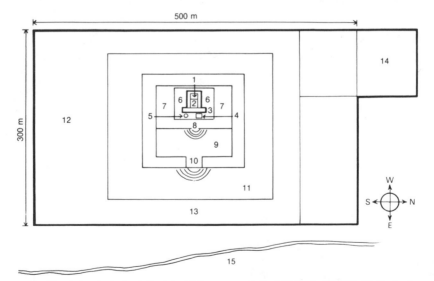

Plan of Herod's Temple showing, 1. The Holy of Holies, 2. The holy place, 3. The porch, 4. The altar of burnt offering, 5. Water basin, 6. The priests' court, 7. Courts of Israel, 8. The gate between the courts, 9. The Women's Court, 10. The Beautiful Gate, 11. The Court of the Gentiles, 12. The royal portico, 13. Solomon's Portico, 14. The fortress Antonia, 15. The Kidron Valley

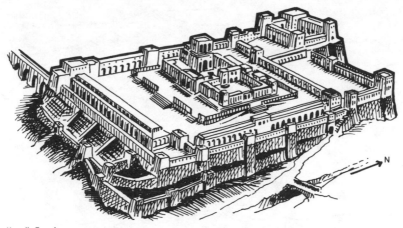

Herod's Temple

that for non-Jews to enter these courts was prohibited and would be punished by death.

The temple building was constructed in white marble and decorated in gold. The new Temple, like that of Solomon, consisted of a porch with annexes, the Holy Place and the Holy of Holies. Between the Holy Place and the Holy of Holies there was a drapery, known as the 'veil' of the Temple.

Temple in Epistles. Jewish religion thought of the Temple and worship of God in terms of a magnificent building. After the resurrection of Jesus Christ and the events which followed – the Ascension and Pentecost – Christian teaching about the Temple took on a completely new dimension. The Temple ceases to be just a special and holy building, but is now described in spiritual terms. The human body is the temple of the Holy Spirit. 'God's temple is holy and that temple you are' writes Paul to the Corinthian Christians, in 1 Corinthians 3:16. The church, meaning the worldwide body of believers, is also described as growing into a holy temple with Christ as the corner-stone of the whole structure (Ephesians 2:16–22).

When we see how the first Christians gradually grasped the implications of Jesus' death and resurrection (at first they still worshipped in the Temple), then the Old Testament forerunners take on a new significance. No longer is the place of worship confined to bricks and tent cloth, man can now worship with the heart, mind and body. Other references on this theme are 2 Corinthians 6:16–7:1; Hebrews 9, 10; Revelation 3:12; 21:22; 11:19; 21:3.

See also Ark of the Covenant, Bread of the Presence, Lamp, Tabernacle, Treasuries, Worship.

TENT

The patriarchs Abraham, Isaac and Jacob lived in tents (Genesis 12:8; Hebrews 11:9). The Israelites lived in tents during the wandering in the

First stage in the erection of a tent

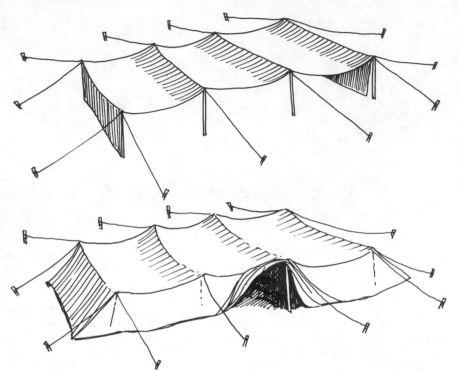

wilderness (Exodus 18:7). The tents were made of animal skins or woven from goats' or camel hair. The material made the tents dark brown or black in colour.

The interior of the tent was divided into two sections, one of which housed the men and the other the women and children. The fireplace and the household utensils were usually found in the women's part of the tent.

During the wandering in the wilderness the Israelites had a tent sanctuary, the tabernacle. There the Lord God dwelt, and there services were held to his glory (Exodus 33:7).
See also: Tabernacle.

TEREBINTH

The terebinth is a large tree which grows especially in the northern part of Palestine. The growth of the terebinth is not

unlike that of the oak. It offers pleasant shade to both people and animals. People often built altars and made sacrifices under the large shady terebinths.
See Hosea 4:13.

THANK-OFFERING SEE SACRIFICE

THEFT

To steal was to break one of the commandments in the Law (Exodus 20:15). If a theft had been committed, the most important thing was that the person who had been robbed was given back his property. That which the thief had stolen, had to be returned, at several times its original value. If he was unable to do this, he was sold into slavery (Exodus 22:3).

He who had stolen money or other

goods had to repay twice the amount (Exodus 22:7).

He who had stolen one ox was to return five oxen, and he who had taken one sheep was to return four sheep as compensation (Exodus 22:1).

THESSALONIANS, LETTERS TO

Written by Paul and Timothy, with Silvanus (Silas) as scribe, these two letters were written to answer questions asked by a young church, who had not benefited from Paul's teaching because in AD 50 Paul had to make a quick exit. A church had been formed, but Paul was not able to stay long enough to see it established (Acts 17:1-10). Timothy returned there to find a stronger church than before (1 Thessalonians 3:6). But they had problems on moral behaviour and worries that Christians were dying before the expected return of Christ. Paul reassures them that those who die before Christ's return are not at a disadvantage; they meet him 'in the air' when the day comes for his return. In the second letter this imminent expectation of Jesus' coming back was producing laziness and apathy. Paul reminds them that many things must happen first, and in the meantime, they are to live a Christlike life – advice that holds true today.

THESSALONICA

was the capital of the Roman province of Macedonia. It was a large seaport and an important centre of commerce and trade, situated at the place where the roads from Italy to the East and from the Aegean to the Danube meet. The apostle Paul visited the city during his second missionary journey (Acts 17:1-9). The two letters to the Thessalonians in the New Testament were written by Paul to the Christian church which he had founded in the city during an earlier visit there.

THRESHING SEE AGRICULTURE

THYATIRA

was a city in western Asia Minor, to which one of the letters in the Revelation to John was addressed (Revelation 2:18-29). Lydia was a native of this city (Acts 16:14).

TIBERIAS

was a city on the western shore of Lake Gennesaret. (This lake is also known as the Sea of, or Lake, Galilee or Tiberias.) The city was built by Herod Antipas and was the capital of the province (or tetrarchy) which he governed. A thoroughly Gentile city apparently never visited by Christ.
See John 6:1; 21:1.

TIGRIS

The Tigris is a river which joins the river Euphrates and flows into the Persian Gulf.

TIME

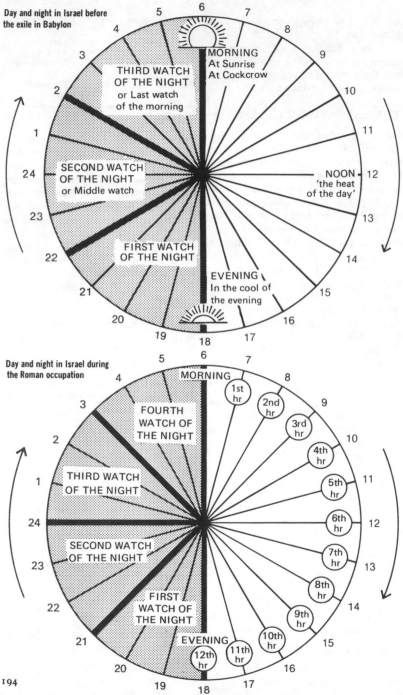

Day and night in Israel before the exile in Babylon

MORNING
At Sunrise
At Cockcrow

THIRD WATCH
OF THE NIGHT
or Last watch
of the morning

SECOND WATCH
OF THE NIGHT
or Middle watch

FIRST WATCH
OF THE NIGHT

NOON
'the heat
of the day'

EVENING
In the cool of
the evening

Day and night in Israel during the Roman occupation

MORNING

FOURTH
WATCH OF
THE NIGHT

THIRD WATCH
OF THE NIGHT

SECOND WATCH
OF THE NIGHT

FIRST
WATCH OF
THE NIGHT

EVENING

1st hr
2nd hr
3rd hr
4th hr
5th hr
6th hr
7th hr
8th hr
9th hr
10th hr
11th hr
12th hr

TIMES AND SEASONS

All calendars are controlled by the movements of the sun, the moon and the stars. In addition the Jews were strongly influenced by their great national festivals and by the agricultural cycle. The year was divided up into months determined by the phases of the moon. This must have involved some adjustment as twelve lunar months of twenty-nine or thirty days result in a total of 354 days which is less than the 365 of the year based on the earth's rotation around the sun. Probably an additional month was included every few years (similar to our modern practice of an extra day every leap year).

The week was also very important for Jews and every seventh day (Sabbath) was a rest-day used for worshipping God. The Jews normally regarded the day as running from evening to evening. Initially, there was no division into hours. The night was divided into three watches and the day roughly divided following the position of the sun and other natural phenomena. In New Testament times the Roman practice of dividing the night into four watches and the day into twelve hours was followed.

The Jewish year

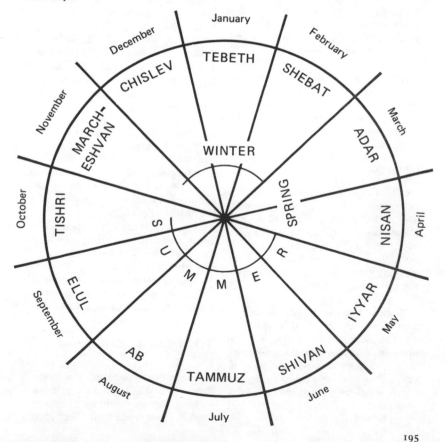

TIMOTHY, LETTERS TO

Timothy was the apostle Paul's co-worker and his companion on the second and third missionary journeys. Timothy was born in the city of Lystra in Asia Minor. His mother was Jewish and his father Greek (Acts 16:1-3).

Paul regarded Timothy as his most dependable assistant. He used him for special tasks and writes in one of his letters about him: 'I have no one like him...' (Philippians 2:19-22). Much of the letters concerns church organization: women, bishops, deacons, order in the Church.

The two letters to Timothy belong to the latter period of Paul's life. When he wrote the Second Letter to Timothy Paul was a prisoner, and realized that he would soon have to leave his work and his responsibilities to others.

The letters were addressed to Timothy, who visited different Christian churches on Paul's behalf. In the first letter Paul gives advice and regulations concerning life in the Christian church at Ephesus.

TITHES

In Old Testament times, each Israelite was expected to tithe and had to make a solemn declaration that he had done so (Deuteronomy 26:12-15). This meant giving one-tenth of his crops, herd or flock to God. As the animals were counted, every tenth one was withdrawn and given to God (Leviticus 27:30-33). The tithes were paid to the Levites (Numbers 18:21-24). Only cereals and fruit crops are mentioned in Numbers 18. The offering of the tithe was the occasion of a ritual meal (Deuteronomy 12:7, 12). Jerusalem was the place to offer it, though one's own locality was permitted every third year (Deuteronomy 14:28).

See also Malachi 3; Matthew 23:23 ff; Luke 11:42.

TITUS, LETTER TO

Titus was one of the apostle Paul's co-workers. He had been of great help to Paul in the Christian church in the city of Corinth. When Paul wrote the Letter to Titus he had just left him on the island of Crete. In the letter Paul gives advice to Titus concerning the organization of the Christian churches in Crete.

TONGUES, SPEAKING IN

Speaking in tongues was one of the particular spiritual gifts which were given to the Christian church.

Speaking in tongues might consist of speaking another language without ever having been taught it.

On the first day of Pentecost in Jerusalem the disciples spoke foreign languages in this way. The audience, whose members came from different countries could each listen to the apostles' sermon about Christ in their own languages (Acts 2:1-13).

Speaking in tongues could also be speaking a language which was incomprehensible to other men. The apostle Paul writes about this: 'One who speaks in a tongue speaks not to men but to God; for no one understands him, but he utters mysteries in the Spirit' (1 Corinthians 14:2).

However, these 'mysteries in the Spirit' could have a direct message to the church, because there were individuals who possessed the particular spiritual gift of interpretation, and could tell the church what the speech in tongues meant (1 Corinthians 14:28).

TOWER OF BABEL

In Genesis 11:1-9 the story is told of how men began to build a tower which they intended to reach the sky, 'a tower with its top in the heavens'. Verse 7 describes how God affected their speech

The great temple tower in Ur, a Ziggurat

so that they could no longer understand one another, and work on the tower had to stop. We cannot tell how far the tower resembled the later Babylonian ziggurat mounds.

TRADE

Before the time of King Solomon very few Israelites were merchants, making their livelihood from trade.

The Canaanites, who lived in the country before the Israelites, took care of trade and commerce. Caravans of camels or mules came from other countries carrying merchandise which was sold in Palestine. Most of the major trade routes of the time went across Palestine (Genesis 37:25). During the reign of King Solomon, the Israelites began to devote themselves to trade. From Phoenicia Solomon bought cedar wood and other materials needed for the construction of the Temple and other buildings. The Phoenicians were happy to buy wheat, oil, honey, balm and oak wood from the Israelites. Solomon ordered a fleet of merchant ships to be built at Ezion-Geber on the Gulf of Aqaba (1 Kings 9:26). His vessels brought back precious stones, gold, silver, ivory, spices, peacocks and monkeys (1 Kings 10:22).

At Ezion-Geber smelting-works have been found, where Solomon melted the copper ore which was mined in the nearby hills. Copper was a highly desirable commodity. King Solomon bought horses and chariots from Egypt (1 Kings 10:28-29).

The trade within the country was concentrated in the cities. The rural population brought their goods into the city.

The open space inside the city gates was similar to our market-places (Nehemiah 13:15, 16), and here the goods were sold and bought. In Jesus' day people had to pay customs duty on goods which were brought into the city.

Buying and selling often took place in the street. A baker's shop

In the larger cities there were special business blocks or bazaars, where little shops were side by side along the street (1 Kings 20:34). The whole shop front was open to the street and it was easy to see what goods the merchant had to offer. There was no fixed price, and after a great deal of haggling the seller and the buyer agreed on a suitable price.

TRAVEL

There is an Oriental proverb which says 'In the world there are three terrible misfortunes: disease, fasting and travel.' In the ancient world, travel was always a dangerous and difficult undertaking.

One might be attacked by robbers, the roads were usually very bad, and there was a risk that one would find nowhere to sleep at night, except in the open air.

In spite of these difficulties, thousands of travellers came to Jerusalem every year in order to take part in the great festivals which were celebrated there.

Most roads were nothing but stony and uneven paths, or wheel-tracks, which the traveller had to follow. In desert areas, the road was marked by stones placed at intervals along the way. No one was responsible for looking after or improving the roads.

The Romans built roads in order to be able to move their troops more quickly from one place to another. Their method was to place blocks of the local stone side by side, to a width of perhaps

yard, where the travellers could keep their pack-animals. Although guests could sleep in the buildings round the yard, every traveller had to prepare his own food. As a rule an inn would be built near a spring of water or an oasis (see Inn). There were different ways to travel.

The commonest and simplest way to travel was to walk. Otherwise, travellers could ride on asses or mules, animals which were also used for the transport of baggage. Donkey-drivers would also carry baggage for a fee. On longer journeys across waterless deserts, camels were used.

One way of increasing security on such journeys was to join together to form larger groups, called caravans.

When transporting heavier goods, use was also made of ox-carts.

Part of an old Roman road

An Assyrian ox-cart

20 ft. These roads were so well made that parts of them are still to be seen today. Whenever necessary the Romans also built bridges over the rivers.

When the winter rains came, it became practically impossible to travel along the waterlogged roads. Where there were no Roman bridges, travellers were forced to wade over the rivers at fords. And after heavy rains, it could be impossible to cross even at these places.

Along the major roads there were inns or taverns, where travellers could find lodging for the night (Genesis 42:27; Luke 2:7; 10:34). These consisted usually of buildings grouped round a

Travel was very slow. From Jerusalem to Gennesaret was about 75 miles (120 km.), and this took a person walking or riding on a donkey three days. A normal day's journey was no more than 25 miles. A riding-camel could cover 110–120 miles (170–180 km) during the same period, and a pack-camel carrying 300–550 lb (150–250 kg) could cover about 30 miles (50 km).

In Bible times horses were mainly used by the army, and came into use as pack-animals and for transport only later. When going into battle the horse was ridden by an armed soldier or pulled an armed chariot.

An Egyptian ship

The oldest boats or ships we know were used in the 4th millennium BC by the Egyptians.

In the ancient world, the best ship-builders and sailors were the Phoene-

chor; lifeboat; cables, which were passed around the hull so that the storm would not open the planks; sea-anchor; lead and line for checking the depth of the water; a foresail and a mainsail. The

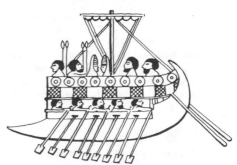

A Roman ship

A Phoenician ship

cians, who lived on the coast of the Mediterranean north of Palestine.

The Greeks were a sea-faring people, and the Romans built vast numbers of both war-ships and merchant-ships. There was an extensive traffic by Roman ships in the Mediterranean. The Israelites, however, knew little about the sea. Most of the ships mentioned in the New Testament were Roman ships.

The apostle Paul often travelled by sea. The ship in which he travelled as a prisoner to Rome was a Roman corn-ship which carried 276 passengers and crew.

The ship's equipment included: an-

mainsail was the sail which propelled the ship forward. It was difficult to sail against the wind. The foresail was a small sail in the bow of the ship, which made steering easier.

The story of Paul's sea-voyage in Acts 27 is the most detailed account of such a voyage which has been preserved from the ancient world.

See also Inn, Domestic Animals

TREASURE

In one of his parables Jesus compares the Kingdom of Heaven to a treasure which has been hidden in a field (Matthew 13:44). The Israelites, like many other peoples, would often bury their large sums of money and valuables in times of peril and war.

Through systematic excavations, and also by coincidence, people have found treasures which have been hidden in this

Treasure from the 7th century BC found in a field in Syria

way. They have often been placed in clay pots and Paul compares this to the new life in the body of clay (2 Corinthians 4:7). Treasures were also stored in a rich man's house (Proverbs 15:6; Matthew 13:52).

TREASURIES

At the time of Jesus there were in the Jerusalem Temple 13 treasuries (or large collection boxes), placed in the Court of Women. At the top they were shaped like a funnel and they narrowed towards the base.

The money collected in these treasuries was used for the upkeep of the Temple. It was here that Jesus observed the poor widow, who put all that she possessed in one of the treasuries (Mark 12:41–44).

THE TREE OF KNOWLEDGE

To eat of this tree in Eden meant disobedience to God's command and the consequent claim to be one's own arbiter of right and wrong. This act set the processes of death working in the body.

There was no magic in the fruit itself, but the significance lay in the act of eating (Genesis 3).

THE TREE OF LIFE

The tree of life is mentioned in Genesis 2:9; 3:22–24. After Adam's and Eve's disobedience against God, when they had taken fruit from the tree of knowledge, they were driven out of Paradise. In this way God wanted to prevent them from taking fruits from the 'tree of life', since this would have made them immortal sinners.

In the last book of the Bible, in Revelation 22:1–2, the tree of life is mentioned, which gives healing to the people of God. This tree is for those whose sins are washed away (22:14); they are not immortal sinners.

TREES

There have never been many large forests in Palestine. In Old Testament times the Lebanon mountain range was afforested. Mount Lebanon is situated north of Palestine in the country of Syria. This forest consisted mainly of cedar, but also cypress. In our day there remains very little of the cedar-forests of the Lebanon. Various single trees grew here and there, and occasionally there were small copses. Many different

Almond

kinds of fruit trees were cultivated in orchards.

The commonest fruit trees in Palestine were the following:

Almond tree. The almond tree is a small and hardy tree, which originally grew in India and Persia. The flowers are a pale pink, and blossom very early, before the leaves come out. Almond trees have been seen in flower as early as February. The fruit itself is not edible, but the stone is used for food. By pressing the almonds, almond oil is produced.
See Genesis 30:37; 43:11; Exodus 25:33; Numbers 17:8; Ecclesiastes 12:5; Jeremiah 1:11.

Carob tree. The carob tree was a very common tree in Palestine. It is an evergreen which can grow to a height of 10 m (33 ft). The fruits are 10–25 cm (4–10 inches) long pods, which ripen in April and May. They are used as animal fodder, but are also eaten by poor people. In the parable of the Prodigal Son the fruits of the carob tree are mentioned (Luke 15:16).

Date palm. The palm which grows in Palestine is the date palm. It grows tall and often very old. At the top of the tree there are 40–80 leaves, shaped like feathers, and about 4–6 m (12–18 ft) long. The small and insignificant flowers come out in May. The date palm grows in poor and sandy soil but cannot do without a great deal of water. The dates grow in large clusters. They are used for food, are highly nourishing and contain a large amount of sugar. Fibrous material from the palm leaves was used to make baskets, hammocks, mats, ropes and string. People carried palm leaves in their hands as a symbol of joy during the Feast of Booths, at celebrations of victory, and when welcoming a king. The cities of Jericho and Hazazon-tamar on the Dead Sea were especially famous for their many palms.
See Exodus 15:27; Leviticus 23:40; Deuteronomy 34:3; 1 Kings 6:29, 32; Psalm 92:12; John 12:13; Revelation 7:9.

Fig tree. The fig tree was one of the trees most commonly found near people's houses. The tree has a short trunk with light grey bark, a dense, deep green crown, with branches and leaves which often reach down to the ground. The fruit is pear-shaped. The fig-tree can bear fruit three times a year: (1) Early spring figs, which ripen in June at the time when the new leaves come out. They are eaten fresh. (2) Late figs, which grow on the new young shoots. They ripen in August and September. People usually dried them in the sun, on the flat house-tops. Afterwards they pressed them together into square or round

Carob

Date palm

Fig

Olive

cakes and stored them for the winter. (3) Winter figs are late figs, which have not had time to ripen. They remain on the tree during the winter, when the leaves have fallen. When spring comes, they start growing again.

Besides their use as food, figs were also used as medicine against boils and inflammations.

See Genesis 3:7; Deuteronomy 8:8; Judges 9:10–11; 1 Samuel 25:18; 1 Kings 4:25; Isaiah 28:4; Jeremiah 24:1–10; Nahum 3:12; Matthew 24:32; Mark 11:13; Luke 13:6–9; John 1:48; Revelation 6:13.

Olive tree. The olive tree has a thick, gnarled trunk. It grows slowly, and can become very old. It has a large crown, which gives pleasant shade. The leaves of the olive tree are dark and evergreen,

with a silvery underside. Yellow sweet-scented flowers come out during the month of May. The fruits are the size of grapes or plums. They are harvested during October and November. One third of the olive is oil, which is pressed out of the olives in an oil press.

A full grown tree, 15–30 years old, may yield 50–80 litres (11 to 17 gallons) of olive oil a year. The olives are eaten with bread. The oil was used in cooking, as fuel in oil lamps, in the Temple sacrifices, in treating wounds and for rubbing into and protecting the skin in the hot and dry climate of Palestine.

See Genesis 8:11; Deuteronomy 8:8; 24:20; 1 Kings 17:14; 2 Kings 4:2–7; Psalm 52:8; Jeremiah 11:16; Hosea 14:17; Micah 6:15; Matthew 25:3, 4; Mark 6:13; Luke 10:34; Romans 11:24.
See also Oil Press

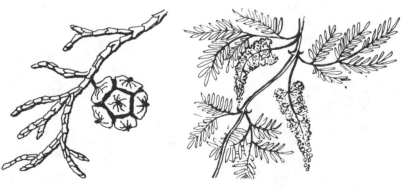

Cypress

Acacia

Pomegranate

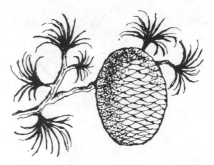

Cedar

Pomegranate tree.

The pomegranate tree is a smallish tree and one of the most beautiful in Palestine. It has a dense crown with shining leaves and fiery red flowers. The fruit ripens in August, and grows to the size of an orange. The juice from the pomegranate was a most popular and refreshing drink during the hot season. The rind of the ripe pomegranate produced a blue dye, which was used in dyeing wool. The rind of the unripe fruit yielded a yellow dyestuff which was used in the dyeing of leather.

See Exodus 28:33; Numbers 13:23; Deuteronomy 8:8; Song of Solomon 8:2; Joel 1:12; Haggai 2:19.

Sycomore tree.

The sycomore tree (in the revised Standard Version called sycamore although not the same as the familiar tree of the maple family) is fairly common in Palestine. It is a large, vigorous tree (50 ft (15 m) and taller) with a thick and gnarled trunk. The trunk divides low down into strong, twisted branches. Its crown can grow as large as 130 ft (40 m) in diameter. The branches grow horizontally from the trunk. It is easy to climb up the sycomore, and it was a sycomore that the tax-collector Zacchaeus climbed into, in order to be able to see Jesus. The leaves are somewhat smaller than those of the fig tree, and the fruits are a greyish green colour and look like small figs. Their taste is bitter. The fruits grow in clusters along the branches and on the trunk, and need to be pierced to help them to ripen (Amos 7:14).

The poorer people who could not afford other fruit used the sycomore fruits for food. The wood of the sycomore is strong and long-lasting and was used in building. In Egypt mummy cases (coffins for the dead) were often made of this particular wood.

See 1 Kings 10:27; Isaiah 9:10; Amos 7:14; Luke 19:4.

Some other trees are the following:

Acacia. The acacia is often mentioned in the Old Testament. This is because the wood of the acacia was especially useful. It is hard and durable and orange-brown in colour. It is very seldom attacked by harmful insects. Such wood is very suitable for fine carpentry. The acacia thrives in dry areas, where other trees cannot grow. Its branches have strong and sharp thorns. The bark is used in tanning leather.

See Exodus 25:10, 13, 23, 28; 26:15; 27:1; 30:1; Deuteronomy 10:3; Isaiah 41:19.

Cedar. The cedar is an evergreen conifer with a thick and solid trunk. The trunk of an old cedar may grow to 2 m (6 ft) thick, and the tree may grow up to 40 m (130 ft) tall. The wood is whitish

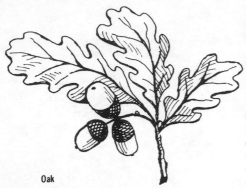

Oak

yellow, compact and very suitable as a building material. In the present day only about 400 cedars remain of the once large cedar-forests on Mount Lebanon north of Palestine.

See Numbers 24:6; Judges 9:15; 1 Kings 4:33; 5:6; Psalm 104:16; Isaiah 9:10; 41:19; Ezekiel 31:3.

Cypress. The cypress is an evergreen conifer, with a short trunk and an elongated narrow crown. The cypress is common in the mountain regions of Syria and Palestine. It has a very long-lasting wood, yellowish red in colour, which is resistant to attacks from grubs and insects. The wood was used for shipbuilding, musical instruments, floorboards and doors.

See 1 Kings 5:8; Song of Solomon 1:17; Isaiah 14:8; 37:24; 60:13; Ezekiel 27:5.

Oak. There were large oak forests in Palestine in biblical times. In our day it occurs most often as a single tree, or with very few together. In Palestine there are several species of oak, including the evergreen holm oak or ilex. One species grows to about the same height as the oak which is native to Britain. On the leaves of one of the other species is found an insect, from which scarlet dye is derived. The oak was a symbol of strength and majesty.

See Genesis 35:8; Joshua 24:26; Isaiah 2:13; Amos 2:9; Zechariah 11:2.

Willow. Common by streams. Their twigs were woven for baskets.

See Job 40:22; Isaiah 15:7; 44:4
See also Tamarisk

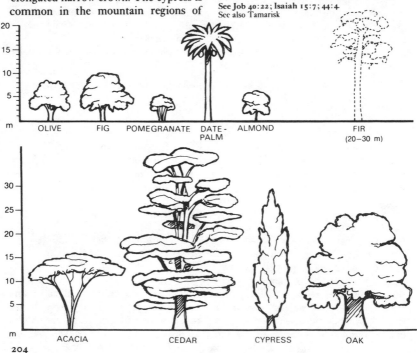

OLIVE   FIG   POMEGRANATE   DATE-PALM   ALMOND   FIR (20–30 m)

ACACIA   CEDAR   CYPRESS   OAK

TRIBES

The Israelites were divided into twelve tribes after the twelve sons of Jacob. When the people penetrated into Canaan after their wandering in the wilderness, the country was divided between the tribes. The tribe of Levi was not allotted a separate tribal area. It was to be a special priestly family within Israel. The name of Joseph was not given to any tribe, but the names of his two sons Ephraim and Manasseh were given to two of Israel's tribes instead.

During the wandering in the wilderness Moses arranged a count of all the adult males in Israel who would be able to carry arms and go to war. All who were 20 years old and above were included. Such a census took place twice, at the beginning and end of the wanderings in the wilderness (Numbers 2:26).

The tribe of Levi was counted on a separate occasion (Numbers 3:39).

Tribe	Number in the first census	In the second census
Reuben	46,500	43,730
Simeon	59,300	22,200
Gad	45,650	40,500
Judah	74,600	76,500
Issachar	54,400	64,300
Zebulun	57,400	60,500
Manasseh	32,200	52,700
Ephraim	40,500	32,500
Benjamin	35,400	45,600
Dan	62,700	64,400
Asher	41,500	53,400
Naphtali	53,400	45,400
Levi	22,000	22,000
All Israel	625,550	623,730

Gradually, the tribes and their areas lost the great importance that they had had earlier. The twelve tribes became divided into the Northern Kingdom (Israel) and the Southern Kingdom (Judah). Some

scholars have reduced the very large numbers above by translating the Hebrew word for thousand by family or by captain or chief. The same Hebrew letters are thus translated in Judges 6:15 and Genesis 36:15 and elsewhere.

TROAS

was a town on the west coast of Asia Minor, through which Paul passed several times. On his first visit he received a call to preach the Gospel in Europe: 'Come over to Macedonia and help us.' (Acts 16:8-9; 20:5-12).

TURN, RETURN

In the Old Testament we often meet the phrase 'turn (or return) to the Lord' and to the covenant with him. Often these words concern the whole of Israel, who have turned away from their God, and are exhorted to turn back, turn around or return to God.

The prophets, and especially Jeremiah, use these expressions (Jeremiah 3:14; 4:1; 31:18).

The prophets also want to stress that the individual must think of returning to God (Jeremiah 15:19; Ezekiel 3:19, 20).

In the New Testament the need of a return to God, or conversion, is also emphasized. Jesus, the Messiah, has come. The Kingdom of God is at hand. Therefore one must turn to Jesus.

Jesus says about this conversion: 'Unless you turn and become like children, you will never enter the kingdom of heaven' (Matthew 18:3).

TURTLE DOVE SEE BIRDS

TYRE

was a city on the Mediterranean coast in the country of Phoenicia. It was an important seaport and a centre of trade, as well as one of the largest cities in Phoenicia.

The city of Tyre was originally situated on an island and was protected by walls (Ezekiel 26). Many foreign rulers tried to conquer Tyre. Nebuchadnezzar subdued it, and Alexander the Great destroyed it after one of the classic sieges of history (332 BC). King Solomon made a treaty with King Hiram of Tyre. During the building of Solomon's Temple the king received help, against payment, from King Hiram and his people (1 Kings 5).

Jesus visited the areas near Tyre during his ministry (Mark 3:8; 7:24).

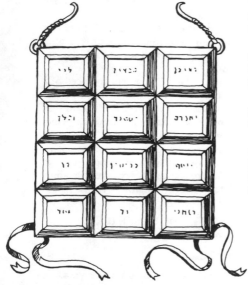

The High Priest's breastplate containing the Urim and Thummim may have looked like this

U

UNCLEAN

When the word 'unclean' is used in the Old Testament, it does not refer to dirt which can be washed away with soap and water. It was a ritual uncleanness (or impurity), which meant that the person was not allowed to participate in worship during a certain period of time. To have touched a dead body (Leviticus 11:39; Numbers 19:11) or to suffer from the disease of leprosy (Leviticus 13), are examples of this kind of uncleanness. After a prescribed period of time and certain sacrifices, the person was regarded as free from his impurity (Numbers 19:12).

Some animals, among them the pig, were unclean and could not be used for food. In Leviticus 11 there is a list of these unclean animals.

Objects, too, such as household utensils and clothes, could be contaminated by uncleanness. They had to be purified in order to be used again (Leviticus 11:29-38). It is often possible to see good hygienic reasons for these regulations.

Jesus distinguished between inner and outer cleanliness (Mark 7:18-23) and Peter was shown in a vision that nothing is unclean in itself (Acts 10:10-16, 28). See also Romans 14:14; 1 Timothy 4:4, 5.

UNLEAVENED BREAD

was bread made without leaven or yeast. Normally a piece of fermented dough from a previous baking was used to ferment the new loaf. Israel celebrated a festival in the month of April which was called 'the Feast of Unleavened Bread'. The Israelites ate unleavened bread during this festival, which commemorated the hurried escape from Egypt at the Passover, when there was no time to wait for the dough to rise (Exodus 12:14–20, 34).

UR

Ur in Chaldaea was the native city of Abraham. Scholars are usually of the opinion that Abraham's Ur is a place situated about 20 km northwest of the Persian Gulf. At the time of Abraham the Persian Gulf probably extended all the way up to the city of Ur.

The city of Ur was dominated by the immense temple tower, which was built in about 2000 BC. It was a centre of worship of the Moon god, Nanna.

Excavations at Ur have yielded many valuable finds. Gold ornaments and vases and richly decorated musical instruments have been found in the ancient royal graves.

The city of Ur was protected by a strong wall. Many of the houses in the city were built in two storeys and contained ten to fifteen rooms.

In Genesis 11:31 we are told that Abraham's father Terah left the city of Ur together with his family and his nephew Lot and moved to Haran.

URIM AND THUMMIM

The Urim and the Thummim were sacred objects which were used for casting lots after prayer on important occasions (1 Samuel 14:41, 42 RSV and other modern translations are almost certainly correct here). The Urim and the Thummim were kept in the High Priest's 'breastpiece of judgement', which looked like a pouch and which he carried on his chest (Exodus 28:28–30). See also High Priest.

VALLEY GATE

The Valley Gate, also called the Gate of Essenes, was one of the gates in the wall surrounding Jerusalem. Uzziah fortified it with towers (2 Chronicles 26:9). It was probably situated in the southwestern corner of the city and opened on the Valley of Hinnom. In excavations on this site the archaeologists have found remains of a gate.

VANITY

1. Emptiness, or pointlessness or frustration. We read in Ecclesiastes 1:2 that 'all is vanity'. This reflects a very deeply pessimistic view of life: whatever man does or accomplishes, he will die. Similarly the whole of creation, including man, is marked by frustration (Romans 8:20–23).
2. Inflated personal pride in oneself, one's appearance or one's achievements. This is a more modern use of *vanity*, and the Hebrew also is different. Translations use *pride*.

VEIL

The 'veil' in the Temple was a curtain made of rich fabric, which separated the sanctuary (the Holy place) from the Holy of Holies. When Jesus died, the curtain in the Temple was torn in two, from top to bottom.

See Exodus 26:31–33; Matthew 27:51; Hebrews 6:19.

VINEGAR

When the grapes had been pressed and their juice had been poured into jars and wineskins, some of the wine was sometimes left in the vat and allowed to go sour. This sour wine was used as vinegar. It was mixed with water and was very good for quenching the thirst. The Roman soldiers at Jesus' crucifixion gave him wine vinegar to drink, and Jesus accepted it (Matthew 27:48; John 19:28-30). Shortly before the crucifixion the soldiers offered Jesus some wine mixed with gall. Jesus did not drink this. Wine mixed with this bitter substance was a painkiller (Matthew 27:33-34).

VULTURE SEE BIRDS

WAILING WALL

The only part of Herod's Temple still standing in Jerusalem is a wall, some 65 ft (20 m) high, which is traditionally called the Wailing Wall. It is a place of worship and prayer for Jews from all over the world.

WANDERING IN THE WILDERNESS

After the Israelites had left their slavery in Egypt and crossed the Red Sea, they began a 40-year-long period of wandering in the deserts of the Sinai peninsula, with many hardships. Many important events took place during this wandering in the wilderness.

Place	Event	Bible
Rameses	The Exodus from Egypt began here about 1290 BC	Exodus 12:37
Succoth	The Exodus continued via Succoth	Exodus 12:37; 13:20
Marah	Moses made the salt water in Marah drinkable	Exodus 15:23-25
Elim	An oasis where there were 12 springs and 70 palm trees	Exodus 15:27
Wilderness of Sin	Thousands of quails were caught by the Israelites. The people gathered manna which could be made into bread	Exodus 16:13-18
Rephidim	Israel fought Amalek and won	Exodus 17:8-13
Sinai	The covenant between God and Israel. Moses received the Ten Commandments	Exodus 19, 20
Hazeroth	Moses' brother Aaron and sister Miriam challenged Moses, and as a result Miriam was struck by leprosy	Numbers 12
Wilderness of Paran	Spies were sent into Canaan. They returned with a discouraging report.	Numbers 13
	The people refused to go in, and were condemned to forty years in the wilderness	Numbers 14
Kadesh-Barnea	Miriam's death	Numbers 20:1
Mount Hor	The High Priest Aaron's death	Numbers 20:23-29
Oboth, Valley of Zered, River Arnon	Israelite camps	Numbers 21:10-13
Nebo	The death of Moses. Joshua became the leader of Israel. The conquest of Canaan began in 1250 BC	Deuteronomy 34

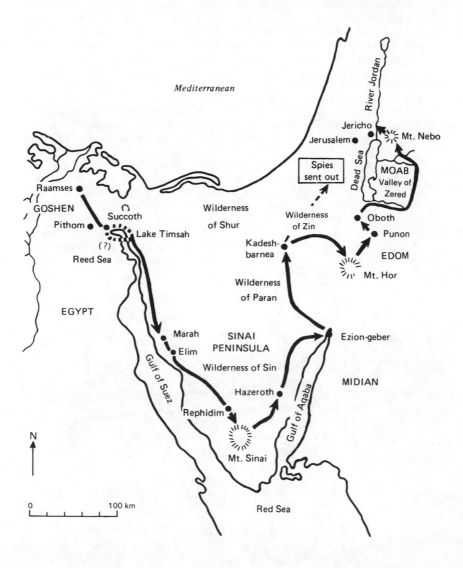

WAR

War was common in the Near East and is mentioned frequently in the Old Testament.

The Israelites were involved in wars during their time in the wilderness and later had to fight their way into Canaan. Under David and Solomon new areas were added to the kingdom through military expeditions. Many of these were lost in subsequent battles. The land of Palestine was strategically placed, lying on several routes and armies frequently marched through it.

Until the time of the Judges war would have been conducted on foot by soldiers armed with a short sword, a spear and a shield. Most able-bodied men would have been expected to fight in times of crisis. King Saul was the first to set up a standing army, and David

employed a number of mercenaries. As Israel learnt from the Philistines and other surrounding nations so warfare became more complicated and weapons were made out of iron rather than bronze. Armour was introduced and cavalry and chariots became more common. As cities became more strongly fortified it became necessary to add catapults and ramps and siege tactics were employed.

Jesus appears to have accepted war as an inevitable result of man's fallen nature (Matthew 24:6) but warned that those who took the sword would perish by it (Matthew 26:52). Christians have always been divided on their attitudes towards war. Some have felt that as it was an inevitable part of human life there were circumstances under which it would be right for the Christian to fight. Others, however, have adopted a

Israelite warrior from the 13th century BC. Drawing taken from a stone tablet at Megiddo

Roman soldier from the time of Christ

Chariot from Egypt

pacifist attitude and have maintained
that warfare is incompatible with the
Christian life.

Paul uses the image of warfare to
describe the Christian life, showing it as
a spiritual battle (Ephesians 6; 2 Timothy 2:3).

See also Weapons

WASH ONE'S HANDS

is an expression which means 'to declare
that one is innocent', or 'to disclaim all
responsibility'. Pilate for instance (Matthew 27:24). For cleansing and ritual
purposes water was commonly poured
over the hands by a servant (2 Kings
3:11) but there was also more formal
washing of the hands (Matthew 15:2;
Mark 7:3).

WATER SEE WELL

WATERS OF BABYLON

The 'waters of Babylon' mentioned in
Psalm 137:1 were the rivers Euphrates
and Tigris.

Jewish captives playing harps or lyres

WEAN

An Israelite mother fed her baby for up
to three years (1 Samuel 1:23, 24). On
the occasion of weaning there might be
a celebration party (Genesis 21:8).

WEAPONS

Weapons and armour of different kinds
were used by the peoples in the lands of
the Bible. The following are mentioned:

Assyrian horsemen with javelin

Roman helmet

club (Job 41:29) **sling** (Judges 20:16; 2 Chronicles 26:14) **spear** (Judges 5:8; 2 Chronicles 26:14; John 19:34) **sword** (Acts 16:27; Ephesians 6:17) **javelin**

Assyrian bowmen

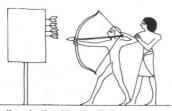

Egyptians shooting at targets with bows and arrows

(Joshua 8:18) **bow and arrows** (Genesis 48:22; 1 Samuel 20:36; Psalm 127:4, 5) **poisoned arrows** (Job 6:4)

flaming darts (Ephesians 6:16) **catapult for arrows and stones** (2 Chronicles 26:15) **chariot** (1 Kings 4:26) **shield** (2 Chronicles 26:14; Ephesians

Roman scabbard with sword found in Germany

6:16) **armour** (1 Samuel 17:38; 2 Chronicles 26:14) **helmet** (Ephesians 6:17).

WEAVE, WEAVER, SEE CRAFTS

WEDDING

A wedding was a great event in an Israelite family. It was not uncommon for the wedding celebrations to last for seven days.

The wedding began with a solemn procession of the bridegroom, his relatives and friends to the bride's home. If it took place at night, the participants carried torches to light their way (Matthew 25:1-13).

In the bride's home the bride had been dressed and adorned with jewels, and she was waiting for her groom together with her maids (Isaiah 61:10). If it was in the evening, a few of the bridesmaids would light the entrance to the house with their oil-lamps. From a distance they could hear the cries of spectators, calling that the bridegroom was coming (Matthew 25:6).

The groom called for his bride, and in a festive procession with singing and exclamations of joy, she was taken to the home of the bridegroom (Psalm 45:10; Matthew 22:1–10). There followed a splendid wedding feast. One of the men at the wedding was called 'friend of the bridegroom'. As 'best man' he was responsible for the success of the wedding feast (John 2:1–10).

The peak of the festivities was the wedding ceremony itself. The bridal couple stood or were seated under a palanquin, made of palm branches and embroidered fabric. There is no reference to this in the Bible, but we gather it from later Jewish custom. Finally the couple were escorted to the bridal chamber (Psalm 19:5; Joel 2:16. See also Tobit 7:16; 8:1).

See also Marriage

WEEDS

Jesus spoke about weeds in two parables, the 'weeds (sometimes called tares) among the wheat' and 'the Sower'.

The weed which grew in the field together with the wheat was a species of grass called darnel. Before this plant forms ears it cannot be distinguished

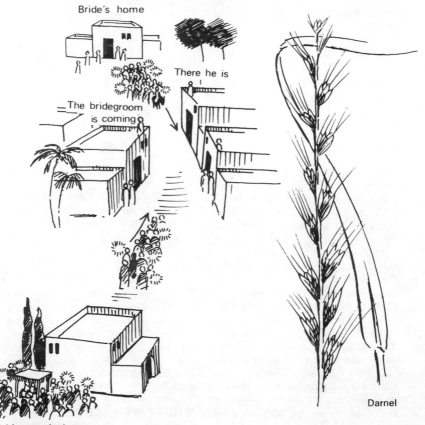

Bride's home

There he is

The bridegroom is coming

Bridegroom's home

Darnel

from the wheat. But when the weed and the wheat have grown to maturity the difference is more apparent, but the darnel cannot be pulled up without disturbing the wheat (Matthew 13:24–30).

The darnel can be poisonous if it is ground up as flour. Other weeds mentioned in the Bible are thorns and thistles. There are many varieties of thorns that grow in Palestine.

There are species in the form of trees, shrubs, and creepers along the ground (Jeremiah 4:3; Matthew 13:7). In a country with as many dry areas as Palestine, these plants flourish.

The thorns could be used for fuel (Ecclesiastes 7:6), or as an enclosure around the vineyard (Isaiah 5:5; Matthew 21:33).

There are species of thistle in Palestine which may grow to a height of 15 ft.

WEEK SEE TIMES AND SEASONS

WEIGHT SEE MEASURES

WELL

Palestine, with its dry climate, was a land lacking in water. The existing springs and wells were therefore highly valuable.

'Living water' was drawn from springs and brooks. There were many wells deep enough to reach the water table, and cisterns were cut in the rock to catch rain water (Jeremiah 2:13). A well at the foot of Mount Gerizim is pointed out as that well of Sychar where Jesus spoke to the woman of Samaria (John 4:6–15). This well is 100 ft (32 m) deep and gives water from the water table. The water was drawn from such wells with leather buckets, attached to ropes. The water was poured into pottery jars and the women carried them home on their shoulders or heads. There were also dug-out cisterns, or tanks where

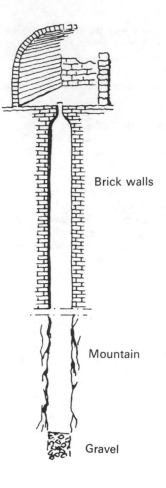

Brick walls

Mountain

Gravel

rain water was collected (Genesis 21:30). These could also be hewn out of the rock or be built of bricks. The water in these tanks will have been unfit for drinking (Jeremiah 2:13). Wells for watering animals were sometimes covered with a heavy stone so that the use could be controlled (Genesis 29:2, 3; Exodus 2:16–19).

WHEAT SEE AGRICULTURE

A simple watchtower built of four poles covered with leaves.

A guardtower built of stone

WINE MAKING

Wine making was a very important part of Israelite agriculture. The climate and the soil were favourable. It was easy to construct vineyards with terraces on the many hillsides (Isaiah 5 : 1, 2).

Around the vineyard there was often a wall, which protected it against foxes, jackals, robbers or occasional passers-by (Psalm 80 : 12). The vineyard was guarded by a watchman from a tower. This guard-tower might be built of stone, but was mostly of a simpler construction (Isaiah 5 : 2; Matthew 21 : 33).

The vine is a climbing plant with long and thin branches which have to be tied up in order not to fall to the ground. One vine might grow as long as 100 ft (30 m), and can reach a great age. It

Treading out grapes

215

flowers in May. The grape harvest began in August and finished in October. The vines were pruned in December and January.

The grapes were pressed in a special press, which was usually hewn out of the rock. The ripe grapes were put in the tub. One or more men trod the grapes under their bare feet, so that the skins burst and the grape juice ran out (Isaiah 16:10; Jeremiah 48:33). The work was done with song and clapping of hands. The grape juice ran through connecting channels down into a vat where it was collected.

The juice was poured into pottery jugs or wineskins (Matthew 9:17), and left until the fermentation process was completed. The wine was often clarified by pouring gently from one jar to another so that it did not settle on the lees (Jeremiah 48:11; Zephaniah 1:12). Grapes were eaten fresh off the vine, but they were also dried in the sun and made into raisins. Raisins were part of the food during the winter (1 Samuel 25:18; 30:12; 2 Samuel 16:1; 1 Chronicles 12:40).

At Cana when the wine ran out, Jesus miraculously provided more so that the wedding could continue (John 2:1–11). At Pentecost the disciples were so full of joy and bold speaking, that spectators thought that they were drunk with new wine (Acts 2:13). Paul warned the Ephesians against drunkenness (5:18) but told Timothy to take some wine, perhaps for medicinal purposes (1 Timothy 5:23. So also 2 Samuel 16:2; Proverbs 31:6).

WINTER SEE CLIMATE

WISDOM OF SOLOMON

The Wisdom of Solomon is one of the books of the Apocrypha. It may have been written during the period shortly before the birth of Christ. The book is written in praise of Wisdom, which is described almost as if it were a person, as in Proverbs 8 and 9.

WITNESS SEE COURT

WORD OF GOD, THE SEE BIBLE

WORLD

From words and phrases that are used, the following picture is often built up of what the Hebrews believed. The vault of heaven was like a dome placed over the flat and round disc of the earth. Outside and above the dome there was water which fell on the earth from windows in the celestial vault. Above the vault of heaven and the water on top of it was heaven, where God dwelt. Stars and planets were attached to the dome of the sky. The earth was placed on pillars, with the ocean surrounding it. Below the earth was the kingdom of the dead (Genesis 1:7, 14–18; Job 26:5; Psalms 11:4; 24:2; Proverbs 8:27; Isaiah 24:18).

One must distinguish picture language from actual belief. Modern man also sees the sky as a *dome*, speaks of the heavens as *brass* when there is a long drought, and describes the rain as coming down *in buckets*. The sun *rises*, *climbs* to its full height, and *sinks* into the sea, and the stars *travel across* the sky after night has *fallen*. Since no one has ever visualized heaven as below or upon earth, *above* is the only suitable preposition for it. God again is above and beyond all (1 Kings 8:27; Isaiah 40:22). As we bury the body we place it *under* the earth.

A diagram based on factualizing these metaphors would be not unlike what has been deduced from biblical phrases, but neither we nor the Hebrews would claim that we were speaking scientific language. Simple observations show that it is the clouds that hold the waters that are above the earth (1 Kings 18:44, 45; Ecclesiastes 12:2). Windows in heaven are purely metaphorical (Genesis 7:11), and the expression is used of other things besides water (2 Kings 7:2; Malachi 3:10). The presence of wells and springs shows that there are waters under the earth, and the land is obviously *above* sea level (Genesis 1:9).

Wormwood

WORMWOOD

is a name given to a family of herbs or shrublike plants. These have a strong and unpleasant smell and a bitter taste, though one variety is used to make absinthe. It grows in quantity around Bethlehem.

See Jeremiah 9:15; Lamentations 3:15, 19; Amos 5:7; Revelation 8:11.

WORSHIP

The word describes not only those occasions when people turn to God in prayer and sacrifice, but also everything that man does in order to get closer to God. Thus it describes a life in the fear of God, prayer in solitude, and love and helpfulness towards fellow men (Colossians 3:17).

However, 'worship' also means, naturally, the meetings in the Temple, in the synagogues or in the Christian congregations.

The patriarchs Abraham, Isaac and Jacob sacrificed and prayed to God in particular holy places in Palestine (Genesis 13:3–4; 22; 28:10–22). During the wandering in the desert the Israelites had a particular tent set apart for worship. This was called the tabernacle. There they offered sacrifices and prayers to God and received his blessing (Exodus 25:8–9).

In Canaan the Israelites had many holy places where they sacrificed and prayed to God: Shiloh, Gilgal, Shechem, Beer-Sheba, Dan, Bethel and Samaria.

During the reign of King David, the worship and sacrifices of Israel came to be centred on Jerusalem (2 Samuel 6:12, 15, 17). Subsequently, worship took place chiefly in the Jerusalem Temple, following daily and seasonal cycles. Worship consisted of sacrifices of various kinds at different altars, purifications, the singing of psalms, processions, prayers, confessions and blessings. There were various classes of priests and ministers (1 Kings 8:1–14; 1 Chronicles 24–26).

Seasonal festivals were celebrated in the Temple at Jerusalem by large crowds of pilgrims (John 11:55; Acts 2:1, 5–11). After the Babylonian captivity, when the Jews were separated from the Temple, they began to build other places of worship (but not of sacrifice), called synagogues. Jews migrated all over the ancient world, and wherever they went, they built synagogues. These were the Jews of the dispersion, or diaspora. In Jesus' day almost every city had one or more synagogues, where worship took place on each Sabbath and other festival days. Prayers were also held in the synagogue three times a day. Synagogue worship included singing and music, processions, scripture readings, prayers and sermons. There were, however, no sacrifices, and therefore no priests. Jesus and the apostles took part in synagogue services regularly (Matthew 13:54; Luke 4:16).

Worship in the first Christian congregations was very similar to that which took place in the synagogues. There were readings from the Old Testament, and eventually also from the New Testament, followed by a sermon based on the reading. The congregation sang psalms and hymns, and prayers were said (Colossians 3:16). In some churches there was also 'speaking in tongues' (see reference under that heading).

The most important element of worship in the early Church was however the celebration of the sacraments, the Holy Communion and Baptism (Acts 2:46; 1 Corinthians 11:20-34).

See also: Communion, Festivals, Prayer, Priest, Sabbath, Sacrifice, Synagogue, Tabernacle, Temple

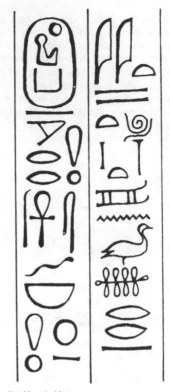

Egyptian hieroglyphics

WRITING

In Egypt, and later Assyria and Babylonia, there was a kind of pictorial writing as early as 3000 BC. Every object or situation had one particular sign. This Egyptian form of writing was called hieroglyphic. The other type of pictorial writing from Assyria developed into the cuneiform script; in this form of writing some signs represented letters or syllables, while others stood for whole words. The cuneiform signs were pressed into soft clay with a wedge-shaped stylus (the word cuneiform means 'wedge-shaped'). Later the clay was dried and hardened.

Cuneiform writing

Later Egyptian writing has also come down to us on papyrus and potsherds.

One of the oldest known examples of written Hebrew is the Siloam inscription from the 9th century BC. This inscription was carved on the rock at a point where the water of the Gihon Spring ran out through a tunnel into the Pool of Siloam.

Inscriptions dating from around 1600 BC have been found in the Sinai peninsula. They resemble Egyptian hieroglyphs and are in a Semitic language. A similar script was used elsewhere in Palestine, and some examples have been discovered. The Amarna letters which are clay tablets of correspondence between Egypt and Palestine, and other archaeological discoveries at Ras Shamra (Ugarit) show that cuneiform writing was also used in Palestine. A linear script was developed for writing with pen and ink, or for carving on stone as in Hezekiah's tunnel. After the exile in Babylon, the Jews began to use a new form of letters, the square script, out of which modern Hebrew has developed. Among the oldest examples of this type of writing are the Dead Sea Scrolls.

The Greeks took over their form of writing from Syria, Phoenicia and Palestine. They created special letters rep-

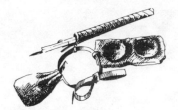

Old writing implements from Egypt

potsherds, papyrus or parchment. The ink was manufactured from soot, water and gum arabic. A knife belonged to the writing utensils, since the pen nib would need sharpening from time to time.

Later on, metal nibs were used, especially for writing on parchment. Writing which it was not intended to keep for a longer period of time was done on wax tablets.

It was not usual for people to be able to write or to possess writing materials. If they wanted to write a letter or send some other written message, they could turn to particular scribes, who would write it down, against payment (Jere-

Κυρίου ’Ιησοῦ μετὰ πάντων

Greek script

𐤀 𐤍𐤔𐤅𐤕𐤐 𐤋𐤈𐤅 𐤈𐤅𐤀𐤋𐤂 𐤎𐤀𐤅𐤂𐤉 𐤃𐤉𐤔𐤂

Hebrew script

resenting vowels – a characteristic which was not part of these languages. The books of the New Testament were originally written in Greek writing.

WRITING MATERIALS

Stone or clay tablets and potsherds were used as materials for writing on in ancient times. The text would be cut or carved into the stone, or impressed into soft clay.

Pens, with nibs made from sharpened reeds, and ink were used for writing on

Egyptian scribes taken from a tomb painting about 2500 BC

miah 36:4; Ezekiel 9:2). Kings and other important people had their own scribes or secretaries (1 Kings 4:3; 2 Kings 12:10).
See also Letters

Y

Z

YAHWEH SEE GOD

YEAR OF JUBILEE

In Israel every fiftieth year was celebrated as a Year of Jubilee.
See under Sabbatical Year

YOKE

A yoke was used when carrying different
kinds of burdens. It was usually made of
wood, and was laid across the person's
shoulders, with the burdens hanging on
each end. It thus became a symbol of
heaviness and oppression (Genesis
27:40; Deuteronomy 28:48; Jeremiah
27:2; Matthew 11:29, 30).

The yoke was also used to harness
two oxen together for pulling a plough
or a cart (1 Kings 19:19; Numbers
19:2).

ZAREPHATH

A city in Phoenicia on the coast between
Tyre and Sidon. Elijah found refuge
here with a widow, whose son he restored
to life (1 Kings 17:9–24).

ZEALOTS SEE PARTIES

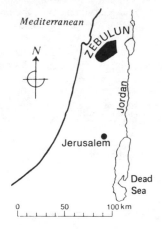

ZEBULUN

was the name of one of the twelve sons
of the patriarch Jacob (Genesis 30:19,
20). Zebulun became the father of the
tribe of Zebulun, which was allotted a
small area in north-western Canaan
(Joshua 19:10–16; Isaiah 9:1). During
the time of the Judges the tribe of
Zebulun took part, with great success, in
the battle against Israel's enemies under
the Judges Deborah and Gideon (Judges
5:18).

ZECHARIAH, BOOK OF

Zechariah was a prophet in Judah. He

returned from the Exile in Babylon and appeared in Jerusalem together with the prophet Haggai. Zechariah and Haggai roused the people to help in the reconstruction of the Temple.

The Book of Zechariah consists of two main parts:

In a series of eight different visions the prophet speaks of the Messianic kingdom, which is to come. The Lord will judge the enemies of Israel, Jerusalem will become a great city, and sin and unrighteousness will no longer be found in Israel.	Zechariah 1–8
This part of the book was probably written later. It contains, among other things, passages of judgement over Israel's enemies and prophecies about the time when the Messiah will appear. In Zechariah 9:9 there is the well-known Messianic prophecy: 'Lo, your king comes to you; triumphant and victorious is he, humble and riding on an ass.' Moreover Zechariah 12:10 contains remarkable prophecy fulfilled to the very detail when Jesus died and quoted by John in 19:37. 'When they look on him whom they have pierced, they shall mourn for him' – written by a prophet in a period of history when death by crucifixion was unknown.	Zechariah 9–14

ZEPHANIAH, BOOK OF

Zephaniah was a prophet in Judah during the reign of King Josiah, 639–609 BC. In the Book of Zephaniah in the Old Testament, the prophet warned his people about the judgement and the punishment which was to come to Israel on the Day of the Lord. Israel had turned to other gods and lived in luxury and unrighteousness. The Day of the Lord would be a day of wrath for Israel, a day of anguish, devastation and darkness. The punishment would be brought down on the neighbouring peoples, too.

But a remnant of Israel would be left, and from this remnant the new people of God would emerge. A new Jerusalem would arise, with the Lord himself as its King. The Book of Zephaniah may be divided as follows.

God's judgement on his people Israel	Zephaniah 1:1–18
God's judgement on the pagan nations	Zephaniah 2:1–15
Continued judgement against Israel	Zephaniah 3:1–8
A righteous people of Israel will one day live in a new Jerusalem	Zephaniah 3:9–20

ZION

Originally Zion was the name of the fortified hill in Jerusalem before the arrival of the Israelites (2 Samuel 5:7). When the temple had been built on a hilltop to the north, this new part of the city was also included in Zion. The name gradually came to apply to the whole of the city of Jerusalem (Psalm 51:18; Isaiah 2:3).

ZITHER SEE MUSIC